A S I A

KYRGYZSTAN

JZBEKISTAN

Beijing ■

khara ■ Samarqand ■

TAJIKISTAN

C H I N A

JRKMENISTAN

Mashhad ■

AFGHANISTAN

erat ■   Kabul ■

Shanghai ■

TIBET

PAKISTAN

Delhi ■   *NEPAL*

■ Karachi

I N D I A

Jacques Anquetil

CARPETS

HACHETTE Illustrated

Contents

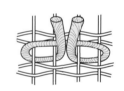

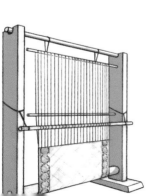

Preface

 he principal aim of this book is to demonstrate how one can 'read' a carpet as one might read a page of text. The analogy is not as far-fetched as it might at first seem, particularly when one considers the etymology of the Latin verb texere ('to weave') and its past participle textus ('woven'), both of which are related to English terms such as 'text', 'texture', 'textile' and 'context'. One can see substantial parallels between, on the one hand, a text and its context and, on the other, a textile and its texture. For the nomad who can neither read nor write, a carpet is, in effect, a text that conveys meaning and so serves as a medium of communication. Just as a written text records the linear sequence of the spoken word, a carpet can be regarded as a woven record of a society or ethnic group – a reflection, as it were, of collective thoughts, experiences and emotions.

As with spoken and written language, the language of the carpet has its own vocabulary and syntax. It is this language that will be explored in these pages – line by line or, we might even say, weft by weft.

It is a language that has several levels of meaning. At its most basic level, the carpet makes a visual impression, the sequence of knots used to form a motif equating to the use of letters to form words. The infinite variations that obtain by virtue of the nuances implicit in the colour palette correspond to the multiplicity of words and phrases that impart

'colour' to a language. What is more, the repeated yet subtly varied arrangement of motifs in a carpet develops a syntax that defines connections and inter-relationships at a general level.

Once this carpet grammar has been assimilated, it is possible to penetrate the meaning of a carpet and decipher the whole spectrum of symbols inherent in its colours, motifs and overall design. This symbolism may have religious significance or esoteric connotations. As we will see, many carpets have a mythology and cosmology rooted in the most ancient beliefs and cultures.

'Decoding' a carpet's specific language and unravelling its individual syntactical structure is only one step on the way to uncovering its meaning and essence. It must never be forgotten that a 'language' can be specific to an entire technique or art form whose underlying principles remain to be understood. Accordingly, this book will examine individual motifs by reference to their origin, evolution and mutation. In other words, we shall consider not only the etymology of the carpet but its current lexicography and principles.

This implies taking a closer look at the carpet-maker's technique in much the same way as one might analyse the linguistic patterns adopted by a poet or novelist to forge his or her own personal literary style. There are guidelines and rules, most certainly, but these are invariably overlaid by individual preferences or social, cultural and religious variants. Thus, each ethnic group imposes its own variations on a style that is 'universal' and on a language that is 'common to all'.

Happily, motifs are like words: they have a past, a present and a future.

This guide examines the principal kinds of carpet and their language by reference to the main geographical centres of production. By definition, carpets are read line by line and phrase by phrase to the extent that, as befits a long oral tradition, each individual carpet has its own melody. The 'song' of the carpet is memorised and handed down as a component of folk memory. It is perhaps for this reason more than any other that carpets exert such a fascination, and that their harmonious permutations of colour and geometrical or figurative motif are a never-ending source of pleasure.

Given the scope of this introductory guide, it is clearly impossible to provide an inventory of every important carpet down through the ages. The finest examples are housed in museums or private collections and have been presented and interpreted in countless specialist studies. That being so, this book focuses most closely on carpets produced in the 20th century and, in particular, on those that are to this day still hand-woven by the nomad tribes of Arabia and Central Asia, or by artisans living and working in major urban centres with a long carpet-making tradition. Inevitably, such an overview will reveal both good and bad, and every effort will be made to guide the new collector through the complexities – and dangers – of buying carpets.

Some carpets are 'authentic' to the extent that their tradition is still vibrant. Others bear witness to an attempt to reconcile traditional design and European expectations. Still others are little more than servile copies of Western models such as the 'Aubussons' reproduced in factories in China and Pakistan. Their charm and sensitivity may nonetheless delight the eye, irrespective of the fact that they are shunned by experts and major collectors. As it happens, this was for many years the case with pileless kilim carpets and rugs, used – among other things – to mark off living areas within a nomad's tent. In fact, the astonishing and seemingly infinite variety and visual boldness of these kilims, woven by nomadic tribes along the ancient Silk Road, never ceases to amaze and delight.

The Silk Road, travelled by nomadic tribes and merchants all the way from Central Asia and Asia Minor to China, played a prominent role in the transmission of textile design and motif. A case in point is the progressive mutation and hybridisation of the 'dragon' motif.

The influence of carpet and rug design on contemporary artists says much for its extraordinary modernity. Paul Gauguin and his close friend Vincent van Gogh were both fascinated by carpets and in particular by their expressive use of colour. Gauguin exhorted his fellow artists to study the carpet-maker's art which, he insisted, contained "all there is to know about colour and its use". Later, Henri Matisse drew heavily on geometrical kilim designs as an inspiration for his positive-negative paper cut-outs, noting how "the East treated pure colour as an expressive vehicle". Matisse was not alone: many other modern painters saw oriental carpets as a model, among them Paul Klee, who interpolated into his canvases the abstract motifs of carpets and tapestries from the western Tunisian city of Qafsah (Gafsa) and, in his Mosque Doorway (1914), employed the chequerboard pattern of an Anatolian kilim.

As we shall see, each carpet has its own extraordinary tale to tell. It is hoped that this book will encourage the uninitiated to embark on a fascinating voyage of discovery.

Carpets through the ages

Pileless corded carpets, or kilims, can be traced back to the most ancient traditions of weaving as practised in Upper Mesopotamia around the fourth millennium B.C.

 The earliest known representation of a loom appears on a terracotta seal from Sumer (present-day Iraq). This shows in stylised fashion two weavers sitting cross-legged in front of a horizontal loom – adopting the same position and employing the same age-old technique that the nomadic kilim weavers of Asia and Arabia perpetuate to this day, some 25 centuries later.

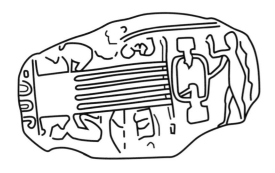

Vestiges of the knotted-carpet technique are also found today in a Mesopotamian weave – known to the Greeks as *kaunakes* – which is described in perfect detail in a passage in Aristophanes' play *The Wasps*. This fabric is often seen on Sumerian statues and figurines, where the cloaks or capes worn by the figures are fashioned from a

thick material consisting of regular rows of tufted wool reminiscent of a sheep's fleece. It is fascinating to note that this long-tuft weave – a distant ancestor of the knotted carpet – can still be seen in Epirus in Greece, where shepherds continue to wear a cape known as a *flocatta*. With the advent of tourism, the production of this 1,000-year-old fabric has flourished in the form of long-tuft multi-coloured rugs hand-crafted in the same manner as velvet, which is to say, with one strand as a base row or warp and a second strand comprising tufted knots. This is a more sophisticated technique than that found in the earliest *kaunakes*, where the tufts were knotted directly on the warp yarn in much the same way as in the spliced warp process used today.

 6

Left: Close-up of flocatta tufts. The effect is similar to that on the reverse of a rug woven by the soumak technique (see next chapter).
Above right: Metsovo/Epirus, Greece: Flocatta rugs drying in the sun after being cleaned and 'fulled' (tightened) to secure the individual knots firmly to the warp and weft yarns.
Below right: Flocatta pile in close-up.

Phrygian ceramic tiles showing a
cruciform motif identical to that in the
field and borders of the Pazyryk Carpet.

Detail of central cruciform motif from the Pazyryk Carpet.

THE OLDEST KNOWN KNOTTED CARPETS

It is perhaps impossible to substantiate this supposed link between knotted carpets and Mesopotamian *kaunakes*. What can be said with certainty, however, is that the precise origins of genuine knotted carpets remained a matter for conjecture until 1949. Until, that is, Russian archaeologist Sergei Ivanovich Rudenko entered the burial mounds (tumuli) of Scythian chieftains in the Pazyryk valley in the Altai mountain range in southern Siberia.

In Tumulus V, dated to the 4th and 3rd centuries B.C., Rudenko made an astonishing discovery. It appeared that the barrow had been opened and *left* open, probably in anticipation of the funeral ceremony for a Scythian chieftain. During the summer months, however, water from the melting snows seeped into the site and, with the onset of the harsh Siberian winter, froze into a solid block of ice that enveloped and protected the precious artefacts in the tomb. By some miracle, this icy sepulchre preserved a large number of materials and fabrics dating from 2,500 years ago.

Among the textiles found in Tumulus V was a fragment of wool fabric – woven into a kind of cord or braid similar to latter-day kilims and to Coptic and Chinese tapestries – whose principal motif was a frieze of high-tailed lions identical to those found on bas-reliefs in the Palace of Susa (south-western Iran). By far the most superb find, however, was a short-pile carpet measuring approximately $6 \times 6\frac{1}{2}$ ft (1.83×1.98 m) featuring 3,600 knots/dm^2 (square decimetre). The Pazyryk Carpet, as it has come to be known, is now preserved in the Hermitage Museum in St. Petersburg.

Various theories have been advanced with respect to the geometrical and floral design of the Pazyryk Carpet and its inherent symbolism. The central field, with its chequerboard design of floral star patterns or rosettes in each of 24 squares framed by 11 different borders, may allude to the Urartian sun motif. On the other hand, this cruciform motif, comprising four buds and four leaves, may also prefigure the 'cross of light' used both by the Phrygians – the same motif can be identified on Phrygian tiles now preserved in Istanbul's

Above: Detail of mounted Scythian horsemen from one of the borders of the Pazyryk Carpet.
Left: Detail of the foreign delegations depicted on the bas-relief at Persepolis. The Scythian horsemen are shown leading their horses by the reins in the same manner as in the Pazyryk Carpet.

Museum of Archaeology – and, much later, by Christian weavers in Armenia.

The outer border comprises winged griffins which, in many mythologies, are recognised as guardians of the dead. In this instance, they are enclosed within beaded medallions that recall those used by Sasanid (Persian) weavers to frame royal hunting scenes. The adjacent border is a frieze with 28 horses and riders, some mounted, others leading their mounts by the bridle.

According to Rudenko, this frieze – in some respects analogous to Persian bas-reliefs from the Achaemenid Dynasty – substantiates the Persian provenance of the Pazyryk Carpet. In fact, the procession of riders and mounts is reminiscent of that shown on a 360-ft (110-m) bas-relief in Persepolis that depicts delegates of the various tribes subjugated by Persia who have come bearing tributes to King Xerxes. This monumental bas-relief, for all the world like an extended cartoon strip, features all the races and ethnic groupings that were destined to emerge as the major carpet-makers of Central Asia and Asia Minor.

The Persepolis bas-relief shows the Scythian delegation leading their mounts by the reins. They are coiffed in the same manner as in the Pazyryk Carpet, their hair knotted below the chin, and sport the same style of beard, the same pointed cape, the same long tight-fitting pantaloons, and the same tunic brought together with a belt, from which dangles a sheathed sword. The heads of the small, thickset steppe ponies are adorned with a sort of plume; their tails are knotted and their saddles are decorated with sinuous branch motifs very similar to those portrayed on the Pazyryk Carpet.

In his remarkable 1991 study of the Oriental Christian carpet, historian Volkmer Gantzhorn sets out to prove that the Persepolis delegation was not of Scythian but of Armenian origin; and that the Pazyryk tombs were not Scythian but Phrygian-Armenian (the Armenians being descendants of a Phrygian-Urartian people). In other words, he accepts this carpet – woven in the south-east Caucasus – as evidence of Armenian manufacture. He is entitled to this theory – after all, there are no limits to speculation, as we shall discover during this sketch of the origins of carpets and their motifs from ancient times to the present. All one can say with certainty, however, is that it would be a further 1,000 years before other well-preserved carpet fragments were found.

THE SPRING OF KHOSRAU CARPET: GARDEN CARPETS

No substantive or material evidence of carpets has come down to us from the 1,000 years or so after the date of the Pazyryk Carpet. All that remains from this hiatus of history are certain stone inscriptions, tiny textile fragments found in various Egyptian and Central Asian tombs, and accounts written by contemporary writers. Among those accounts are those that testify to the celebrated Spring of Khosrau carpet attributed to Khosrau (Chosroes) I, who ruled over the Persian Sasanid Empire from 531 to 579 A.D. This carpet – also known as the Winter of Khosrau carpet, because it was sometimes rolled out for display in winter – was used to decorate the royal audience hall in the Palace of Ctesiphon, the capital of the Sasanid Empire. The walls of the audience chamber were hung with silk draperies depicting hunting and battle scenes in honour of the king. The floor, according to chroniclers of the period, was covered by a sumptuous carpet, woven in a mix of silk and wool, with interspersed threads of silver and gold.

According to the eye-witness reports that have come down through the ages, this was the most magnificent carpet in the history of the Orient. The Spring of Khosrau carpet symbolised 'Paradise on Earth'. It took the form of a vast garden with fruit trees, flower-beds and fields of wheat criss-crossed by irrigation canals, the overall impact heightened by innumerable pearls, emeralds and rubies placed so as to suggest fruits and flowers (hence the generic term 'garden carpet'). Rock crystals added 'authenticity' to the water in the canals and large emeralds intensified the green of the lawns. Irrespective of the time of year, the king would gaze on his carpet, reflecting on the Eternal Spring that would be his reward on his death and inevitable ascent to Paradise.

The Spring of Khosrau carpet met with a tragic end when the first Arab invaders poured into Persia in the year 637 A.D. They were fascinated by the prodigious richness of this garden carpet and, anxious to pre-empt any quarrels as to its ownership, decided that the best course of action was simply to cut the carpet into small pieces and divide the spoils. Sadly, none of those precious fragments has been recovered. We do not even know whether it was a knotted carpet comprising several

A rare and beautiful Persian carpet from the end of the 17th or beginning of the 18th century. A central axis divides the field into compartments holding mirror-image motifs.

panels stitched together, a pileless carpet like a kilim or a *soumak*, or even a huge piece of embroidery.

The garden theme would be reprised by Persian workshops in the 16th and 17th centuries and is perpetuated to this day by wandering Bactrian tribes. A luxuriant garden represented the ultimate vision of Paradise to the ancient tribes of Moslem nomads wandering through the arid desert. Later – in Baghdad, in Damascus, in Granada – caliphs were to lay out magnificent gardens like those evoked in *The Arabian Nights*. Those gardens, like the Spring of Khosrau carpet, conjured up Paradise in the guise of four massive blocks of flowers, shrubs and trees bisected at regular intervals by pools and watercourses, reproducing the formal layout of the four gardens of Paradise described at length in a Persian text on the Koran.

An 18th-century garden carpet can be admired today in the Musée des Arts Décoratifs in Paris. It is attributed to a maker in Kerman. Later garden carpets – those by Kurdish weavers, for example – tend to be less figurative and, on occasion, almost abstract kilims. Good copies are available even today.

OTTOMAN CARPETS AND RENAISSANCE PAINTERS

It was noted in the Preface that a number of important modern artists have found inspiration in the designs used in carpets and kilims. This influence on painting is by no means new. In the 15th and 16th centuries, the painters of the Italian Renaissance and the Flemish School were clearly fascinated by the first knotted carpets which, originating in the sprawling Ottoman Empire, were disembarked by Italian merchants at the ports of Venice, Genoa and, later, Amsterdam.

The first artistic representations of an Anatolian carpet go back to Giotto, whose fresco of the *Vision of St. Francis*, in the church at Assisi, dates back to 1300. Giotto's carpet has a design of crosses enclosed in a circle. It would later form the backdrop to numerous large repesentations of the Crucifixion. On occasion, the star-studded cross is contained within a lozenge-shaped medallion or 'tilted square'.

In his *Madonna with Canon van der Paele*, painted around 1436, Jan van Eyck incorporated a carpet with a ground composed of large star-studded yellow crosses interspersed with dark green 'crosses of light' motifs of Anatolian origin. These are the forerunners of various guls – geometrical motifs set into a hexagon or octagon – which later came to be identified with the individual artist who habitually employed them – for example, the 'Holbein *gul*' or the 'Lotto *gul*'.

In his 1479 painting of the *Mystic Marriage of St. Catherine of Alexandria* and in his *Vase with Flowers*, the Flemish painter Hans Memling reproduced a carpet with a red ground featuring a basic motif in the form of a stepped crotchet or hooked design within a hexagon, a motif commonly known as a 'Memling *gul*'. This same quasi-architectural motif is still found in present-day Anatolian carpets, especially in those from the towns of Obruk and Derbent near Konya, where there is a substantial Armenian community. This self-same stepped-cross motif is also found in various 12th-century Armenian miniatures that may well have served as a model for the carpet painted by Memling.

On his travels through the Seljuq princedoms at the close of the 13th century, Marco Polo was moved to comment on the "most marvellous carpets" and "the silk fabrics in crimson and other magnificent colours". He went on to record the most important towns as Kogni (today's Konya), Kayseri and Sivas – clear proof that the presumed carpet-making centres that inspired Renaissance artists were already well established by the time Marco Polo visited the region in and around 1271.

Left: 16th-century carpet from western Turkey. The central motifs almost certainly reprise a clan emblem or tamga *later known as a 'Holbein* gul'. *The pseudo-Kufic script of the outer border also features in Holbein's painting.*
Opposite page: Hans Holbein's Portrait of Georg Gisze, *painted in 1532. The carpet has* gul *woven on a deep red field and borders in pseudo-Kufic script identical to the 16th-century Turkish carpet shown on this page.*

Ottoman carpets certainly provided inspiration for two celebrated 16th-century painters, Hans Holbein and Lorenzo Lotto. In his remarkable *Portrait of Georg Gisze*, painted in 1532, Hans Holbein posed his subject at a table covered by a deep red carpet with geometrical motifs made up of horizontal rows of hooked medallions set within an eight-point star. A similar carpet 'tablecloth' appears in Holbein's *The Ambassadors*, of 1533. Other paintings – among them Carlo Crivelli's *Annunciation* of 1486 – also portray this same type of Anatolian carpet, albeit used not as a table covering but as a decorative fabric that would have been draped from a window during festivities or processions.

Above: 16th-century Anatolian carpet. The red field is filled with a yellow grid comprising cruciform motifs.
Left: These 'grid' carpets were known as 'Lotto carpets' following their portrayal in several paintings by the Venetian artist Lorenzo Lotto (1480–1556), including that of the San Giovanni di Paola basilica in Venice, depicting St. Anthony, the archbishop of Florence.

The *kotchak* cross that appears in such detail in a Memling *Madonna* (painted in 1494 and now hanging in the Uffizi in Florence) has a long tradition extending at least as far back as Urartian bronzes of the 8th century B.C. As the following pages will show, the motif of the star-studded cross is one that recurs frequently on Anatolian carpets and has done so since the Seljuq period. It is an important term in the vocabulary of carpet design.

The works of the Venetian painter Lorenzo Lotto exhibit a very unusual arabesque *gul* known, inevitably, as the 'Lotto *gul*' (or, alternatively, the 'Holbein Carpet, Type II'). These carpet motifs almost certainly originate in Central Anatolia – most probably in the region around Konya.

Some museums own 'Holbein' or 'Lotto' carpets dating from the 16th century, but most examples were woven later – in the 17th and 18th centuries. Certain commentators believe the latter to have been woven in the workshops of Ushak (Usak). While it is true that Ushak medallion carpets often reveal a design similar to those immortalised by Holbein, some caution is nevertheless advisable when attributing their exact provenance.

THE TAMERLANE CARPET

At the close of the 14th century, the Mongols, under their warrior ruler Genghis Khan, were displaced by the nomadic warlord Timur the Lame (1336–1405), commonly known as Tamburlaine or Tamerlane. Once Tamerlane's military hordes had conquered territories extending from Syria all the way to modern India, only one pocket of resistance remained in Asia Minor – in the person of Yildirim Bayezid, the young caliph of the Ottoman Empire (r. 1389–1402). Their armies clashed on July 20, 1402 at Angora – the present-day Ankara – and the caliph was defeated, taken prisoner and, according to some historians, suspended in an iron cage until he rotted away and died. Others maintain that Tamerlane was so impressed by his adversary's courage that he invited him to his tent to conclude a peace treaty. In his book on Turkish carpets, J. Iten-Maritz subscribes to the latter (and perhaps more plausible) version, adding that

this historic encounter took place "in the middle of the carpet".

Nomadic custom and tradition had long held that a person standing on the central carpet in the tent enjoyed the absolute protection of his host. History does not record if the 'Tamerlane' carpet in question was a double *mihrab* prayer mat or a two-columned *ladik* – a 16th-century example of which is on view in Istanbul's Islamic Museum. Either is possible and, once again, the story is open to different interpretations, not least because Tamerlane was at the time in the heart of Anatolia and within striking distance of several major carpet-making centres.

Iten-Maritz goes on to refer to this "asylum carpet" as an *odchaklik* (or *odshalyk*, a double *mihrab* prayer mat) but declines to specify where it originated – doubtless in Ushak. What we do know is that the carpet was decorated with Tamerlane's *tamga*, the symbol of ownership that nomads used to brand their livestock and identify their tents and household items. The *tamga* motif was commonly woven into carpet designs and, on occasion, was even the principal motif.

Tamerlane's *tamga* was very similar to that used by Genghis Khan. It comprised three small and almost circular octagons with a dentate or jagged red square in the centre, set in a triangle above three ribbon-like clouds. These hooked lines (of Chinese origin) represented lightning and corresponded perfectly with Tamerlane's emblematic device of 'thunder and lightning'. The same symbol for thunder – tiny balls of fire – is also taken up in a brocade caftan worn much later by Sultan Selim I (r. 1512–20) of the Ottoman Empire.

Some experts believe the eight-hooked motif, found to this day on some Turkmen carpets, may represent the eight legs of the tarantula spider – a creature the nomadic tribes viewed with the utmost respect. In the case of Tamerlane's carpet, historical fact and colourful legend thus combine.

Given the reduced space available in the present context, it is not possible to discuss in any great detail every one of the magnificent carpets preserved in museums and illustrated in books. That said, the chapters focusing on the different types of carpet each essay a brief historical overview of the major production centres and attempt to explain the influence of age-old motifs on contemporary carpet design.

Above: A weaver from Qashqai (Iran) dipping different length wool yarns into a pot of vegetable dye (red madder).
Opposite page: A Kurdish shepherd from the region of Van (Turkey) wearing the characteristic wool cape.

Manufacturing techniques

Wool quality is a key factor in imparting sheen and durability to a carpet. The supple elasticity of wool makes it the ideal material for the manufacture of top-of-the-range carpets because individual tufts do not flatten underfoot, with the result that the pile springs back and so retains its shape.

RAW MATERIALS

Sheep wool

Carpet wool comes from different parts of a sheep's fleece. The longest strands come from the shoulders, sides and upper legs, whereas wool from the back, neck and belly is shorter and tougher. The silkiest and most sought-after wool, *kork*, comes from the undersides of eight- to ten-month-old lambs. Wool quality depends on a range of factors – the breed and age of the animal in question, climate, diet, the altitude at which the animal grazes (wool from mountain sheep is tighter and finer than that of sheep from the plains), the shearing season (ideally spring and autumn) and, as noted, the specific part of the fleece from which the wool is gathered. Later on, we shall look at regional variants and peculiarities of wool, highlighting for example the exceptional quality of the supple and lustrous wools of Central Asia, which are used, among other things, to weave the magnificent *Tekke* carpets made by the Turkmen tribe of that name.

Wool shorn from living sheep is first rinsed to wash out impurities – here, as in the dyeing process, water quality is of paramount importance – then soaked in detergent (typically potassium carbonate) to remove the 'suint', a greasy, foul-smelling natural secretion. The wool is then rinsed again repeatedly before being sun-dried and carded.

Carding involves passing the wool strands to and fro between two flat pieces of wood studded

*Weaver teasing hank of hand-spun wool
prior to dividing and sorting.*

with hooked metal teeth. This process frays the wool and, at the same time, helps remove remaining impurities before spinning commences.

Wool from butchered sheep is known as *tablakki* or *tabachi*. It is treated with a caustic solution (quicklime) which renders it hard, brittle and less susceptible to dyeing; it is, quite literally, 'dead' wool.

Camel and goat wool

The nomad weavers' prime source of raw material is their livestock. In Iran and in Central Asia, camel-hair wool is used as the backing for some carpets. Its natural colours, ranging from a raw silk hue to a warm brown, make for attractive carpets that are both soft and durable. Goat-hair wool, by contrast, is drier and, where it is used, is often combined with sheep's wool during the spinning process. Goat wool is also widely used for day-to-day accessories such as horse or camel saddlebags.

Natural silk

Both the warp and weft of some carpets are woven entirely from spun silk, which commends itself on account of its delicacy, suppleness, incomparable luminosity, and remarkable tensile strength. Silk is also often used to pick out a particular motif or salient detail on a wool carpet, highlighting it to brilliant effect by contrasting the two materials. This is particularly true of 'silk flower' *Qum* carpets, where the silk threads also contribute to exceptional durability. In certain cases, inferior grades of 'silk' carpet are produced using artificial 'flock' silk. This detracts from the quality of the carpet and dilutes claims to its being 'hand-made'.

Cotton

Cotton has the advantage of being cheaper than other raw materials and, at the same time, of being hard wearing and capable of retaining its shape. Cotton yarn is used today to weave certain white sections of carpets produced in Turkestan and southern Iran. Less-than-scrupulous merchants occasionally try to pass these off as silk carpets by calling attention to the sheen that is typical of mercerised cotton (which has been treated with caustic soda to improve its strength and its

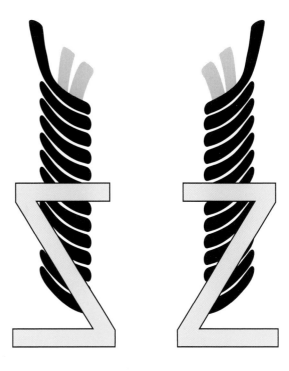

receptiveness to dyes). Both warp and weft threads of wool carpets are frequently made from cotton since it has greater tensile strength than wool. On the other hand, cotton is more difficult to dye than wool and, as a result, is rarely used in knotted carpets.

SPINNING

In certain rural regions, wool is still spun using a spindle or a wheel. As we will see in the section on dyeing, certain aesthetic considerations attach to 'hand-spun' wool thread, not least because of the desirability of 'imperfections' and irregular thickness in the thread.

When a spindle is used, the wool fibres can be spun into yarn either clockwise (to create what is know as a 'Z' twist) or anti-clockwise (an 'S' twist). Warp wool is more tightly wound than the wool used for the pile. Weft wool is wound differently still, and is typically finer and more compact to ensure it can be stretched taut between the rows of knots.

DYESTUFFS
Vegetable and animal dyes

Vegetable dyes have one important characteristic: in general they do not change colour to any great degree over time. In some instances, they even improve with age. Indigo blue is a case in point: far from fading, it becomes deeper and more intense as time passes, especially if it has been dyed repeatedly before the weaving process. Reddish-brown dyes extracted principally from the madder plant lose very little of their original colour with the passage of time; the same applies to carmine reds derived from cochineal. By contrast, yellows obtained from plants such as rocket or saffron crocus tend to lighten with age or, when chemically treated, to turn brown.

Qashqai weaver spinning wool with a traditional spindle.

As a general rule, darker colours are more resistant to sunlight than lighter colours and pastel shades. As it happens, this gradual process of colour change tends to result in heightened contrasts and may well have been what the weaver originally had in mind. Clear evidence of this is found in what is believed to be the sole extant *Seljuq* carpet from the 13th century, a specimen found in the Sultan Ala'ad-Din Mosque in Konya. The script that runs along the borders is woven in lighter tones that have faded over the centuries to soft sky-blues and pinks. By contrast, the indigo field is as brilliant as ever, enabling the Kufic script to stand out clearly against the ground.

One may find it hard to believe the inordinate time and effort that carpet-weavers traditionally put into the selection and preparation of dyes in a bid to achieve perfection. Before the dyeing process begins, the appropriate plants have to be selected and dried, and the wool itself has to be pre-treated to become 'mordant' (capable of 'fixing' the dye when it is applied). These time-consuming preliminaries go a long way towards explaining why vegetable-dye carpets are most sought after – and most expensive.

It is not necessary (given our scope) to explore the various 'recipes' by which vegetable dyes are prepared and applied. In practice, some of these processes are a well-kept secret that has been passed down by word of mouth from one generation to the next. A number of specialist studies have explored these formulae in exhaustive detail, however, and these are recommended reading for anyone wishing to delve more deeply into the mysteries of the dyer's art. In a later chapter on contemporary carpets, we try to indicate wherever possible those villages or workshops where vegetable-dye carpets (and good quality synthetic-dye carpets) are produced.

Over and above the specific formulae used by individual weavers in different regions, the key feature of a dyestuff is what is termed 'mordancy' – the 'fixing' or 'setting' quality. Depending on the region in question, weaver-dyers typically use alum – a hydrated sulphate of aluminium and potassium – in one form or another, possibly as chrome or ammonium alum, or frequently – and principally because they are easier to apply – ferric or tin alum. In other words, an astringent with a high tannin content is added to the dye-bath solution in order to 'set' the colour and give it a new intensity.

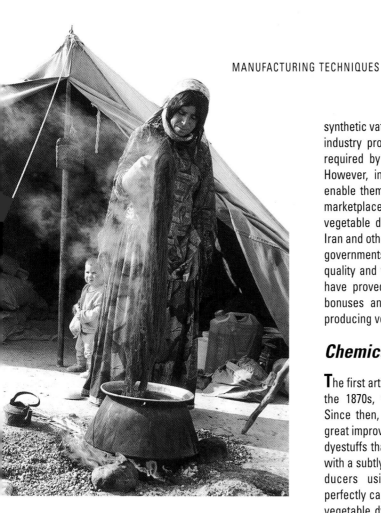

Qashqai weaver dipping wool into a pot of red madder dye. Dyeing wool in small lots results in uneven and irregular colours (known as abrash*).*

synthetic vat dyes are increasingly the province of textile industry professionals for whom the limited quantities required by individual craftsmen are of little interest. However, in order to supply craftsmen weavers and enable them to meet growing demand in the European marketplace, specialist workshops for the production of vegetable dyes have now been established in Turkey, Iran and other producer countries such as Morocco. The governments of those countries – anxious to sustain the quality and viability of the indigenous carpet industry – have proved supportive to the extent that they grant bonuses and subsidies to workshops that are again producing vegetable dyes.

Chemical dyestuffs

The first artificial aniline-based dyes, which appeared in the 1870s, were demonstrably coarse and unstable. Since then, however, the chemical industry has made great improvements, to the point where it can today offer dyestuffs that are stable, highly impervious to light, and with a subtly diversified colour range. Industrial dye producers using chromium-based fixatives are now perfectly capable of reproducing the colour spectrum of vegetable dyes. To the trained eye, however, there are appreciable differences in quality between vegetable and industrial dyes.

The celebrated carpet historian and collector Ulrich Schülmann may have been guilty of exaggeration when he remarked in 1974 that the beauty and charm of a *Khotan* or a *Kachgar* woven before 1860 are incomparably superior to that of the "grotesque caricatures produced fifty years later". On the other hand, it has to be conceded that vegetable dyes *do* have a depth, brilliance and fascination to which chemical dyes – irrespective of the progress they have made in the interim – will never aspire. A striking vegetable-dye mauve and a brilliant vegetable-dye green can exist in harmony side-by-side despite the audacity of their juxtaposition. The same cannot be said of the same colour contrast achieved by chemical means: there, the colours emerge as garish, offensive, even vulgar. This explains why, at the end of the 19th century, growing European demand for light-coloured carpets that appeared 'old' resulted in chemically dyed carpets being put through an alkaline or chlorine wash before they were exported.

Inevitably, perhaps, each weaver-dyer has his or her own 'secret' solution, but the most commonly used astringent in Iran, for example, is an extract of crushed pistachio shells and leaves.

Back when the carpet weavers of Asia Minor and Central Asia lived a purely nomadic existence, there was ample time for the preparatory steps outlined above. Today, however, there are external pressures that are alien to the traditional nomadic way of life. Faced with the need to increase output, today's weavers find it increasingly difficult to prepare, spin and dye their own raw materials. As a result, the current trend is towards buying yarn produced in industrial quantities in nearby urban centres or, failing that, towards using cheaper aniline-based dyes.

Itinerant craftsmen still exist in certain regions, plying their trade in the bazaar and *souk* (weekly market) and offering their services to craftsmen weavers. That said,

LOOMS

The two traditional types of loom have not changed appreciably over the centuries.

The horizontal or flat loom

This type of loom is used above all by nomadic weavers because it is easy to put together and take apart, even when a carpet is still in the process of being made. The loom proper consists of two parallel beams staked directly to the floor. The warp yarns are held taut between the two beams and the mechanism for raising and lowering the weft yarn to be subsequently threaded and knotted is a movable tripod. The weaver squats at the loom (on the carpet as it develops) and operates it by the simple expedient of moving the tripod into the required position (see right).

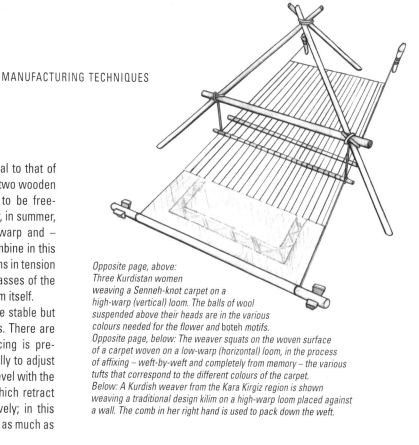

The vertical or upright loom

The principle of the vertical loom is identical to that of the horizontal loom except that it comprises two wooden uprights that allow the whole mechanism to be free-standing – against an indoor wall perhaps or, in summer, outside in the open. The tautness of the warp and – progressively – the weight of the carpet combine in this (at times rudimentary) loom to cause variations in tension and in weaving width due to the irregular passes of the weft and to the inherent instability of the loom itself.

Metal looms available today are clearly more stable but produce aesthetically less attractive carpets. There are also fixed-roll looms where the warp spacing is pre-regulated; this requires the weaver continually to adjust his or her position in order to remain at eye-level with the weave. Other looms have rotating rollers which retract the warp from the top, coiling it progressively; in this case, the length of the finished carpet can be as much as double the height of the loom.

Opposite page, above:
Three Kurdistan women
weaving a Senneh-knot carpet on a
high-warp (vertical) loom. The balls of wool
suspended above their heads are in the various
colours needed for the flower and boteh motifs.
Opposite page, below: The weaver squats on the woven surface
of a carpet woven on a low-warp (horizontal) loom, in the process
of affixing – weft-by-weft and completely from memory – the various
tufts that correspond to the different colours of the carpet.
Below: A Kurdish weaver from the Kara Kirgiz region is shown
weaving a traditional design kilim on a high-warp loom placed against
a wall. The comb in her right hand is used to pack down the weft.

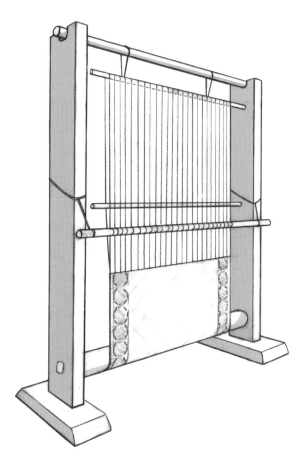

KNOTTED CARPETS

The warp

Different types of knot are applied to the yarn stretched across the frame of both horizontal and vertical looms. As we have seen, prior to weaving the warp yarn is held taut by tent stakes affixed to the floor. The weaver calculates the number of warp threads that correspond to the desired dimensions of the finished carpet and the number of knots required, the classic ratio being two warp threads to a knot. In effect, the finer the weave, the greater the number of warp threads. Thus, in the case of some very delicate silk carpets, there may be as many as 50 warp threads per inch of width (20 per cm).

As a rule, the warp yarn is a cotton thread strong enough to take the considerable pressure exerted by the weaver during the knotting process. In the absence of cotton, nomad weavers use wool mixed with goat hair. Very fine silk carpets made in urban workshops may also use warp yarn made of corded silk.

Selvage

Before starting to knot, the weaver creates an edge or strip, essentially a lower border against which the weft is secured. In Turkmen carpets in particular, this border – called 'selvage' – may be up to 28 in (70 cm) in length and, typically, will feature decorative motifs. Warp yarn fringes that extend below the selvage are subsequently trimmed using a variety of techniques.

Borders at each side of the carpet play a key role in imparting rigidity to the extent that the weft yarns come to rest against them. As a rule, the edges will comprise up to two or four threads that are thicker and stronger than the warp threads proper. Depending on how the weft yarn is interlaced with the border, different effects are obtained, notably flat or rounded edges. Some left and right edges are finished with a narrow flat-weave kilim strip (in the case of Turkmen carpets, for instance).

Knots

Once the lower selvage is finished, the weaver commences the knotting process proper. In fact, the term 'knot', though habitually used, is imprecise: strictly speaking, it is not a 'knot' but merely a looped connection between the warp yarn and the tuft of wool attached to it.

Suspended on a bar above the weaver are various balls or bobbins of wool arranged in sequence to correspond with the desired motif. The weaver selects the wool as required, inserts it between the warp threads and knots it into place, pulling the two ends downwards. The thread

is then cut with a small knife held permanently in the palm of the weaver's right hand. The weaver then moves on to the next knot.

In some regions, knot tufts are pre-cut with the aid of a baton whose circumference is equal to the length of knot required. A central groove carved into the baton allows the individual tufts to be cut off and stored in small boxes according to colour.

In certain high-output workshops, weavers – often young children – use not their fingers but a small hook into whose centre a blade has been inserted to enable the wool to be cut quickly. This speeds up the process considerably, though it has to be said that an experienced weaver can in any case average 15,000 knots every day.

The weft

Generally speaking, the weaver leaves two weft threads between each two rows of knots. The weft thread runs the entire width of the carpet weave (picking up each alternate warp thread). Two movable shuttles are used to divide the even and odd warp threads, starting from the bottom of the weave. The first weft thread is stronger and tauter than the second. Some weavers insert three threads for additional rigidity, and it is the weft threads pressing up against the knots that determines the relative tightness or slackness of a carpet as a whole. The weft thread may be in cotton (as in the case of *Nain* silk carpets) or in silk (as in an *Isfahan* silk carpet). In some fine-weft carpets such as those from Tabriz, the weft threads are fed through only after every fourth row of knots. The weaver uses a wooden or iron 'beater' or 'comb' to push each weft thread firmly down against the row of knots. The teeth of the comb are inserted between the warp threads and the new knots are pressed firmly into place with a series of forceful downward strokes.

Pile

Once the knots have been pushed firmly into place every three to eight rows or so, the tuft ends are trimmed with scissors to obtain an even pile. The height of the individual strands typically varies between ⅛ in (4 mm) in the case of flat pile to ⅝ in (15 mm) or so for raised pile. The shearing operation is carried out once the carpet is finished but before it is removed from the loom. In urban workshops, this procedure is usually assigned to a specialist (known in Iran as a *pardachei*); in today's high-output carpet factories, the procedure is also carried out using electrical shears. By contrast, some nomad tribes use a sword to trim the pile, with uneven (but by no means undesirable) results.

Types of knot

Knot types may vary from one region to the next, but the two types most commonly used are the symmetrical Turkish or 'Ghiordes' knot and the asymmetrical Persian or 'Senneh' knot. Although both knots are designated by reference to a specific country, they are in fact used across many different regions. Thus, the Persian knot is employed widely in India, China and even in Turkey, while the Turkish knot is used in Iran. As may be seen from the illustration below, the Ghiordes knot brings both tuft ends to the surface symmetrically, whereas the Senneh knot brings each end of the tuft to the surface separately. Both types of knot can open to the left or to the right. The Turkish knot is the more solid of the two, but the Persian knot makes for a finer, 'rounded' finish, facilitating the transition from straight lines to curved.

A third knot type – the so-called 'Jufti' knot – extends over four rather than two warp threads, thereby reducing the number of knots overall and saving both material and time. As a result, however, it makes for a carpet structure that is slacker and inherently less stable.

Cheaper machine-made carpets have 'knots' formed by a wool thread passed through the canvas base and glued on the reverse. Hand-knotted carpets, by contrast, exhibit considerable irregularities. To ascertain whether a carpet is hand-knotted or machine-made, just look at the reverse.

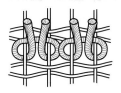

1. Turkish (Ghiordes) knot

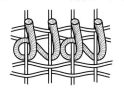

2. Persian (Senneh) knot

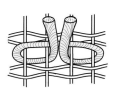

3. Jufti knot (double Turkish)

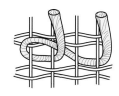

4. Jufti knot (double Persian)

PILELESS CARPETS

Kilims

The process used to weave kilims is identical to that used today to manufacture Gobelin or Aubusson tapestry. The word 'kilim' is derived from the Persian term *gelim*, which means to 'fashion' or 'weave', and the pileless kilim may be said to represent the classic art of weaving *par excellence*.

The kilim is a flat-weave floor covering hand-woven by tapestry techniques. The corded surface effect – the 'rep' – comes about in essentially one of two ways: when the weft thread completely covers the warp thread, the kilim is described as 'weft-rep'; conversely, when the warp thread completely covers the weft thread, the resultant kilim is described as 'warp-rep'.

The surface texture of a kilim becomes increasingly delicate in direct proportion to the number of warp threads and their proximity to one another. The finest kilims, from Dehna in north-west Iran, boast up to 10 warp threads and as many as 114 weft threads per inch (4 warp and 45 weft threads per cm). The result is a floor covering that is thin but extremely dense and hard-wearing. The thickest kilims have about 7 warp and 25 weft threads per inch (3 warp and 10 weft threads per cm).

Kilim motifs are woven in such a way that the weft threads never completely cover the entire width of the

Left: A kilim in close-up. Note the vertical relays separating each motif.
Right: A soumak in close-up. Note the 'geometrical' style of the animal shapes as a result of this technique using interposed additional weft yarns.

warp but only the width of each individual pattern or motif. Thus, threads of each colour and motif are tied off either vertically or horizontally. Weavers are adept at closing off each vertical design from the next, and the gaps between motifs are reduced to an absolute minimum to ensure overall stability. When finally taken off the loom, the kilim is finished by means of a virtually invisible needlepoint stitch.

Weft threads are usually joined in saw-tooth fashion, but many regional variations exist. Sometimes, additional weft threads are inserted to correct any variations in weft thickness, a technique that creates a heightened impression of weave density, particularly at the top of curved motifs.

Cicim

Skilled weavers also employ a technique – known *cicim* in Persia, *zili* in Anatolia and *driadi* in Europe – which consists of creating small raised patterns on the underlying kilim framework. This is achieved by inserting additional weft threads above and below the warp in a process that is, in essence, identical to that used to create brocade motifs. The superimposed weft threads are continued behind the warp without being cut.

Soumak

Soumak and *cicim* techniques are very similar, differing only to the extent that the former is applied over the entirety of the woven surface area. Weft threads are gathered around every three or four warp threads and fed back through the following two warp threads to create what is, in effect, a series of connected loops. Inevitably, the *soumak* technique implies geometrical patterns comprising oblique (diagonal) lines. Tuft ends are left loose on the reverse and the loose ends are snipped off.

The *soumak* variant is highly reminiscent of the 'tangled' coloured tufts that appear in Greek *flocatta* rugs. Bedouin nomads use this technique in their pileless *Hanbel* rugs and carpets.

A type of kilim known as a *Verbeh* is produced in certain regions of Azerbaijan and the Caucasus. Its characteristic feature is its mixture of superimposed and tucked weft threads.

Exploring designs and motifs

For those passionately interested in carpets, one question is of fundamental importance: How does one identify the intrinsic melodies and rhythms of an individual carpet?

Each carpet or kilim has its own 'sub-text', its own wealth of inherent intellectual, artistic, emotional and sensory messages.

To arrive at fuller appreciation of what a carpet actually 'means', a first and obvious step is to talk to experienced carpet merchants who, as a rule, will have a keen and informed interest in every item in their gallery. Alternatively, one might do worse than turn to Garry Muse's sensitive interpretations of the Anatolian kilims in the Caroline and H. McCoy Jones Collection, currently housed in the Museum of Fine Arts in San Francisco. His reflections on carpets and their meaning drive home the point that even the most modest kilim cannot be viewed merely as a simple and essentially 'decorative' floor covering or bedspread but, instead, must be seen for what it is – "an expression of abstract art at the most creative and profound level".

Knotted-pile carpet from Tabriz (Iran) with the portrait of Rumi (1207–73), the Sufi mystic credited with establishing the Whirling Dervishes. Rumi was originally from the Turkish city of Konya, where his commemorative mausoleum is a place of worship that attracts pilgrims from throughout Asia Minor.

To appreciate a carpet and what it means, it is essential to look both at its component motifs and at the whole that they form. Over time, one's knowledge and appreciation will be honed to the point where perceptions become more acute and one slowly but surely acquires a genuine understanding. To embark on a voyage of exploration into the complex and hypnotically fascinating universe of textiles is to engage in a dialogue that evokes atavistic memories and triggers long-lost awareness.

The 13th-century Persian (Sufi) mystic Rumi, who was one of the founders of the confraternity of Whirling Dervishes, speculated that the 'musical' cadences of the weaver's art are shrouded in mystery. "Were I to unlock that mystery," he once wrote, "it would stand the world on its head."

Appreciating a carpet presupposes a firm grasp of its many interconnected components, as well as an ability to respond

Weaver from the Isfahan region, Iran. Note the 'cartoon' template on the high-warp loom and the eye-level cartoon detail corresponding to the section of carpet she is in the process of weaving.

velours. The use of traditional dyes was deemed too time-consuming, and they were substituted by aniline-based synthetics. Moreover, the Jufti knot, the double knot tied on four threads instead of two, was increasingly used to cut the number of knots by half. As a result, the overall quality of design diminished and carpets sacrificed their strength and durability.

Worse, carpet merchants in Istanbul and Tehran began to commission carpets that were intended to service the expectations of an expanding foreign clientèle. As a result, carpet dimensions were adapted to accommodate the size and layout of Western drawing rooms: carpets were woven square instead of rectangular, and floral patterns and central medallions appeared, motifs that were alien to local and regional tradition. It is only now that we are beginning to appreciate the damage caused since the 1870s by these purely commercial considerations.

That said, some nomadic and semi-nomadic tribes continued to produce carpets and kilims that exemplified traditional skills and reflected traditional cultural and spiritual values.

CARPET COMPOSITION

The template

Although carpets are 'composed' in appreciably different ways from one region to the next, a weaver will always be able to decipher their message by 'reading' them as one might follow a musical score. There is a particular form of annotation which enables a Persian carpet design to be slavishly copied in every detail in, say, China or Pakistan; all that is required is to follow line by line – 'note for note' – the precise directions contained in the design template (see opposite).

The weaver first makes a rough sketch of the carpet that has been commissioned, developing a general impression of its composition and colours. Subsequently, each individual motif is redrawn in precise detail and transposed to squared stencil paper, with the colour of each individual knot carefully and accurately indicated. From that point on, the weaver's task is straightforward: all he or she has to do is to follow each line.

emotionally to its implicit musicality. For this experience to be meaningful, however, it is imperative that the carpet in question be genuine. A carpet made on a high-yield production line will never exhibit the same sensitivity as one hand-made by a nomad or urban weaver who works to his or her own interior rhythm.

At the end of the 19th century, when Oriental carpets began to enjoy increasing popularity in the West, order books were full. To respond to this surge in demand, traditional workshops organised themselves into quasi-industrial co-operatives and established spinning mills to turn out various grades of warp and weft yarn and

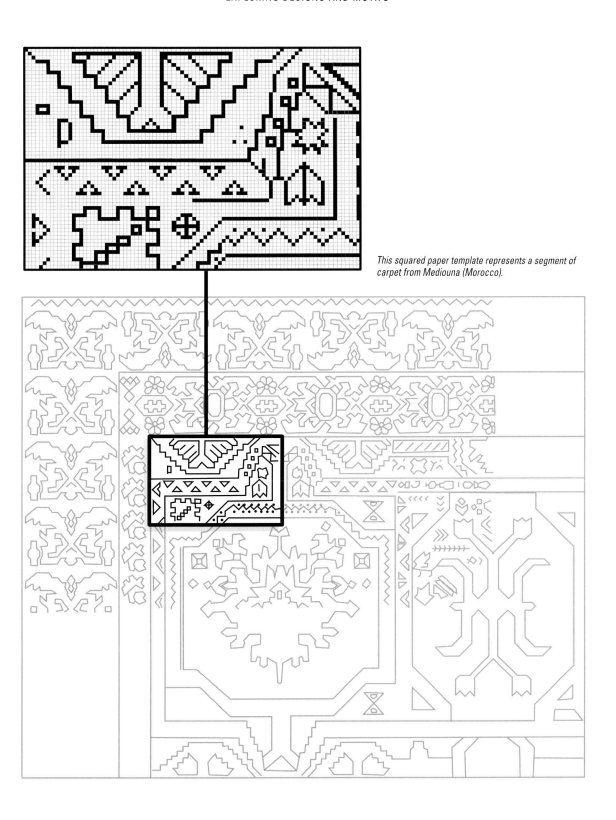

This squared paper template represents a segment of carpet from Mediouna (Morocco).

The process boils down in the final analysis to the equivalent of computer programming. To the extent that the weaver can track the design line by line and knot by knot, the entire operation passes out of the domain of the 'hand-made' and into the realm of industrial production, as on a Jacquard loom.

The song of the carpet

For nomadic or semi-nomadic carpet and kilim weavers, however, there were no universal templates. They alone were responsible for the choice and arrangement of motifs and colours. Here, oral tradition played the key role, with mothers passing on to their daughters their own intimate knowledge of how every carpet was woven and named. From a very early age, young girls would learn the 'song' of the carpet and its component motifs. A Berber weaver from Morocco once confided that she knew by heart the 'music' for over 100 carpets.

The principle is deceptively simple: it is sufficient to commit to memory – as one might a nursery rhyme or song – the specific succession of wool colours. Thus: "blue-blue-blue-red-red-yellow-yellow-yellow-yellow-green-green" and so on will be chanted as the carpet takes shape, inch by inch, until the 'song' ends and the carpet is finished.

Repeated motifs

Many carpets are decorated comparatively simply. One, two or three basic motifs are established and repeated across the surface. In isolated villages in Iran, for example, women entrusted with weaving carpets still use to this day a reference pattern known as a *waghireh* which displays exactly how a particular motif should be woven. By turning the reference pattern over, the weaver can also see clearly the tufted ends of the polychrome (multi-coloured) knots. From that point on, it is merely a question of carefully observing the sequence of colours. Over time, the weaver finds she has no further need of the *waghireh* inasmuch as she has memorised the 'score' of each individual motif.

So the weaver is 'programmed' – but only to a degree. As far as the overall composition of the carpet is concerned, it is she who orchestrates the motifs and selects the colours in which they are to be woven. She is free to insert, as and where she deems appropriate, such other smaller motifs as are available to her from her repertoire of designs. As a result, stylised silhouettes of people and domestic animals are frequently incorporated into the overall design, as is the case with *Kirwan* and *Shiraz* weavers from the Caucasus and southern Iran respectively – two regions, incidentally, where master-pieces are the rule rather than the exception.

The master class

In the Orient and in those parts of North Africa penetrated by Islam, a prerequisite of urban carpet production – invariably more richly decorated than its tradition-based 'repetitive' rural counterpart – is a much broader knowledge of mathematics and geometry. In order to develop carpet designs with new and richer motifs, such as floral patterns and medallions, a new class of designer emerged – the master craftsman.

Typically, the master craftsman would be a town dweller who was better educated than the female weavers of the villages. This class of craftsman – known as *ma'allem* in Arabic and *ustad* ('carpet-master') in Iranian – would routinely rough out more intricate designs and, on request, would travel to rural districts in order to execute specially commissioned projects (such as weaving a carpet intended as a wedding gift). The host family would offer hospitality and would compensate him at a predetermined rate for each measured length of carpet he wove. As part of the arrangement, the head of the family would also make provision for delivery of wool in the quality and quantity required and ensure that the wool was dyed in the colours specified by the *ma'allem*. Typically, the *ma'allem* would work on the upright loom belonging to the family in question, and would call on various qualified family members to assist him. Needless to say, the *ma'allem*, like the nomadic weavers, would have committed to memory the 'scores' of hundreds of carpets, each with its own name. As a rule, he would take a stick and trace out in the sand the outline of the carpet model he proposed to make. As in an urban workshop, he would then call out the colour scheme, slowly chanting the individual colours one by one to allow the nomadic weavers to recognise and follow his intentions knot by knot. Clearly, as many carpets could be worked on as there were looms available.

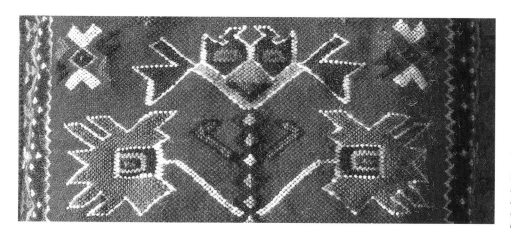

Detail of a stylised Tree of Life motif that clearly illustrates the rhythmic and colour patterns used.

Hanbel *design showing rhythmic variations.*

The musicality of the carpet

A. V. Pop, a connoisseur of Persian art, wrote in 1926 that one of the salient features of carpet design was "its similarity with melody and with poetry". One can only concur, bearing in mind that, to the extent that every mode of Persian music boasts its own melodic repertoire, there are clear analogies between melodic rhythm and the spatial organisation of a carpet.

Although weavers may employ different carpet-weaving techniques, they all work essentially from a common vocabulary and with a common store of basic rhythmic effects designed to achieve compositional harmony and overall coherence. As M. Messaoudi has noted with regard to the weavers of the Middle and High Atlas in Morocco (who, to this day, still design carpets without a pre-established template), "the art of weaving is visual when one considers the end-product, but essentially musical in terms of its conception and execution".

In short, a carpet is composed on the basis of several 'melodies' that are introduced as a traditional arrangement of motifs, each with its own specific tonality and variations. This melodic line is played over an underlying rhythm that subtly shifts and changes, so that the chromatic and rhythmic interplay of the finished carpet emerges, at times, as a work of almost symphonic proportions. The schematic of a *Hanbel* (left) provides a clear illustration of this.

One cannot emphasise too strongly the close parallels between carpet weaving and music. The 'performer'

A Kurdish grain pouch with hooked gul patterns typical of Anatolian kilims. Repetition of the identical gul in a range of colours develops a 'musical' score that is built up from a series of juxtaposed motifs.

A carpet's rhythms

Various elements are subsumed into the term 'rhythm' as it applies to carpet design. It covers the rhythm inherent in the repeated movement of knotting each tuft; the rhythm dictated by changing colours and their respective tonalities; the counterpoint achieved by contrasting raw materials (such as the apposition of silk and wool); the rhythm that ensues from repetition and inversion of individual motifs; the changing rhythms imposed by the interplay of different techniques within the overall compositional framework (knots, pileless or corded weave); and the all-embracing rhythm intrinsic to the finished product as a whole.

A textile 'score' emerges from the linear and sequential development of a set of signs. Thus, a carpet can be read 'line by line' (weft by weft) in much the same way as a melodic line can be tracked over a musical score. Certain motifs emerge over and over again, like the repeated verse and refrain of a piece of music.

In sum, the various motifs in a carpet are assimilated as one might assimilate a musical composition – movement by movement. It is no coincidence that the two genres are so often compared and described in almost identical terms: 'alternation', 'variation', 'inversion', 'rhythm', 'harmony', 'colour'. The weaver's art is a musical act both in its execution of rhythmic sequences and fragments and their juxtaposition and in the basic melodic perception invoked by the tonality of contrasting colours. At times, what predominates is the rhythm that derives from permutations of motifs; at other times, it is the creative potency of colour that prevails.

(the individual weaver) is free to interpret his or her score by imparting 'pitch', 'volume', 'intensity' and 'sonority' to an individual note (which is to say, colour) but is not free to change or depart from it arbitrarily. In the case of the carpet, the melodic line of the 'score' comprises the coloured knots that make up the design. That said, there is still scope for variation and improvisation. Here, the parallel might be with jazz or with certain aspects of Bach counterpoint. To the extent that most rural carpets and kilims are made without recourse to a template, improvisation is perhaps as inevitable as it is important.

Kilims produced by nomadic weavers may be said to equate to folk music, an authentic art form often derided or even ignored. In the case of nomadic weavers, rhythm prevails over melody and geometrical design over pictorial content. In villages and small towns, by contrast, the sedentary weaver also has traditional folk roots and is required to comply with specific technical and artistic requirements mandated by the tribe, family or ethnic group to which she belongs. But she is comparatively free to specify her own colour palette and the size, disposition and sequence of traditional motifs. The rhythmic sequences will tend to be shorter and more orchestrated around a central theme or *leitmotif*. In this case, the pictorial will tend to prevail over the graphic rhythms preferred by the nomadic weaver. Above all, the technique and execution of sedentary as opposed to nomadic weavers differ in terms of how the design space is organised and filled.

What is particularly striking in the case of weavers from throughout Asia Minor and Central Asia is that they use virtually identical elements drawn from the same basic repertoire, but are capable of remarkable variations on the same theme, organising space and deploying design motifs with an astonishing degree of individuality and creativity.

In other words, the carpet is more than an unthinking juxtaposition of traditional motifs and colours. It is a synthesis of emotions – hopes and fears, pleasures and hardships, doubts and beliefs – that reflects the personal thoughts and feelings of its creator. As such, looking at a carpet should invoke in the viewer thoughts and emotions that are as intense as those experienced when contemplating any other genuine work of art, be it painting, sculpture or music. Messaoudi offers an excellent illustration of a carpet's melodic line in the case of a simple woven cushion from the Zaer region of the Middle Atlas.

Carpets currently manufactured in major urban workshops exhibit a musical form that approximates more closely to a symphony. As in music, however, everything depends on the composer. Attentive reading of the carpet's score will ensure that each knot is in its designated place, with each member of the 'orchestra' (the artisan weavers) playing his or her part. In essence, however, it is the composer/designer who is the principal figure, the conductor, as it were, the one who guides the weaver in the precise choice of pre-selected colours. The senior weaver is the leader of the orchestra who, in some workshops, may even perch on a raised platform and call out, knot by knot, the colours specific to each row. The weavers themselves are members of the orchestra. They each work to the same rhythm as their neighbours, following the score and fashioning the carpet. They are paid on the basis of completed knots per day. This is production-line work that reduces the weaver to the role of a skilled worker who has, however, no say in matters of creativity and improvisation.

The workshop owner, who is often a carpet merchant, is now increasingly conscious of growing Western demand and, as a consequence, is concerned more with quantity than quality. Sometimes he will not hesitate to exploit child labour – both girls and boys – whose small and nimble fingers expertly tie the finest of knots, notably in silk. Output from these workshops is regularly claimed to be 'hand-made'; perhaps so, but the designation glosses over a considerable quotient of human exploitation and misery. In sum, it is better to acquire a high-quality industrially manufactured carpet, particularly in the case of designs by a contemporary artist, than to give implicit support to this form of surrogate artisanship carried out by a workforce that is shamefully over-exploited and underpaid.

As we shall see, however, a number of countries have finally taken appropriate measures to safeguard their textile heritage. Among those measures are stringent controls imposed on workshops to ensure that they produce genuine quality products and encourage fresh creativity. When all is said and done, the creative tradition is *always* contemporary.

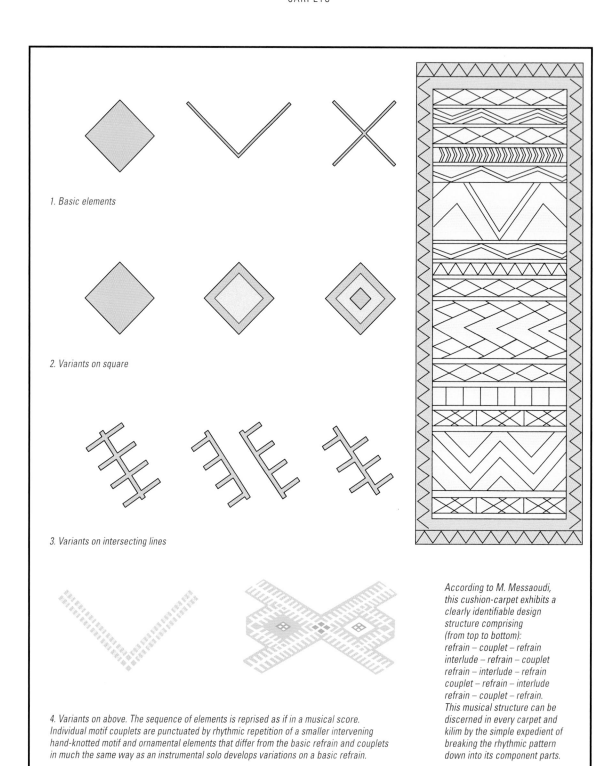

1. Basic elements

2. Variants on square

3. Variants on intersecting lines

4. Variants on above. The sequence of elements is reprised as if in a musical score. Individual motif couplets are punctuated by rhythmic repetition of a smaller intervening hand-knotted motif and ornamental elements that differ from the basic refrain and couplets in much the same way as an instrumental solo develops variations on a basic refrain.

According to M. Messaoudi, this cushion-carpet exhibits a clearly identifiable design structure comprising (from top to bottom): refrain – couplet – refrain interlude – refrain – couplet refrain – interlude – refrain couplet – refrain – interlude refrain – couplet – refrain. This musical structure can be discerned in every carpet and kilim by the simple expedient of breaking the rhythmic pattern down into its component parts.

SYMBOLS

Another and perhaps equally rewarding way to approach a carpet is by reference to its principal motifs and symbols. The individual signs and symbols are those that mankind has used since time immemorial to express thoughts and emotions and, above all, to communicate those thoughts and emotions to others. In a carpet, image and expression coincide. The carpet tradition is based on a process of oral transmission of motifs and their meaning, a vital component of what French author André Malraux once called the "boundless universality of form".

The notion of 'form' extends throughout the arts and crafts, but it is perhaps in the carpet that symbolism has been preserved most vigorously and prodigiously. The decorative vocabulary of carpets and kilims has ancient roots reaching as far back as the Neolithic period, though their symbolism is not always easy to interpret, particularly where the thread of oral tradition has been broken. The words of the celebrated Fulani philosopher Ambate Ba come to mind: "In our tribe, when an ancestor dies, it is a library that burns."

In carpets, as in cinema, meaning is found in the interstices between images. In other words, there is more to be gleaned *between* images than directly from the images. Essentially, meaning is conveyed through the vehicle of an abstract image. A carpet merchant and aficionado from Lyons summed this up succinctly when he famously said: "Ultimately, a carpet is a pretext." This formulation is acute and perceptive, because it is only by 'reading' a carpet attentively that one can hope to unravel the tiny puzzles that go to make up the greater puzzle of the carpet itself.

Left: Inkok basketwork vessel from Burundi (Central Africa) with chevron motifs made up of small lozenges.
Right: Ibiklmayi vessel from Burundi with zig-zag chevron motifs symbolising lightning (rain and fertility).
Below: Pots from the Neolithic site at Hacibar (Turkey) dating back to 5000 B.C. The chevron motifs are identical to those on the African vessels and are habitually used in the design of Anatolian kilims. The chevron is a universal symbol derived from one of the most ancient Egyptian hieroglyphs representing water, the source of all life.

Symbolism and mysticism

The overriding factor in understanding a carpet lies in appreciating its composition as a whole – its beauty, rhythms, harmonies, geometricality, colours and symbols. The last of these reflect a spirituality that has its roots in a profound faith in God as the creator of all things. It is of paramount importance to the weavers that their carpets find favour in the eyes of the Creator. Failing that, weavers will lose that intimate bond between themselves and their faith and its symbols and, should that happen, the carpet itself will lose its 'soul'. (Tradition holds that each carpet must contain a small imperfection, since God alone is perfect. This represents an interesting lesson in humility that some contemporary artists might well take to heart!)

The basic artistic motifs are archetypes to which can be sourced individual motifs and the variants and permutations dictated by ethnic tradition and cultural preference. This universal language of symbols also occurs repeatedly in bas-reliefs, in gold and silver jewellery and in pottery. Needless to say, it is a language that permeates the discipline of weaving and the textile arts. As the Persian mystic Mahmud Shabestari wrote in his classic *The Mystic Rose Garden* (published around 1311 and arguably the major work of Sufi or Islamic mysticism): "Non-being is a mirror, the world an image and Man the eye of the image in which the person is hidden. You are the eye of the image and God is the light of the eye. Who has ever seen the eye through which all things are seen? The world has become Man and Man the world."

Symbolism and syncretism

The language of the Oriental carpet, with its hermetic origins in religious confraternities, is the ideal medium to convey a religious message. Avicenna, the early 11th-century Arab philosopher-scientist from the renowned carpet-weaving region around Bukhara, reasoned that "the symbol is the mediator because it is silent, saying and not saying and thus enunciating precisely what it and it alone can express". That, in a nutshell, is the essence of the language of the carpet.

The trade routes that carried silk, spices and porcelain from the Orient to the West also spread knowledge of new motifs and symbols that were to influence craftsmen and artisans of every artistic persuasion. Accordingly, it is important to consider the carpet not as an essentially ethnic phenomenon but rather as an amalgam of all the major textile civilisations that met and commingled in that part of the world. Patronage, successive invasions and spontaneous or enforced migration all played a part in stimulating inter-ethnic, inter-cultural and inter-religious contacts. These are reflected in the hybrid motifs which, in the 2nd century B.C., saw the light of day in the China of the Han Dynasty, penetrated Sasanid Persia, and were ultimately disseminated throughout Islamic Persia.

So the symbolism of carpets needs to be interpreted carefully. The fact that a carpet features a cross (or any of the many variations) does not necessarily mean that it was woven by a Syrian or Armenian Christian. Moslems also employ the cross motif to convey religious or other esoteric meanings. This is a prime example of religious syncretism – the fusion of different, even opposing beliefs and their attendant symbolism – that is typical of Silk Road culture. It should never be forgotten that the Silk Road was not only a conduit for commerce and trade, it was also a highway of tolerance and mutual acceptance.

Times change. Thus, from the very earliest times until the beginning of the 20th century, nomadic or semi-nomadic weavers regarded the pomegranate not only as a decorative motif but as a symbol of fertility or, to be more precise, fecundity. Today, now that the oral tradition has largely lapsed, this progressively abstract motif can be

The Sufi 'divine breath' symbol is built up from four elements:
A. The basic form (the square)

interpreted in many ways. As a result, great care must be taken to avoid certain pitfalls and misconceptions when attempting to look through a particular abstract motif to discern its hidden symbolism. This is especially true when the symbol has lost its original significance.

The profusion of abstract geometrical designs in kilims and in certain carpets, allied to the exuberant colour schemes and the emotional – even mystic – meaning they imply, suggests that the weaver inhabits a 'parallel' universe of signs, symbols and colours, a universe that cries out to be explored in all its complex detail.

The magic of symmetry

That symmetry and mirror-image forms are key components of carpet design is self-evident. Visually, these effects impart a balance to the whole composition, creating a sense of continuity and coherence by reiterating the same motifs in different permutations. Aesthetically, these reciprocal motifs heighten the sense of movement and create a link between a carpet's 'field' and its decorative elements or, as Parviz Tanavoli noted in his benchmark study of nomad kilims, "a polyphonic field capable of developing greater depth and meaning". It has long been recognised, however, that the 'mirror image' effect is substantially more than a convenient and self-evident technical device. Far from it. The technique has philosophical and religious connotations for the weaver to the extent that the implicit juxtaposition of day and night, of plenitude and emptiness, is of divine

inspiration. To put it another way, the mirror image is an ideal device through which the 'non-material' nature of the invisible world can be communicated effectively.

In effect, the perfect symmetry of motifs to which kilims aspire has a specific function as a key to another 'hidden' cosmology common to many faiths. Symmetry is the key that unlocks the gateway to the spiritual world. The images seem to be temporarily suspended, almost as if the weaver has attempted to compress time or even to achieve an inversion of space and time by juxtaposing positive and negative images. In short, it is a world that has indeed been 'stood on its head'.

The circle that is the universe represents both the 'cosmology' of our primary physical relationship with the visible world around us and, on the other hand, the profound spiritual relationship between us and the invisible world, where the inner self aspires to attain the divine. It is this primordial relationship between the visible and invisible worlds – symbolised also in the Tree of Life – that enables us to visualise inner truths, to perceive unity in multiplicity, and to apprehend the ultimate 'meaning' behind the most abstract symbols of trees, birds or flowers.

At times, stylised animals are also arranged back to back, one mirroring the image of the other. To the weaver, this duplication of motif connotes the unity that underlies multiplicity, the essential continuity that underpins creative diversity.

Paradoxically, a perfect circle – with all its primordial symbolism – is rarely found in carpets or kilims

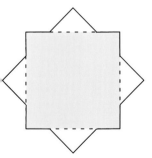

B. The extended square (breathing out)

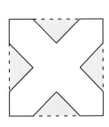

C. The closed square (breathing in)

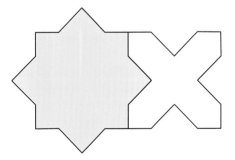

D. The two variants juxtaposed, with inhalation and exhalation combined to represent the 'divine breath'.

(with the exception of the medallions that feature on Persian carpets or the arches on prayer rugs). Reasons for this are primarily technical, since linear weaving techniques inhibit the creation of curves and circles. Accordingly, the circumference of a circle is usually indicated by a series of contiguous steps softened into a curve by a succession of very tight knots. As a result, the circle – usually bisected by a symmetrical axis symbolising primordial Man's essential dichotomy – remains a basic motif.

It is interesting to note that the burial mound where the most ancient knotted carpet of all was found – the Pazyryk Carpet – also contained examples of tapestries where stag and mythical bird motifs were cut from pieces of felt and leather folded in two, exemplifying the principle of mirror-image symmetry.

Every faith needs a language to communicate the transition from unity to multiplicity. In the case of carpets, the weaver uses numerals and geometrical forms to translate and communicate this sacred language. The hourglass motif is a case in point. Typically, this appears in the guise of two triangles, one inverted over the other. The overall effect is to create a mirror image where two worlds are juxtaposed – the ethereal or divine world above and the 'human' or natural world below. The forms and the light of divine inspiration in the upper triangle are reflected in the lower triangle. This special hourglass motif symbolises the notion of time running from one world into the other; it is also a symbol of relativity and ambivalence, since all that is needed to reverse the flow of time is to invert the hourglass, in other words to view it from the opposing direction. This invokes the concept of perpetual – eternal – motion, a concept that occurs particularly frequently in Kurdish prayer rugs, as shown here.

What this all adds up to is that those who work with textiles, irrespective of their individual speciality (knotted carpets or silk carpets, for example) have always formed a closed society, a sort of cabal with its own secret language of signs, symbols, myths and cosmologies of various ethnic origins. Theirs is a society to which there has been attributed an affinity with the divine. This spiritual heritage is conveyed from mother to daughter by transmitting the skills necessary to make a carpet 'sing'.

There is thus an underlying spiritual dimension to carpet-weaving that presupposes passionate commitment and intelligent dedication. If this commitment and this dedication are no longer in place, the end-product – the carpet – will still be decorative, but it will constitute little more than a lifeless artefact, a pale copy of its illustrious predecessors.

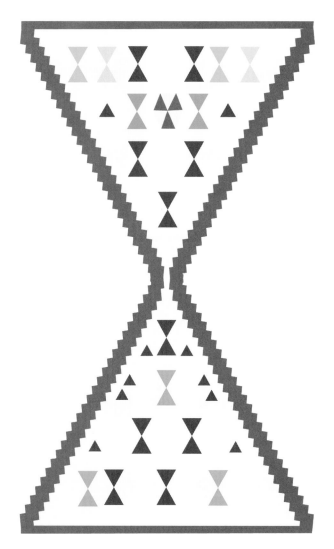

The hourglass motif.

Detail of a garden-carpet design that exemplifies the concordance between image and symbol. In the Moslem world, Eternity is expressed not only via the architecture of the miniature but also, as has been noted in the case of the Spring of Khosrau carpet, by decorating the carpet to evoke Paradise (the Garden of Eden). In the Koran, Paradise comprises four gardens which Sufi mystics called The Garden of the Soul, The Garden of the Heart, The Garden of the Mind, and the Garden of Being. These four gardens correspond to the four stages of Sufi initiation; they are also the four essential qualities that must be present in the 'perfect' carpet.

THE PRINCIPAL MOTIFS EXPLAINED

The illustrations on this and the following pages identify the principal motifs that have symbolic significance. The motifs are to some degree open to interpretation and are often wrongly attributed, their original connotations having been lost over the centuries. Nonetheless, they persistently recur in many designs as essentially decorative motifs that may vary from case to case. Being able to identify them is important not only as regards their original form, but also in terms of the variations and distortions which have ensued.

The geometrical composition of carpets or kilims, with their squares and chequerboard patterns, demonstrates the weaver's preoccupation with a 'modular' perception of the material world as a manifestation of a temporal and spatial universal order.

The cross and its variants

The motifs of the cross and its star-based variations are illustrated opposite and serve as points of reference for both carpets and Christian or Moslem kilims.

The cross is perhaps the universal symbol *par excellence*; it appears in virtually every ancient culture. The cross stands in close relation to the centre, the circle, and the square, all three of which have intrinsic symbolic value. The intersection of the arms of the cross corresponds to the centre; the cross is divided into four segments that are circumscribed by the circle; and it forms a square (two triangles) when its outermost points are linked by four straight lines to represent the cardinal points of the compass – and, by extension, the totality of the cosmos.

The cross reunites the four elements. The apex of the triangle represents fire and the male principle, whereas the lower points represent water and the female principle. The confluence of a triangle on the left represents air and that on the right, water. When the centre of the square coincides with the centre of the circle, this common point connotes – for Chinese weavers – the ultimate 'crossroads' of creativity.

Variants on the star cross (from top to bottom and from left to right):
Line 1: Simple eight-branch stars elaborated progressively to produce a 'crab' pattern.

An almost infinite number of carpet designs can be woven by incorporating the geometrical modules of the square, the rectangle, the triangle or the hexagon; that said, the cross module is a strikingly recurrent motif. As noted previously, the stepped cross is known as a *gul*. It is a motif that is found in Hans Memling's painting *Vase with Flowers*. The rows of the *gul* are separated by intersecting rhomboids. When the cross is set into a hexagon, all manner of overlapping becomes possible. The octagonal central medallion, for example, can be linked horizontally or vertically by short lines at each corner to form a new cross. Certain stepped-cross carpets have no crotchets, and other crosses can be floral or star-studded. The 'Lotto *gul*' is one form of the floral cross and is capable of being varied *ad infinitum* (see illustration on page 14).

The star cross

The eight-branch star is to all intents and purposes a four-arm cross lengthened by the addition of four triangles of equal dimensions. It has the basic configuration of the eight-branch medallion-star *gul* and can be composed asymmetrically. The basic configuration can accommodate a vast array of star shapes that can be compressed in width or extended in length. Accordingly, they may be:
– Stars in the form of a cross ('star crosses'), with or without crotchets, which suggest inward-turning rays of the sun.
– Classic eight-branch stars in the shape of a crab, but with crotchets added at each perimeter point. Among the many variants possible is the eight-legged tarantula spider motif.
– Stars in a lozenge configuration.
– Stars in a comb-shaped pattern.
– Stars in the form of a stairway ('stepped stars').
All the above variants are woven to fill out a given field. They may be superimposed in square or octagonal compartments or even overlap in order to fill the field completely. One classic design takes the form of a cross set in another formed by compartments, where the cross-shaped lozenges are diagonally divided into four.
Turkmen and Armenian weavers from Central Asia use most if not all of the possible variants and

Line 2: Hooked stars or bent rays.
Line 3: Crab and lozenge-form stars.
Line 4: 'Comb' or 'stepped-cross' stars and octagonal gul *star.*

permutations of this single central motif, either to complete the entire individual field or to flesh it out by adding alternating diagonal cross arabesques and *guls* which themselves create new crosses in the shape of star-cross rosettes.

In the final analysis, it does not matter whether the star cross is set into a hexagon, a square or a triangle, or whether those figures are themselves set into the star cross: the resultant 'negative' design matches the positive. What is more, it does not preclude any differentiation of the cross in terms of its colour.

To Christian Armenians, the cross motif was originally a sacred symbol. Over the centuries, however, it lost that significance and degenerated into what is, in essence, an embellishment used to fill out an individual carpet field.

The gul

The *gul* is an age-old motif in carpets and kilims that corresponds to the motif known as a 'rosette' when the latter is polygonal in shape. The Persians referred to the *gul* as *herati* or *fergham* when it was inscribed within a lozenge whose points were each embellished by a smaller rosette with a stylised leaf at each corner.

Iranian weavers use the term *gul* to refer to a motif inscribed within a hexagon and bearing a caption. For the Turkmeni, as we shall see later in the case of the magnificent *Tekke* carpets, the *gul* is a tribal motif known as a *tamga* (*niscian* in Persian). The Tekke also refer to these hexagonal motifs as 'elephant feet' or 'bird feet' to symbolise at one and the same time a leader's power and fragility.

The *tamga* serves to identify each individual tribe. Thus, the motif known as *tsin tamani*, or 'thunder and lightning', was the *tamga* of Genghis Khan. It comprises three small balls set into a triangle. Further examples of Turkmeni tribe *guls* will be referred to later, in the section on Central Asian carpets.

Several different types of *gul* can be identified, although the two most common are 'stepped *gul*' and 'crotchet *gul*' varieties. This does not preclude differentiation by colour, however, or by the insertion of various crosses that can also be stepped or lozenge-shaped. Once again, each basic form can be compressed or extended, and

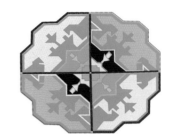

Tekke

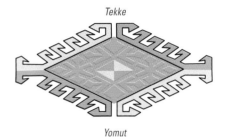

Yomut

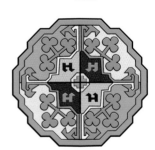

Salor

Ersaris

one form may be inserted into another. A chequerboard polychrome square set into the centre of a cross symbolises an enclosure or sacred place in the case of *Kasak* carpets in particular. Here, the 'magic square' is divided into nine compartments.

The crab or spider

The 'crab' symbol, derived from star-cross motifs, has several geometrical variations. The crab often features on the splendid kilims woven by the Shahsavan, an ancient nomadic tribe from Iran. Certain weavers insist that this motif, featuring a crotcheted lozenge contained within a hexagon, is the 'magic' symbol for an eight-legged spider, the deadly tarantula; moreover, that its inclusion in a carpet design – as in the case of the scorpion – is intended to protect it (and, presumably, its owner).

The spider is also a 'cosmic' symbol, its form echoing that of the sun and its rays. It is also, as a spinner of webs, the symbol for 'weaving' itself. In Central Asia, this motif represents the soul leaving the earthly body; in other regions, its thread establishes a link between Creator and created, between – effectively – Heaven and Earth. One variation of the crab motif is now commonly called the 'tortoise', an indication of how difficult it is to know today the precise significance of various motifs and their derivatives.

The cockerel

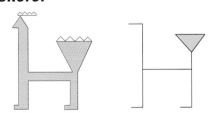

The 'cockerel', usually represented in heavily stylised form, is a Zoroastrian 'solar' symbol whose 'song' heralds sunrise and the break of day. To a Sasanid Persian *magus*, the cockerel was the creature which woke believers in order to recite their morning devotions (compare carpets from the Shiraz region) and this symbol has been taken up in Islam. It also has Christian relevance, the cockerel being a symbol of the resurrected Christ.

The swastika

This symbol – notoriously adopted by Germany's National Socialist Party – is in fact a universal one that appears as a decorative element on countless carpets. It is at one and the same time a symbol of good health and fecundity. Originally, this motif would have been placed in the centre of an eight-branch star and would have symbolised the rays of the sun in its implied rotational movement around a central point. The figure can be rotated in either direction and as a twin spiral, a symbol of cosmic energy.

The dragon

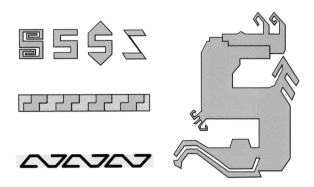

The 'dragon' motif appears in various stylised and abstract forms that are at times difficult to identify. To Oriental eyes (and, particularly in its place of origin, China), it connotes power, representing the creative life force of nature (*yang*) and the person of the emperor. There are many variants, including the flying or rain dragon, and the sea or marsh dragon (the creature is generally perceived as a guardian of water). Each dragon watches over a hidden treasure. The dragon motif is also used to denote happiness and wisdom.

By far the most stylised dragon motifs are those of the dragon *levant* and the dragon *couchant*, represented by a highly abstract 'S' shape woven either vertically or horizontally. To Armenian weavers, however, the 'S' motif might arguably have stood not only for a dragon but also for the first letter in the Armenian words for both 'God' and 'Jesus'. This connection may well be tenuous and even far-fetched, but interpretation often requires imagination.

The comb

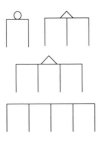 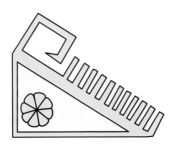

The 'comb' or *tarak* motif is a stylised representation of the weaver's comb. When it has five teeth, it can represent to Moslems the Hand of Fatima, a 'magic' amulet that is still worn today to ward off evil spirits and witchcraft.

The Tree of Life

  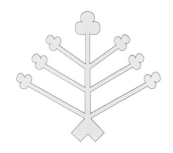

The many-branched tree is a cosmic symbol linking Earth and Heaven, the present and the hereafter. At the same time, however, it also stands as a symbol for the weaving process itself, where the union of warp and weft corresponds to the vertical element representing the trunk of the tree and the horizontal elements representing its branches. The Tree of Life nearly always appears in the *mihrab* woven into the prayer rug.

Whatever the species, the mythological sacred tree is always connected to immortality (as in the case of the 'tree' on which Christ was crucified before being resurrected). And, whatever the configuration of the motif, it is without exception composed on a vertical axis around which the branches are displayed in mirror image.

The boteh

The 'flowering bush' or *boteh* motif is a regular feature of floral compositions and is magnificently illustrated in the medallions that dominate the central field of Persian carpets. Originally, the *boteh* was a Zoroastrian flame symbol connoting immortality, and frequently appeared side by side with the cockerel motif in carpets from the Shiraz region. Together, these two motifs symbolised Paradise.

The 'flowering bush' motif usually appears in extremely stylised form – sometimes woven as a floral motif such as a small palm or rose bush, or as a violet or tulip. Its shape has been interpreted variously as deriving from an almond, a leaf, a fig, a pear, an inverted teardrop or even as a distorted representation of a (Zoroastrian) cypress motif. The 'bush' typically extends over the entire central field of the carpet (as in *Qum* carpets, with their multiple rows of regular *boteh* motifs) and is occasionally combined with other motifs.

These examples of motifs do no more than hint at the complex process involved in interpreting a carpet and deciphering its various levels of meaning, irrespective of whether one is a believer or a non-believer, Christian or Moslem, Buddhist or Taoist.

CARPET GEOMETRY

Basic principles

A carpet is a vast chequerboard of multi-coloured mosaic compiled stitch by stitch or knot by knot on the basis of specific motifs that integrate to create the overall design. Its two basic orientations – horizontal and vertical – are dictated by the vertical warp and the horizontal weft, the intersection of which creates an axis that is the point of departure for each ensuing stage of the weaving process.

The technique of weaving is actually very similar to that used in pointillist painting. The French artist Georges Seurat, a prime exponent of that style, felt that everything in the universe could, in essence, be reduced to 'vibrations' triggered by the juxtaposition of an 'infinite' number of small dots of colour.

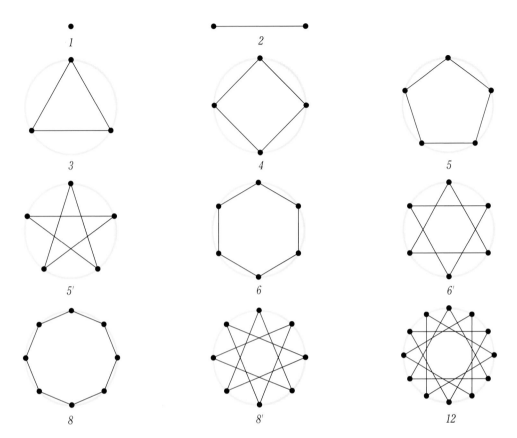

The earliest weavers sensed precisely this. They perceived the universe as either infinitely vast (clouds, stars, and so on) or infinitely small (the hidden substructure of materials visible to the naked eye, such as wool itself). They also knew that, while the world might be essentially 'modular', it was infinitely varied and never repeated itself. As a result, their carpets were made up of a seemingly infinite number of modular stitches and motifs.

The stitch or 'point' symbolises infinity and is effectively non-dimensional in the sense that it is perceived as no more than the intersection of dotted or continuous lines. The point and its repetition and permutation are the basis for every motif.

Though many weavers may not have been well-versed in formal geometry, they had an innate sense of it as an extension of their own feeling for rhythm and harmony. They wove instinctively, developing their own carpet language stitch by stitch and motif by motif. This is not to suggest that the process was haphazard. Far from it:

weavers developed a subconscious rapport between the language of geometry and the language of numbers. Thus, as the illustration above clearly indicates, 1 corresponded to a point, 2 to a line, 3 to a triangle, 4 to a square, 5 to the pentagon or five-branch star, and 6 to the hexagon or six-branch star. The latter, the 'Seal of Solomon', encapsulated all the elements in the universe as a synthesis of opposites: fire and water, earth and air, hot and cold, dry or wet, and so forth.

Similarly, in the case of two equilateral triangles superimposed to form a 'chromatic circle', the apex of the triangle pointing upwards would be rendered in red and its baseline points in blue and yellow, whereas the corresponding points in the downward-facing triangle would be in violet, orange and green respectively. The number 8 connoted the octagon or eight-point star and so on up to the twelve-point star corresponding to the twelve signs of the zodiac. Thus, although the design of a carpet invariably reflects the individuality and interpretative improvisation of each weaver, its formal components are archetypes that employ a common vocabulary and exemplify a common set of beliefs.

As noted earlier, the basic principle of inverted motifs is derived from a single unity, the square or rectangle, inscribed within a circle divided vertically or horizontally into two equal halves, each with a left or right diagonal that yields two triangles. A large number of distinctive motifs can be derived using these diagonals and parallels. As the illustrations below clearly show, the square module can accommodate left-to-right or right-to-left diagonals and inversions. Meanwhile, upward or downward extension of the basic motif offers ample scope for the creation of new motifs.

As a general rule, four-cornered motifs such as squares or crosses represent the male principle and three-corner motifs (the triangle) the female principle or deity. This basic vocabulary is capable of almost infinite expansion – just as the letters of the alphabet can be combined to form words that not only facilitate day-to-day communication but are also the vital building blocks of literary and poetic expression.

The base motifs can be articulated by size (small or large), by form (triangular, square, hexagonal, and so on), by position and by colour. For example, base elements 1 and 2 can be combined to create a *gul* (A) or a stylised flower (B); similarly, base elements 1, 2, 3 and 4 can be combined to form a more complex motif as in (C).

A square may be divided by one or two diagonals (5) or by one or two medians (6) or by two medians and two

Base elements

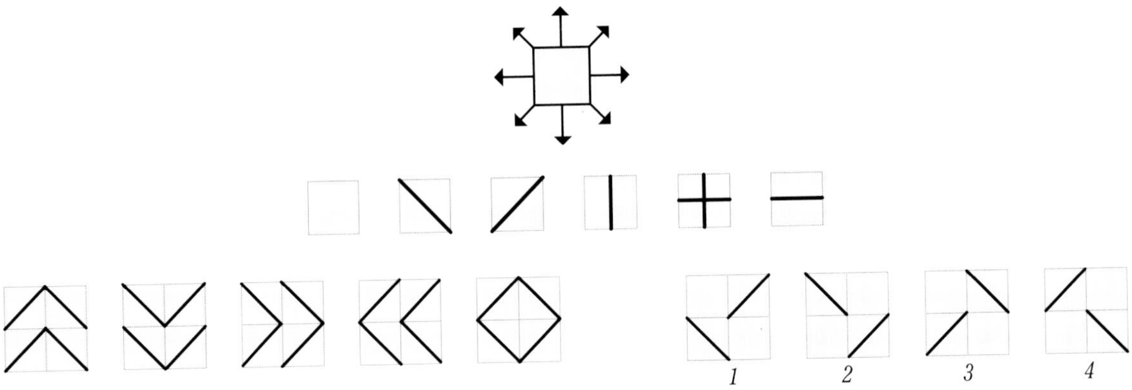

1   2   3   4

Permutations of base elements

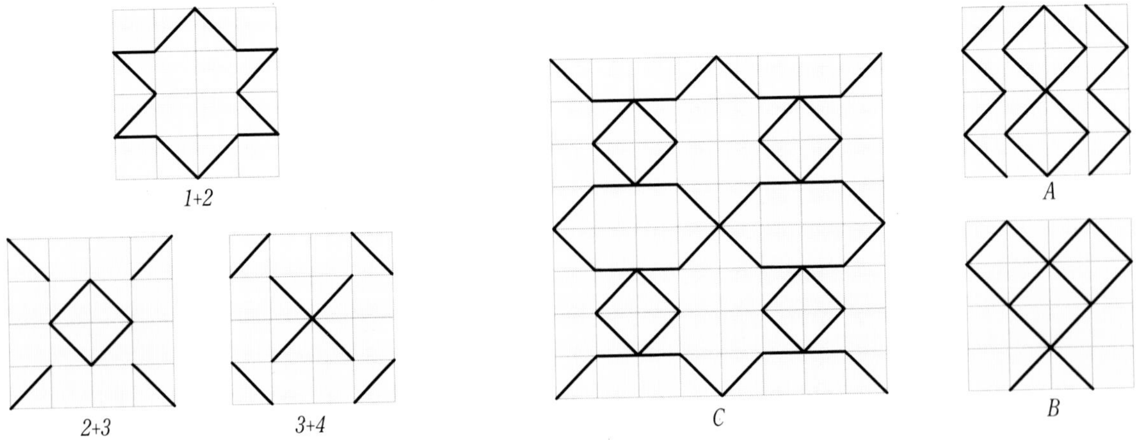

1+2

2+3   3+4   C   B   A

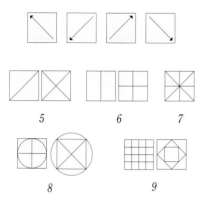

diagonals (7). Combinations of circle and square (8) are readily achieved, as are multiples of squares or diagonals within a square (9). This illustrates the potential of the square, but similar patterns and variants apply in the case of the rectangle.

Modular principles

Design modularity is based on four basic elements:

a) The repetition of one or more motifs.

b) The repetition of a single motif in each and every direction (vertically, horizontally, diagonally), the effect being to fill out the entire carpet field with a trellis-work of square or lozenge-shaped motifs picked out in different colour combinations.

c) Multiple use of a single motif (such as a rectangle) which is dentate or 'saw-toothed' at one extremity. This is typical of friezes or pavements where the modules fit into and against each other and occurs in the case of the kilims from Central Persia that feature a small square with saw-toothed edges. This simple motif can be geometrically or chromatically varied to create distinctive variants repeated horizontally, vertically or diagonally and in different colour combinations. The possibilities are infinite and are exploited by weavers with remarkable virtuosity.

d) The juxtaposition of motifs implies a series of lines that interlock to form a grid within which the individual motifs are positioned more or less equidistant from one another.

Static and dynamic motifs

Geometrical forms have an inherent duality in the sense that they can represent motifs that are 'static' or 'dynamic'. A case in point is the hexagon, a polygon with six equal sides: in terms of 'pure' geometry, this is a static form, but it becomes dynamic when viewed as a six-point star. Bringing the static and the dynamic together in this way yields a third formal element that can be developed to create further dynamic forms. The form is implicit in its geometry, just as (as will be described later) the arabesque develops across an infinite surface.

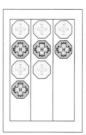
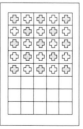

Inverted motifs

A motif can be changed dramatically by the simple process of inverting it as one might invert an hourglass.

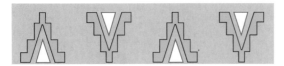

1) Inversion can take the form of repetition of the same motif or colour in different positions. This makes for considerable compositional variation, for example when a triangular motif is positioned upside down in a frieze. Motifs can be oriented toward the top or bottom, or toward the right or left.

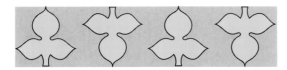

2) Combination and rotation of a simple motif can be used to create new motifs, as in the case of a simple square bisected by two diagonals comprising four basic motifs.

Alternating motifs

Alternating motifs are common in Moroccan carpets, but the technique can be seen in other regions. The process of alternation, like inversion, is used to accentuate the rhythm and to impart variety to the carpet design. This can be achieved by:
1) Simple repetition of a motif while changing its colour sequence and orientation, i.e. ranging left or right, or turning upside down.

2) Regular insertion of a blank field between one or more motifs.
3) Alternating straight lines and curves.
4) Alternating flat or raised surfaces.
5) Inverting colours or textural values.
6) Introducing contrasting geometrical motifs.
7) Switching between geometrical and floral motifs.
8) Switching from one weaving process to another, e.g. from knotted pile to cordless pile, a technique typical of certain bags woven by the Lur and Bakhtyari tribes in the Luristan region of Iran (see photograph page 67).

Superimposed motifs

Superimposition is the term commonly used to describe a number of techniques that impart additional variety to the surface texture:
1) A relief texture can be achieved by the application of raised motifs using embroidery or other procedures such as tufting or brocading. An example of this is illustrated above, where an Anatolian kilim has been decorated in relief with ears of wheat.
2) A new motif can also be superimposed by interlocking two different motifs; equally, two identical motifs can be combined to create a third, e.g. dentate motifs (small

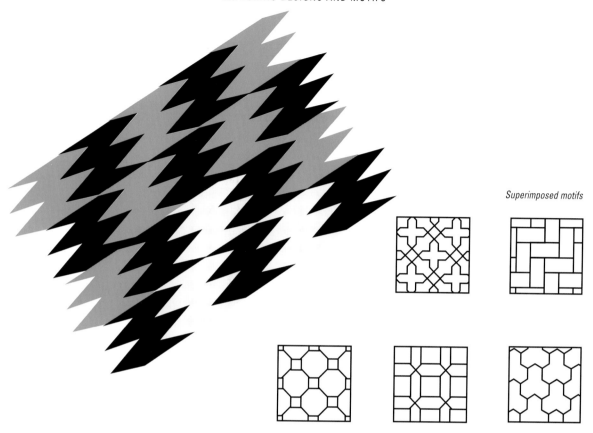

Superimposed motifs

squares with saw-toothed edges), offset slightly one against the next to create an optical sense of superimposed or interlocking lozenge shapes. A typical example is shown on pages 88 and 89.

3) Interlacing is achieved by bringing together knotted or braided motifs arranged in straight lines, curves or broken patterns (see illustration above).

Interplay of positive and negative images

On occasion, the surface texture is enriched by juxtaposing an image with its negative. An example of this might be a design woven in red on a yellow field set off against its 'negative' woven in yellow on a red field. Alternating colour contrasts in this way changes the overall appearance of a given motif. The balance achieved by alternating positive and negative images can be striking in its visual impact. An example of this is the ancient kilim shown on page 70, with its alternating positive and negative ('full' and 'empty') spaces.

Positive and negative motifs

Frame variants

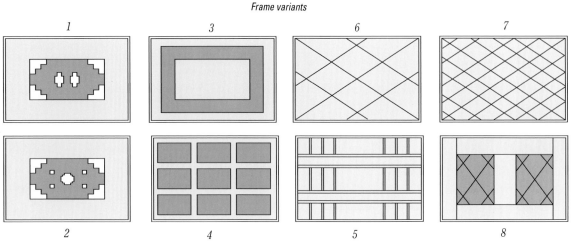

BASIC CARPET STRUCTURE

The basic framework

The surface area of a knotted carpet is divided into several distinct sections. The basic structure, of both rural and urban design, is inevitably dictated by the vertical warp and the horizontal weft. Outer and inner borders frame a design surface that can be woven at will. Thus, the carpet may have one or more central medallions set off against an underlying monochrome (as in figures 1 and 2 above); or it may feature square or rectangular blocks running vertically or horizontally (figures 3, 4 and 5); or it may have diagonals that can be worked into lozenge shapes (figures 6, 7 and 8).

In the case of a medallion carpet (see illustration right), the decorative borders are indicated as the 'frame' (A); the central area is known as the 'field' (B); the design of the central motif is indicated as the 'medallion' (C); and the field is delineated at each corner by a 'quartile' or quarter-circle (D).

What is particularly striking about the carpet structure is its double symmetry. In effect, only one quarter of the carpet has to be drawn in order for its entire design to be reproduced.

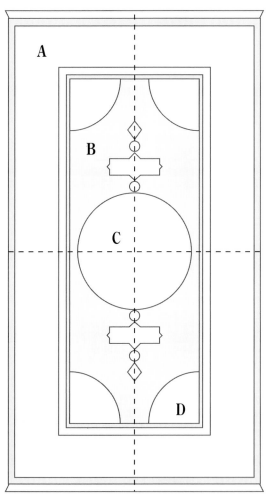

Variations in field motifs

Decorative motifs sometimes fill the entire field (as in the case of *Senneh* carpets with a *boteh* motif), and are typically classified under three general headings:

1) Floral motifs such as *boteh*, tulip, marigold, vine or twined leaf, garden carpets or *mille-fleurs*;

2) Abstract and stylised animal motifs that include representations of crabs, dragons, cockerels, goats, scorpions, two-headed birds and hunting scenes; and

3) Geometrical motifs such as squares, rectangles, lozenges (including *guls*, usually set within hexagons), hooked *guls*, stepped *guls*, etc.

Urban carpets also feature compartmentalised squares and rectangles of identical or divergent dimensions; these are commonly known as 'multiple-field' carpets.

The abundance of motifs noted above, together with the emotions they convey, permit one to postulate a carpet 'cosmogony' that alludes to the origins of the universe. What one may say with certainty, however, is that the vision of 'universe' implied in the Pazyryk Carpet (not to mention countless *Seljuq* carpets now lost to us forever under the sands of the Silk Road) appears to have been sustained at the level of the collective unconscious. One should add, however, that centuries of popular migration and persistent cross-fertilisation of cultures and traditions are such that the geographical and ethnic provenance of a particular carpet cannot be determined with any great degree of accuracy on the basis of designs and motifs alone.

There is an infinite variety in the form of geometrical motifs such as the cross or the star, whose origins pre-date Christianity. These motifs were later adopted in the Christian era by the Nestorians of Central Asia, the Byzantines, the Copts and the Armenians and, as a consequence, have mutated into hybrid forms that reflect the shifting social and religious values encountered along the way. Finally, the cross (starred or otherwise) started to be used in the geometrical compositions of Islam, where it was incorporated into the most sophisticated arabesques. What we have here is Sufism in its purest state: multiplicity in unity and unity in multiplicity.

For the mystics of Islam, there is a clear link between a 'passive' form such as a simple hexagon, and an 'active' form such as a star composed of two offset triangles that

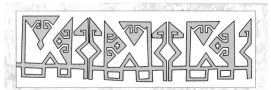

Carpet inscriptions

Frequently, labyrinthine motifs in Arab script combine with decorative arabesques to create a complex narrative that can be interpreted on many levels, depending on the horizontal or vertical sequence of letters and interstices. Arabic script lends itself to almost infinite variation, particularly in the case of 'geometrical Kufic', where the letters are arranged in squares and rectangles that combine to build a mosaic of text much as bricks are assembled to build a wall.

The earliest example of this is the 13th-century Seljuq carpet found in Konya (in Turkey) that was discussed in an earlier section. In effect, the Konya sultans of Kufa were the first to have angular Umayyad Dynasty Kufic script incorporated into their carpet designs. Over time, however, this rigorously geometrical script degenerated into what has come to be known as 'floral Kufic', where the ends of the letters were embellished and rounded off by the addition of leaves ('lobes') in much the same way as cross motifs were 'softened' into more ornate guls such as the 'Lotto gul' illustrated on page 14. In time, Kufic script gradually became purely decorative – developing into a 'pseudo-Kufic' that is at best only vaguely analogous to the real thing. An example of this is the carpet border design we now know as 'Holbein' (see pages 12 and 13).

Many carpets – and prayer rugs in particular – have sacred italicised texts woven into 'cartouches' or decorative scrolls. These are clear professions of religious faith, typically extolling Mohammed as the servant of Allah and his true prophet. One contemporary silk Hereke prayer rug carries a decorative Arabic inscription which, in the interests of design symmetry, can be read in both directions, whereas conventional Arabic is always read from right to left only. Other carpets feature cartouche inscriptions which contain specific imprecations extolling Allah or (even) secular figures. Signatures in Latin script are often appended to Turkish carpets from the Hereke region made during the reign of Kemal Atatürk (1923–38), the great Turkish reformer who decreed that Arab script should be suppressed and substituted by its Latin equivalent.

comprise a complete form that can be connected vertically or horizontally so as to constitute a new motif that fills the entire field. Here, each triangle stands for the number three, the symbol of the 'holy trinity' of divinity, harmony and proportion.

As we have seen, the vocabulary of geometrical forms is restricted to the square, rectangle, triangle, hexagon and lozenge (itself an essentially square or rectangular form). But the variations and permutations that these base modules admit and their interaction with the warp and weft are without limit: superimposed triangles, inter-connecting upside down motifs, crotchets extending out from the sides of a hexagon, and the alternation of positive and negative images – all of these are powerfully evocative and capable of producing remarkable effects when allied to the creative force of colour. This is a theme to which we shall return later.

MOTIFS AND RELIGIOUS CONSTRAINTS

Arabesques and interlacing

Images that reproduce human and animal forms are proscribed by the imams of Islam on account of their supposed idolatry. The Koran contains no such specific proscription, however, being content to observe only that the creation of a likeness is reserved to God and that the artist who seeks to emulate God in this respect is guilty not of a breach of law but of unacceptable presumption and arrogance. Moslem clergy have always been critical of the figurative arts, advocating representations of trees, flowers and inanimate objects in preference to portrayal of the human form. As a result of this intransigence, the decorative arts of Islam are essentially non-figurative in nature. This holds true of carpets and their designs.

To the kilim maker, as we have seen, colour and motif do not exist as an end in themselves, but as a means to an end, as a form of expression. Wherever Islam prevails, the arabesque replaces images as the fundamental decorative form. As such, the arabesque employs highly stylised motifs drawn primarily from botany, using undulating meanders and sinuous curves to evoke the whorls and scrolls of ivy or the vine.

In short, the arabesque (as the word itself indicates) is the universal decorative language of every country that has embraced Islam. Moslem weavers of Chinese, Indian, Persian, Turkish, Coptic and Arab origin speak this common tongue, itself a language written within a language, whose symbols and calligraphy – as Kufic script clearly illustrates – become progressively embellished and hybrid. To read arabesques is to decipher the force lines that connect and interconnect them, echoing the interminably subtle modulations of Arab poetry and music.

The interlace, by contrast, is decidedly more geometrical in nature. It comprises a set of lines that come together and cross, complementing and reinforcing each other by repetitive rhythms and impeccable symmetry. The square and the circle are the essential elements; the former is subscribed in the latter, which is always invisible.

The characteristic rhythms of the interlace derive from a subtle but aesthetically pleasing balance between detail and lack of detail, a symmetry based on a series of axes around which a motif is allowed to develop and invert. The motif is continuous and infinite: the viewer's eyes are attracted not to a specific detail but to the complex overall rhythm generated by arabesque and interlace.

The gateway to paradise: the prayer rug

To the earliest Judeo-Christian and pre-Islamic civil-isations of the Mediterranean Basin, an arch symbolised the doorway to the Great Beyond, to Paradise, in whatever form it might take. To this day, Islamic prayer rugs are designed with a prayer 'niche', a sacred part of the design that is always oriented towards Mecca when the rug is placed on the ground. It is the equivalent of the *mihrab* niche in the mosque.

Saf rugs, which with their arches and slender columns are used as prayer rugs at home or in the mosque, are usually made in workshops in Ushak and Anatolia. Occasionally, one comes across a nine-row *Saf* that faithfully reproduces the *mihrab* niche in the mosque.

These knotted or pileless prayer rugs are a substantial part of Oriental carpet history and production. They typically evoke Paradise in their use of the Tree of Life as their principal motif. The two columns supporting the arch form part of the tree: they are 'rooted' in the earth,

Prayer rug variants

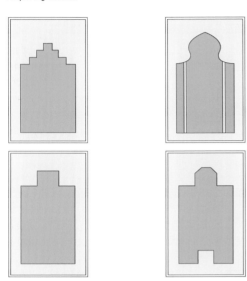

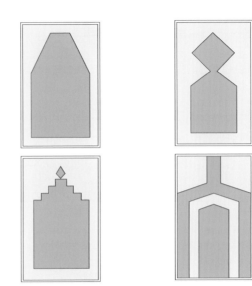

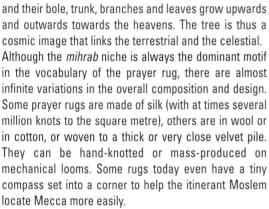

and their bole, trunk, branches and leaves grow upwards and outwards towards the heavens. The tree is thus a cosmic image that links the terrestrial and the celestial. Although the *mihrab* niche is always the dominant motif in the vocabulary of the prayer rug, there are almost infinite variations in the overall composition and design. Some prayer rugs are made of silk (with at times several million knots to the square metre), others are in wool or in cotton, or woven to a thick or very close velvet pile. They can be hand-knotted or mass-produced on mechanical looms. Some rugs today even have a tiny compass set into a corner to help the itinerant Moslem locate Mecca more easily.

In urban centres, master craftsmen knot prayer rugs. The decorative motifs are extremely varied to the extent that each weaver seeks to add a personal touch to the design, though traditionally venerated motifs are the norm. Each weaver has his or her own colour spectrum and repertoire of original motifs that combine to impart originality to prayer rug design. Thus, the actual shape of the *mihrab* may vary, appearing as round, conical, triangular or lozenge (the last-named symbolising the immortality of the soul). Prayer rugs from Konya boast geometrical *mihrab* designs: the 'arrowhead' motif, where three successive arches are supported by twin columns, is typical. Elsewhere, the 'Turkish triangle' motif is common; this has a 'magic triangle' with its

mihrab in a saw-toothed or stepped configuration (see illustration above).

On occasion, the columns may be surmounted by a stylised ewer or water jug that refers to the ritual ablutions that are mandatory before prayer. The columns may also be adorned with thuya blossom, which symbolises immortality and the links between life on Earth and in the Hereafter. Lamps suspended by a chain from the top of the niche denote God and His divine light. Garlands and arabesques fill out the field with tulips, marigolds, hyacinths and rose designs that offer a foretaste of the Garden of Paradise. The hourglass motif common in Kurdish carpets points to the ephemeral quality of human life. Prayer rugs also exhibit a symbolism based on colour. Green (the colour of the flag of Islam) is used extensively to honour the Prophet and as the colour each Moslem recognises as symbolic of individual salvation.

Mention should also be made of Islamic prayer rugs exclusive to Anatolia. These are used to honour the dead and are placed over the body of the deceased prior to burial. Tradition dictates that each family member contributes to their manufacture by, at the very least, adding a few knots. This sacred burial rug is handed down from one generation to the next and is often presented to the mosque. In the Kula region, they are known as *Mazarlik* (prayer rugs), whereas in Turkey they are called *Mezar* or 'cemetery rugs'. A typical rug of this kind will contain three distinct symbols: the niche, which indicates piety in the face of death; the weeping willow, which stands for sadness and mourning; and the cypress, the Tree of Life, which (like the thuya) connotes immortality, of which it is the symbol *par excellence*. These prayer rugs also carry images of mausoleums and mosques with stylised minarets (see illustration on page 76).

In villages and semi-nomadic communities, it is the women who weave prayer rug kilims. These are discussed in more detail in the section below on kilim motifs.

The Oriental Christian carpet

The term 'Oriental Christian' can be applied to any carpet woven by Christian weavers, irrespective of the denomination to which they adhere: Eastern Orthodox, Armenian, Syrian or Greek. These sumptuous carpets are adorned with essentially Christian symbols and are used to decorate and impart beauty and dignity to church interiors. In paintings by Jan van Eyck, for example, this carpet type is often shown at the feet of the Madonna.

In Anatolia (and in other regions where there is a strong Armenian presence), carpets and rugs featuring an arch or gateway symbol of Christian origin are common. In this instance, the arch connotes the triumphant power of God and access to His Kingdom (Paradise). Frequently, the letter 'S' – the first letter of the Armenian word for 'God' – is woven into the central field or into the border around the niche. It is often accompanied by a stylised lily, intended to symbolise God's mercy on the Day of Judgement.

At times, the Tree of Life fills out the entire niche. Vases are placed below it. The background colour is red, the colour representing Christ. An oil lamp suspended below the centre arch recalls those that hang in churches to indicate the presence at the altar of the Holy Sacrament as shown on this page.

It has already been pointed out that the cross motif, starred or otherwise, was Phrygian in origin and was subsequently adopted by Armenian carpet-makers. Carpets comprising various forms of cross symbolise the Christian faith and the Crucifixion. In some arch-and-column carpets, a star cross fills the centre of the niche. The ground plan of Greek, Eastern Orthodox and Roman churches is usually in the form of a cross – a 'Greek' cross of four equal branches in Eastern Orthodox places of worship, and a 'Latin' cross in the West.

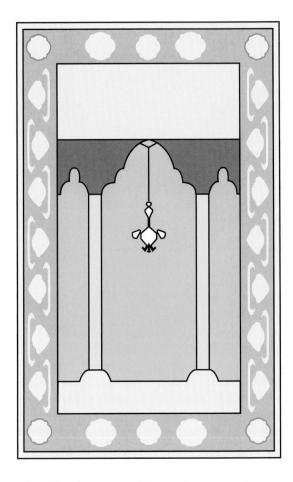

Central Anatolian prayer rug of Armenian Christian make. The two columns represent the gateway to Paradise, the portal to God 'through which only the righteous and just shall pass'. The lamp suspended in the centre symbolises in this instance the presence of God in the tabernacle.

This brief digression may suffice to show how tenuous the distinction is between 'Christian' carpets and their 'Moslem' counterparts. This is especially true to the extent that many non-Christian prayer rugs deploy the same 'Christian' symbols: the columned arch, the Gate of Paradise, the oil lamps, the star-cross motifs, and flowers such as marigolds, hyacinths and roses which adorn the path to Paradise. As Volker Gantzhorn has noted in his work on Oriental Christian carpets, there continue to be many grey areas when it comes to distinguishing the specifics of Christian as opposed to Islamic decorative art and practice.

KILIM MOTIFS

Origins

The kilim is a special case and deserves to be considered as such. In effect, the kilim goes to the very roots of textile manufacture. It is woven with the same rep stitch tapestry technique used by Ancient Egyptians and Copts, pre-Columbian weavers, Navajo blanket-makers of North America, *k'o-ssu* tapestry-weavers of China's Tang Dynasty, and the 'classical' tapestries of the late Middle Ages and the Renaissance as exemplified by the 14th-century *Angers Apocalypse* or the celebrated 15th-century *Lady with the Unicorn*, now preserved in the Musée de Cluny in Paris. In short, the kilim technique has a long and venerable history that has seen it migrate across continents.

It has been suggested that the geometrical compositions favoured by kilim-makers in Central Asia and Asia Minor were already known to the Phyrgians, a people regarded in antiquity as the most accomplished weavers. They are believed to have handed on the geometrical technique to nomadic Bedouin weavers whose encampments were located next to Phrygian trading outposts in Tyre.

Traces of the Phrygian civilisation in west-central Anatolia (in the heart of Asia Minor) are found in monuments such as the palaces built by the legendary King Midas in the 7th century B.C. The most spectacular of these is the Palace of Midas at Yazilikaya, the nearest town to the ancient Phrygian capital of Gordium, where Alexander the Great famously cut the Gordian Knot.

The facade of the palace was carved directly out of the rock and decorated with geometrical motifs that correspond exactly to those used to this day in some Anatolian kilims. In his history of art, French historian Georges Périot describes this facade as being completely covered with carvings and light reliefs, its entire circumference decorated with lozenges arranged in star-shaped groups of four with a tiny square set into the space at which they converged. The gable ends of the facade were adorned with other, larger saw-toothed lozenges. Within the parallelogram formed by these there was a more complex rectilinear motif, "a sort of continuous meander".

Périot's description of the six-branch star and stepped or saw-toothed lozenges covering the entire rectangular field corresponds in every detail to the design of kilims from the eponymous Kula and Ghiordes regions which may have served as prototypes for innumerable carpets made throughout Anatolia. The kilims woven by the Yürük nomads, who winter in villages in this part of Central Anatolia, exhibit identical texture and decoration.

Other nomadic tribes helped disseminate these motifs through Asia Minor until Islam arrogated this geometrical vocabulary by conferring religious significance on what was originally a pagan 'language'. Seductive as this theory may be, however, it cannot be said with any great certainty that this notion of a common ancestor takes full account of the diversity of kilim design and manufacture extending from the Caucasus to Central Europe.

Field variants

Kilim designs are composed using the same grids as in knotted carpets: lozenges, rectangles within rectangles, rectangles set into lattice-work, hexagonal motifs repeated across the entire width of the field, horizontal or vertical bands, and so on. The kilim field is frequently enclosed within one or more borders.

The simplest and most commonly used technique – to the extent that it follows the direction of the weft – is that employing horizontal (weft) bands of various widths, often separated by narrower secondary bands, very much along the lines of Middle Atlas *Hanbels* described earlier.

The fragmented and juxtaposed graphics of a rural or nomad kilim are in marked contrast to the more pictorial and spatially unified central axis design of urban kilims. This may be explained by the fact that the two types reflect an entirely different concept of space and time. Kilim geometry, which is to say, the expressive compositional balance between form and colour, evokes 'perfection' and 'immortality'. (The Dogon tribe in Mali demonstrate a perfect understanding of this principle by weaving shrouds in a simple black-and-white check to symbolise their dead and the resurrection that awaits them. The same duality as regards space and time is also exemplified in the work of the Russian Constructivists, notably in that of Kasimir Malevich of the Suprematist school of abstract painting, whose celebrated *White on Black* is an example of the ultimate geometrical abstraction.)

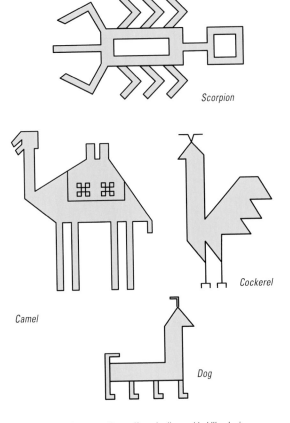

Scorpion

Camel

Cockerel

Dog

Stylised zoomorphic motifs typically used in kilim design.

technical considerations, however, environmental factors have exerted a profound influence on kilims produced by nomadic or semi-nomadic weavers.

Kilim prayer rugs are subject to the same design principles as knotted prayer rugs; they also feature a prayer niche but their geometrical composition is more abstract. The most frequently recurring pattern is that of a simple triangle surmounted by a rectangle. Many kilim prayer rug niches are also stepped, either in standard format or with hooks (crotchets) as in individual *guls*. Each weaver has his or her own decorative style and colour palette, in much the same way as each writer has his or her own 'personal' vocabulary.

A particularly striking feature of the kilim is the manner in which colour is deployed. According to the Prophet Mohammed, "the colours that the Earth spreads before our eyes are manifest signs to those who give thought to them". For urban weavers, green is the colour sacred to the Prophet; for nomadic weavers, on the other hand, green has a secular significance as the colour that represents and epitomises hope and joy, the colour of the brief flowering of the desert after rain.

Some kilims from the Shiraz region are distinguished by the use of zoomorphic elements in the guise of highly stylised camels, lions, ducks, horses, and so on (see left). Examples of these will be shown in subsequent chapters.

Motif variants

Irrespective of where they are made, all kilims adhere to a number of common design principles including symmetrically proportioned motifs, a perfectly balanced structure, alternation and repetition of motifs and colours, and saw-toothed elements forming small cross-shaped blocks or lozenges. That this appears to be the universal language of the kilim is perhaps confirmed by the fact that the same design principles govern the weaving of Navajo blankets.

The 'slit' or *relais* technique used in kilims is closer to the pointillist technique than is the case with knotted carpets inasmuch as the design is developed stitch by stitch. This *relais* technique gives rise to motifs that are more abstract and more disjointed, generally in triangular, hexagonal or lozenge form. Quite apart from these purely

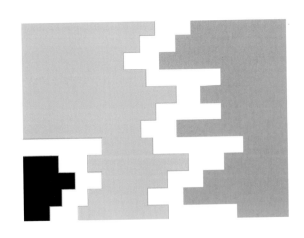

Form variants

Nomadic weavers use the *relais* or 'slit' technique to weave to this day all the fabrics that their way of life demands – a large tent kilim to separate the living quarters of men and women, floor coverings, and the various pouches and saddle-bags to hold food and clothing.

By way of example, the *khorjin* is a saddle-bag and occasional cushion woven in a variety of formats, but essentially comprising two identical pockets with straps that are slotted through apertures and secured in place by a central woollen cord. The larger models are used to store wheat or other cereals, while medium-sized bags are used to carry clothes and household utensils. The *namakdan* is a bag used exclusively to transport salt during the long journeys following flocks from one grazing ground to another. The Shahsavan *mafrash* is in three sections that are folded together and stitched into the shape of a trunk. The base and the rear panel are woven in a dense, almost rigid weave and only the front and side panels are decorated with geometrical motifs very similar to those of a kilim. The *chanteh*, meanwhile, is a specially shaped bag that is used to hang wooden cooking spoons in one corner of the tent. With its section of tightly gathered mesh, it is curiously reminiscent of contemporary tapestry (see photograph on page 154).

Nomad womenfolk also weave horse and camel blankets made of a double-layer felt-like fabric designed to be soft and warm. In addition, they weave 'occasional' kilims, known in Persian as *soffrai*, small rugs that serve to decorate the tent and complement the larger carpets. The overall result is a veritable textile 'culture' closely linked to *in situ* gathering, dyeing and weaving of sheep, goat or camel wool.

The loom is simple in construction. Four stakes are driven into the desert floor, the warp thread is stretched horizontally at floor level, and the weft is attached at the two ends by wooden poles. It is effectively the self-same loom that appears on Mesopotamian seals.

Marriage is a social and economic event of capital importance to nomadic tribes. The giving of a dowry seals the union between two families. The kilim plays a key role in this respect, inasmuch as a family's social standing and reputation are judged on the basis of the quality and quantity of kilims that go to make up the dowry. The so-called *kis*-kilim is personally woven by the bride-to-be, and is characterised by the pronounced finesse of its weave. It is stored in the *mafrash* trunk as a symbol of the perennial nature of the bond that unites husband and wife.

Inevitably, these centuries-old traditions are under threat from contemporary society. Until very recently, weaving was essentially a family affair and the resultant fabrics were only very rarely made available to third parties. In addition, carpet merchants were primarily interested in the commercial potential of knotted carpets and tended to look down their noses at these utility kilims. Over the last 30 years or so, however, increasing interest in this populist art form has been shown by Western collectors. This has accelerated demand to the point where the principal concern must now be to safeguard authentic examples remaining from some of the remoter regions of Central Asia and Asia Minor. Both these regions are under increasing threat as communications improve and tourist travel to and within those parts of the world becomes more frequent. That said, some merchants are alert to the value and importance of quality kilims and have taken steps to ensure that they continue to be made. Subsequent chapters this book indicate where this is the case.

The 'Song of the Carpet': Qashqai weaver (Iran) seen composing a carpet solely from memory.

Classification

Carpets have been woven for centuries in far-flung parts of the world, from China to North Africa by way of the leading production centres in Central Asia and Asia Minor. Becoming familiar with their vast range and diversity can prove a daunting task. Accordingly, this chapter sets out some helpful guidelines for classification.

Political and geographical frontiers have never held any real meaning or represented any real physical barrier to the nomadic or semi-nomadic tribesmen, whose most pressing need has always been, first and foremost, to move their livestock to fresh pastures. This was particularly true, for example, of the various scattered Kurdish tribes who travelled freely though areas of Turkey, Iran and Iraq. Over the centuries, however, this incessant process of ethnic migration has played an important role in the history and development of carpet-making.

In the following pages, we list major towns and villages that have acquired a reputation as present-day centres of carpet production. This must not be taken to mean that no other centres exist or that they are of no importance; merely that there are too many to allow inclusion in this overview.

Carpets take on the name of the town (Shiraz), village (Ushak), or the central bazaar that brings together output from a specific catchment area (Bukhara). They also are identified in generic terms by reference to an entire region (the Caucasus) or to a nomadic or semi-nomadic ethnic category (Qashqai).

Western buyer emphasising a detail for a carpet he is on the point of commissioning.

Additionally, as noted earlier, certain ancient types of Turkish carpet are referred to in Europe by the name of the (European) painter who first portrayed them, such as Lotto, Holbein or Memling. An added complication is that certain carpet types have, for commercial reasons, come to be known by reference to the particular technique involved in their manufacture or by reference to their intrinsic structure or dimension. Examples of this might be *soumak*, which refers to a particular technique; *Gabbeh*, which is used to denote a specific type of long-pile carpet made in and around Shiraz; and *Nim Baff*, a composite carpet assembled by stitching together smaller sections of carpet or rug.

Not least, a carpet may also be identified by its specific use as, say, a prayer rug, or by reference to its unusual format – as is the case of the *Dozar*, a type of long, narrow carpet.

No attempt will be made to gloss over the considerable uncertainty that attaches to the origins and provenance of a particular carpet. Manufacturers in some towns and cities are resolutely oriented towards the export market and, as such, unreservedly capable of turning out carpets named after another region entirely. As we have seen, carpet templates are like sheet music, in that they indicate 'notes' in the form of each knot and motif. As a consequence, they travel well. Carpet manufacturers in China and Pakistan, for example, are today perfectly capable of producing substantial quantities of *Shiraz* carpets which are virtually indistinguishable from (and distinctly cheaper than) those made in their original homeland of Iran. With this sort of thing in mind, we will attempt, wherever possible, to identify and indicate both quality and authenticity.

The golden rule about carpets is and will remain that their provenance is not automatically synonymous with good *or* bad quality. Every weaver in every village, however remote, has the potential to turn out excellent or shoddy work. The same holds true for every urban workshop, irrespective of its implied reputation, and for every state-owned carpet manufacturer.

The sole factor dictating the quality of a carpet is its authenticity. It is what it is, no more and no less. Like a precious stone or an Old Master, a carpet is either genuine or fake. It was either made as a labour of love or duplicated on a production line for purely commercial reasons. To which one should add that the latter type will be no more than a pale copy of an original design or, worse still, an industrially manufactured carpet that purports to be 'hand-made'.

In order to familiarise the reader with the principal towns, villages and regions concerned, a brief historical overview of each centre is given in this chapter. There is also a

Greek

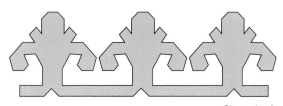

Clover-leaf

Running dog

Boteh

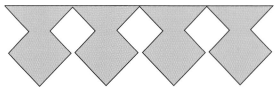

Geometrical motifs

Classification by reference to specific border decoration that indicates provenance.

capsule review of the carpets produced there, listing salient features, current output and, where possible, technical specifications in terms of knots per dm² (square decimetre) per m² (square metre) or by running metre (rm), with dimensions also being given in imperial measures.

Before proceeding to a systematic inventory, however, it is appropriate to add some general observations that will flesh out the geographical data by examining certain cultural, religious, social and economic factors that affect carpet classification.

Classification by dominant decorative structure

The principal categories include those with:
– A geometrical design (page 88)
– A floral design (page 118)
– Illustrations of scenes, animals and people (page 27)
– Central medallions (page 77)
– Prayer motifs (*Nemazlik* in Turkish, *Dja-namas* in Persian, *Selahak* in Turkmeni, *Sedjadé* in Arabic) (page 66)
– Wedding motifs, such as the small Turkmen *Khalik* used as a camel blanket on ceremonial occasions and at weddings (page 101)
– Burial motifs or *Ayatli* (page 76).

Classification by individual motif

Classification is possible by reference to a particular and distinctive motif, for example the *gul* so characteristic of *Tekke* carpets made by Turkmen nomads. In effect, each region has its own carpet 'language' that has evolved as a function of:
– Variation of motifs and the introduction of new permutations of traditional motifs. Here, one may cite reciprocal influences resulting from the absence of genuine geographical frontiers during the Persian, Mongol and Ottoman empires, together with specific technical constraints attaching to a particular carpet type.
– Variation imposed by religious constraint. Here, one might cite the geometrical abstraction that predominates in Moslem carpets.
– Variation resulting from social and economic factors. Here, the contrast is between 'grass-roots' output from nomadic and sedentary rural communities and the more sophisticated carpets of urban workshops.

Gendja *gallery carpet from the Caucasus, woven in the format known in Iran as* kenaré. *The narrow field is completely filled by three traditional Kazak medallions.*

Classification by use and format

Here, the primary distinction is between nomadic and urban production:
– In the case of nomad carpets, the main carpet types are those used to mark off spaces within the tent, together with *Joval*-type saddle-bags, and *sofreh*-type fabrics.
– In the case of urban carpets, specific formats apply to *Dozar* (*Dozer*) household rugs (typically 7 ft 4 in × 4 ft/ 2.20 m × 1.20 m), known in Turkey as *Seccade*, and to large format *Miam Farsh* carpets intended as floor coverings in the main room of a house (a category known in Turkish as *Taban* (6 ft 7 in × 11 ft 10 in/2 m × 3.50 m) or *Büyük Taban* (8 ft 3 in × 11 ft 10 in/2.50 m × 3.50 m). Smaller long and narrow carpets placed around each side of the large central carpet are known in Iran as *Kenaré* (approx. 10 ft 2 in × 5 ft/3.10 m × 1.5 m) or *Kelley* (approx. 9 ft 10 in × 5 ft/3 m × 1.5 m).

Modern-design (geometrical) carpet from a workshop in Konya, Turkey.

Classification by major purchase category

In essence, there are three principal carpet categories on the market:
– 'Old' or 'antique' carpets: at the moment, those produced prior to the 1890s (in other words over 100 years old). These are 100% vegetable-dyed, but vary in technical and aesthetic quality according to their precise origin, the specific date of manufacture, and the skill and inventiveness of the weaver.
– 'Semi-old' carpets: those produced largely between the two World Wars (1919–39). Some are vegetable-dyed, but the majority use poorer grade chemical (aniline) dyes in the interests of mass production. Artificial chlorine discolouration ('ageing') is frequently used to attenuate the harsher colours, and the weaving process is accelerated by using the four-strand Jufti knot described earlier. What this implies in practice can be exemplified by reference to Ushak and its surrounding villages, which produced on average 400,000 m² of carpet annually in the years between 1927 and 1930, the period when demand for Oriental carpets was at a peak. Comparable figures for 1932 to 1934 show an annual average of some 20,000 m², and this falls off sharply to 4,000 m² for 1935 and 1936. Many workshops shut down when Western markets dried up at the outbreak of World War II, and production started to pick up again, albeit slowly, only after 1945.
– Contemporary carpets: improved-grade chemically dyed carpets, the result of considerable strides made by the chemical industry, notably with the introduction of tincture of chrome and vat dyeing. These carpet grades gradually approximate to ancient vegetable-dye quality, particularly where the most advanced (and most expensive) dyeing processes are used.
Several governments, including those of Turkey and Morocco, have taken steps to ensure that top-of-the-range labels of quality are granted exclusively to manufacturers that are again using vegetable dyes and superior grades of wool and, moreover, working closely from ancient models and traditional motifs. Output from the countries in question has since proved substantial on a region-by-region basis. Certain governments also encourage contemporary design of the highest quality on the grounds that the carpet-weaving tradition has always been driven by innovation rather than imitation.

Classification by geographical or climatic factors

Geophysical and climatic factors exert a key influence on how a carpet is designed and woven, not least with regard to the colours used. As we have seen, a carpet is a narrative that recounts its own history not only in terms of *why* but also of *where* it was woven.

It will be recalled that non-literate ethnic groups have habitually used the carpet as a 'text' to record their culture in signs and symbols that are familiar to the group yet also have a 'universal' significance. In his discourse on the 'universality of forms', the French writer André Malraux once argued with reference to Byzantium that there is a clear parallel between Chartres and Samarkand, which is to say, between the art of stained glass on the one hand and the art of the carpet on the other. He went on to argue that the essence of a

Close-up of a deep-pile Gabbeh.

carpet lies not in its colours but in its total abstraction. In this respect, Malraux is wrong: the essence of a carpet lies both in its colours and in its value as an abstraction, whereby either of these two qualities may predominate at one time or other.

It is self-evident that the colour palette in the north of a country or region will inevitably differ from that of the south. The Caucasus is a case in point: by virtue of its geographical location between Russia, Iran and Turkey, the region is an ethnic mosaic. Knotted-pile carpets woven in the mountain valleys where the winters are severe are typical of the Caucasus; their principal design function is as blankets to ward off the cold. Accordingly, their compacted pile is garish, often trimmed coarsely with a sword or knife, with the result that their geometrical motifs are often blurred – as typified by *Derbent*, *Kazak* and *Karabagh* carpets. There are exceptions to this rule, however, inasmuch as these mountain people also turn out short-pile *Choucha* carpets (not to mention others from the Kouba region, also made in Azerbaijan) which exhibit a highly sophisticated knotting technique and are woven in remarkably delicate and sombre colours.

It is often possible to determine the provenance of a carpet by reference to the geophysical environment in which it was made. In other words, to define carpets by

major geographical or climatic category, allowing in each instance for the widest possible interpretation. By way of an illustration, we can consider the case of a weaver living and working in the monotonous desert wastes; typically, such a weaver will opt for bold and lively colours. Some nomadic tribes living in particularly arid desert are inexorably drawn to floral and garden-carpet format and design. Some will see a watercourse in the shape of a central medallion. As M. Ivanow has said, some carpets from Sistan are "smooth as the desert itself, bisected by the green ribbon of the Helmand River (in today's south-west Afghanistan and eastern Iran) and bordered by the reddish hue of the mountains".

There can be little doubt on one score: weavers are profoundly influenced by nature generally and by their immediate environment. The higher into the hills one climbs, for example, the thicker and deeper the pile of blankets woven to provide increasing warmth.

A carpet reflects not only images, however, but also an inner vision. Weavers who spends months or even several years creating a design are affected not only by their physical surroundings, such as the colours and contours of the countryside, but also by the religious creed to which they adhere, as well as by myth, ritual and superstition and the cultural influences exerted by traditional pursuits such as music and dance. It is only to be expected that a weaver will turn to and be inspired to reproduce, in either realistic or stylised fashion, those aspects of the environment that are most immediate: trees, shrubs and flowers; domestic animals such as the ass, the horse, the camel, the cockerel; dangerous creatures such as the tarantula, scorpion and snake; mythical creatures such as the winged dragon and the phoenix; or watercourses, mountains, clouds or gardens; together with everyday objects such as weaving combs, shears for cutting knots to the desired pile, gourds, tea urns and so forth. Little wonder then that, when the weaver's environment is under threat, it is by no means unusual today for carpet designs to reproduce in one form or other another the machinery and hardware of battle:

Contemporary Afghan Baluchi carpet reflecting the impact of the Afghan War.
Traditional boteh motif borders have been replaced by bomb motifs, and the borders proper are decorated with armoured tanks. The field comprises scenes of modern warfare, complete with helicopters.

helicopters, tanks, machine guns, and bombs (see illustration on page 64).

Carpets from urban workshops or state-owned mills draw on more sophisticated influences from a more complex cultural and socio-technical environment. The town of Iznik in Turkey, for example, is renowned for its porcelain; it comes as no surprise therefore that *Iznik* carpets have frequent recourse to motifs and colours inspired by local porcelain, notably in terms of floral designs featuring tulips, marigolds, roses or hyacinths.

Any attempt to classify or categorise carpets must also take account of cultural influences linked to ethnic history. The history of a carpet is frequently bound up with historical events, never more so than when an ethnic mix emerges in the wake of war and deportation. Miscegenation is so prevalent in the sprawling territories of Central Asia and Asia Minor that certain villages in Anatolia and Iran today are of extremely diverse racial origin. For example, weavers from some villages in the Karasi region near Bergama (the former Pergamum) in

western Turkey are directly descended from a tribe who in the 13th-century captured the fortress of Pergamum. To this day, local weavers have preserved the tradition (or, better still, the collective memory) of Turkmen motifs (typically, octagons with red or dark blue crotchets with a cross in the centre), with designs and motifs handed down from mother to daughter over the ensuing centuries. In some carpets from the Bergama region, for example specimens from the village of Kozak, one can still detect significant Caucasian influences imported by immigrant Caucasian ethnic groups. Similarly, an admixture of ethnic groups on the western side of Asia Minor has also resulted in highly original hybrid motifs which intrigue (and sometimes confuse) the specialist.

The motifs found in many carpets today are essentially the same as those handed down and transcribed with varying degrees of success from centuries-old models. Despite all external influences, however, they still exhibit continuity in terms of composition and execution.

Classification in terms of dyes

An earlier section on dyes and dyeing touched on the very real differences that exist between a vegetable-dyed carpet and one dyed by artificial (chemical) means.

The fascination exerted by vegetable dyes can be traced to the variety of shades and tonal effects that can be achieved within one and the same colour. A principal reason for this is that the weaver usually dyes wool in modest batches or skeins, dipping each batch as required into a small vessel containing the vegetable dye solution. Depending on how the dye has been mixed and how long the wool is immersed, the colour of each batch will inevitably vary, however subtly. These variations in tone (known as *abrach*) may not be immediately apparent to the weaver (and may not become so until the entire carpet has been finished or, indeed, until several years afterwards). These almost imperceptible tonal differences not only impart a particular charm to a carpet, they are also a clear indication that it has been vegetable-dyed.

There are other tell-tale signs, not least because fibres of uneven quality used in the weave tend to absorb vegetable dyes to a different degree. The resultant colour nuances, virtually invisible to the naked eye, are an integral part of the fascination of hand-woven and hand-coloured carpets. These nuances – part and parcel of the Impressionist painter's technical repertoire – impart an incomparable and almost indefinable richness to the finished product.

Despite the inroads made by modernisation and improved communications, some isolated regions have continued to use predominantly vegetable dyes. There are two main reasons for this, the first geographical, the second economic. Firstly, distances between these remote weaver villages and the nearest town where chemical dyes are available are often considerable. Access to chemical dyes is even less practical for nomadic tribes in the process of moving their livestock to mountain pastures during the summer months. The second reason is cost. Top-quality chromium-based dyes are expensive, whereas roots, leaves, bark, mosses and other organic materials are freely available, even in the most inhospitable of desert regions. What is more, any semi-nomadic or sedentary weaver worth her salt will be familiar with vegetable dye compounds and recipes.

In towns, weavers working at home on behalf of an agent will use the industrially produced raw materials placed at their disposal to complete an order.

In the final analysis, however, a choice may have to be made between, on the one hand, a good quality, tightly hand-knotted carpet with industrially processed wool and dye and, on the other, a coarser hand-knotted carpet with vegetable-dyed hand-spun yarn.

To the uninitiated it is disconcerting to learn that the bright and vibrant colours achieved by vegetable dyes will gradually fade to the softer muted tones of a century-old carpet. The whole notion of artificially 'fading' chemical dyes to make a carpet look 'old' thus falls by the wayside. Any doubts on that score are effectively dispelled when one considers the current vogue for rustic *Gabbeh* carpets.

Carpets of Asia Minor

The vast region that is Asia Minor exhibits common cultural influences. For the sake of simplicity, a distinction is made here between the two major countries that comprise the region: Turkey and Iran. The following section reviews carpets and kilims made by semi-nomadic and sedentary tribes in rural regions and also output from urban artisan workshops.

Yürük prayer kilim (late 19th century) from the Taurus Mountains. A 'double-portal' effect is achieved by the use of off-white ('negative') for the main borders.

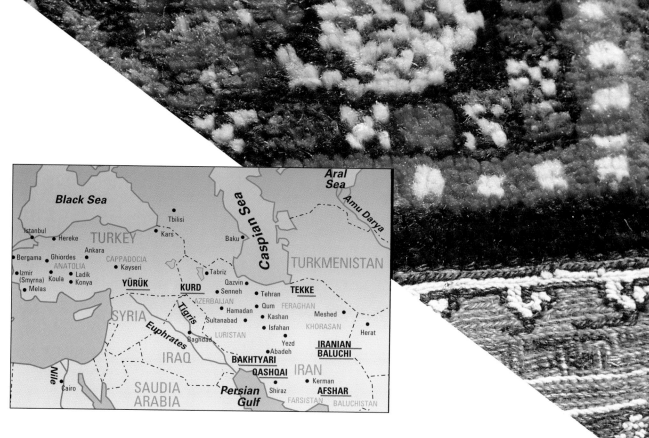

Close-up of a Kurdish pouch featuring a permutation of weaving techniques: knotted pile, soumak and kilim.

THE NOMADS OF TURKEY

Yürüks

The nomadic way of life has almost disappeared in modern Turkey other than in certain parts of central Anatolia and in the Taurus Mountains.

The term *Yürük* (from the Turkish verb *yürümek*, meaning 'to walk') is commonly applied to nomadic peoples and, in Anatolia, is taken to refer to all nomadic tribes, including Kurds, Turkmens and others who range across eastern Anatolia. An attempt is frequently made to distinguish between the various ethnic groups by reference to their origins, the region or village where they habitually winter, or the area where they put their herds out to summer pasture. *Yürük* carpets are often named by reference to the town or village closest to the tribe's annual summer pasture, because the locality often influences carpet pattern and motifs. This is the case, for example, with *Konya-Yürük* carpets, because semi-nomadic ethnic group use motifs commonly found in *Konya* carpets. Although the nomad-produced versions tend to be coarser, the differences are slight to the point of being imperceptible to the unschooled eye.

Key features

– Warp and weft wool yarn mixed with goat hair.
– Fine, silky pile.
– Knot density from 500 to $1,000/dm^2$, yielding a rather coarse but dense and soft pile.
– Vegetable dyes on a predominantly red or blue ground.
– Motifs: luminous and harmonious, with rare tonality; frequently geometrical, and 'spontaneous'. The Yürük has no distinctive ethnic repertoire but borrows freely from surrounding traditions. As a result, some Yürük carpets are similar to nomad Turkmen carpets from Central Asia, with a field filled by a gul like that of the Tekkes; others draw on kilim patterns with large crotcheted lozenges with smaller lozenge-shape inserts.
– Dimensions: small: 3 ft 3 in × 6 ft 6 in (1 m × 2 m) or 4 ft 4 in × 9 ft 10 in (1.30 m × 3 m).

Yürük carpets are much sought after by collectors on account of their rarity and their silk-like lustre. They are comparatively expensive. *Yürük* kilims are coarser and more rustic, yet exhibit the same silk-like luminosity. *Yürük* prayer rugs are distinguished by an arrow shape set into the centre of each arch at the apex of the stepped *mihrab*. The borders are frequently decorated with a meandering 'T' motif or with dentate, stylised leaves separated by a band of beads.

The *Yürük* kilim is often confused with its Kurdish counterpart to the extent that both Yürüks and Kurds live an essentially identical nomadic pastoral life. In the Kasak region, semi-nomadic shepherds produce thick wool carpets with vividly contrasting colours.

Kurdistan Kurds

Although often referred to by the generic term Yürük, the Kurds are of Iranian stock. For centuries preceding the currently difficult political situation, the Kurds roamed freely and far – across the extended Armenian region of the Caucasus, and as far as the extreme south of Azerbaijan, along the frontier between Turkey and Iran, up the western slopes of Mount Ararat in Anatolia, into the Iranian provinces of Kurdistan and Kermanshah, and through north-eastern Iraq. The Kurdish majority is now largely sedentary, but certain groups are still semi-nomadic, spending their winters in mountain villages and their summers in the upper mountain pastures.

Carpets are the Kurds' most prized possessions, particularly the dominant kilims. A family's prestige and prosperity are judged by reference to the size and quality of the carpets and kilims displayed in its home, tent or clay and straw hut. Until quite recently, carpets and kilims were woven exclusively for domestic use, but financial pressures have resulted in some being offered for sale, albeit with the greatest reluctance.

The largest Kurdish community is found in Anatolia. There, sedentary weavers turn out carpets that reflect their cultural identity but frequently incorporate other ethnic influences. Most of their output is in the form of kilims in a wide variety of styles, yet featuring the standard formats and geometrical motifs derived from ancient Persian carpets, for example the *herati* motif that originated in the former Persian capital of Herat. In the Diyarbakir region, kilim weavers regularly incorporate

highly stylised scorpion motifs into their designs in the belief this may help prevent them from being bitten.

Kilim borders often comprise octagons ringed by 'beaded necklace' motifs. The border motif of the Armenian 'S' is common, as is the hourglass motif that the Kurds venerate as a symbol of the transience of all living things.

Kurdish carpets are found in the marketplaces of Malataya in eastern Anatolia. In Sivas, 160 miles (250 kilometres) to the north-west, there is a bazaar offering ancient and modern Kurd or *Yürük* carpets. A major Kurdish carpet-making region exists within the triangle formed by the towns of Diyarbakir, Hakkari and Van.

Opposite page: Reverse of a soumak *pouch showing variegated tufts reminiscent of Greek* flocatti *carpets.*
Below: Kargisman *prayer kilim from north-west Turkey. Note the* hooked *mihrab and the two* guls *in the field. Woven in muted tones with a rich madder red predominating.*

Key features

– Warp and weft yarn in cotton but occasionally in goat hair mixed with coarse and lustrous sheep and camel wool.

– Dense, closely woven pile.

– Depending on specific region, Persian or Turkish knot density between 280 and 390/m (700 to 1,200/dm²).

– Vegetable-dye colours of pink, raw silk and pale blue, with graded intervals of black and white.

– Design varies from one tribe to next, although grounds are typically in beige wool or camel hair with stylised motifs extending across the entire field.

– Top and bottom edges are finished in kilim strips of various lengths, woven in plain colours or in stripes of contrasting colour.

– Dimensions: large rectangles, 13 ft × 6 ft 6 in (4 m × 2 m) ranging down to 6 ft 6 in × 3 ft 3 in (2 m × 1 m).

Sadly, current output of carpets and kilims is greatly jeopardised by civil war, notably in and around Diyarbakir, the large commercial centre for the Kurdish population in Turkey. This high-plateau region of Anatolia is highly unstable at present and the authorities strongly advise against visiting it.

Kurdish and *Yürük* carpets are very similar and can be told apart only on the basis of minor variations. In and around the town of Siilt, large quantities of kilims continue to be produced, but the region is best known for its prayer rugs woven locally on hand looms from silky and lustrous angora wool, first imported from Kashmir when cashmere scarves were the height of fashion. Similar output is recorded for the towns of Kerman and Yezd in Iran.

Turkmen tribes living in and around Balikesir

Balikesir lies in today's western Turkey between the towns of Bursa and Bergama and is the centre for a type of kilim known as a *Bergama-Balikesir*, woven by the descendants of ancient nomadic tribes of Turkmen origin who settled the villages of this mountainous region. Designs are highly distinctive, featuring motifs set into interlocking loops or linking with slightly undulating vertical strips. Elsewhere, in Konya-Nigde, Turkmen descendants produce similar kilims featuring borders decorated with herringbone patterns.

An extremely beautiful ancient kilim from the early 18th century made by the Yüncü tribe from the Balikesir region of north-west Anatolia. The design employs interlocking 'latch' motifs typical of the region to juxtapose positive and negative effects to the point where it is virtually impossible to determine where the field ends and the motifs begin. This audacious design hints at a succession of decidedly abstract Tree of Life motifs.

URBAN WORKSHOPS IN TURKEY

The following section profiles carpet towns and regions and traces the development of urban workshops and factories.

The Dardanelles Strait

The Kumkapu (Kumkapi) quarter of Istanbul

Istanbul – the Byzantium of old – is justly renowned for the excellence of the carpets made during the sultanates of the Ottoman Empire, some of which are displayed today in the famous Topkapi Museum. That collection boasts Persian carpets and rugs, together with Egyptian models from Cairo, notably an assortment of 30 or so regional prayer rugs dating variously from the 17th to the 19th centuries and decorated in brilliant colours with extracts from the Koran.

Today, however, carpet manufacture in Istanbul is restricted to the suburb of Kumkapu, an area settled by Armenian emigrants towards the end of the 19th century that stretches along the banks of the Bosphorous between the Museum of Turkish and Islamic Art and the Arch of Theodosius.

When in Istanbul, a visit to the Museum of Turkish and Islamic Art is a must, not least because of its magnificent collection of 13th- and 14th-century *Seljuq* carpets. Equally mandatory is a visit to the Carpet and Kilim Museum that adjoins the Blue Mosque. Directly behind the mosque is a bazaar that is devoted entirely to the sale of carpets. If you do visit the bazaar, try to go with a specialist; this holds true also of visits to the carpet section in the Grand Bazaar, where a great number of serious and competent merchants ply their trade. They will be pleased to arrange for your purchase to clear customs and be sent to your home. Payment by credit card is accepted.

A sumptuous silk Kumkapi *carpet (end 19th century) comprising 13 mihrab prayer niches with animal and Tree of Life insets. The weaver's intention is to conjure up Earthly Paradise (complete with flowers, deer, snakes, etc.). The soft colours and elegant design are perfectly co-ordinated.*

Hereke

Hereke is located on the southern bank of the Sea of Marmara about 38 miles (60 kilometres) east of Istanbul. It was a major manufacturing centre during the Ottoman Empire and, as of 1843, started to produce beautifully coloured silk carpets with an exceptionally fine finish (at times, with some 20,000 knots/dm²). In the main, these *Hereke* carpets exhibit Persian floral or Indian *mille-fleurs* motifs, but Hereke also produces classic *Ushak* carpets and rugs (intended as a rule to be presented by the Sultan

to visiting royalty and dignitaries from all over the world) and carpets inspired by Savonnerie models.

In 1922, when the Ottoman Empire was dissolved, the production of carpets in Hereke ceased. It was not until 1955 that a consortium of foreign investors and Turkey's Sümerbank were able, with the help of the Turkish government, to re-open the former factories and effect a renaissance of high quality carpet-making as it had flourished under the Sultans. As a result, Hereke now turns out silk carpets of irreproachable finesse and delicacy, at times with something approaching a million

A contemporary saf (in Turkish, 'row' or 'band') carpet with three mihrab prayer niches. The stylised animals and Tree of Life, inspired by Persian designs, are evocative of Paradise. The carpet is clearly Armenian: a Moslem weaver would never have infringed to such a degree the Koran injunction against depicting human and animal forms. A highly original prayer rug, not least in view of the owl and giraffe figures.

The Aegean Sea and hinterland

Bergama

The ancient Attalid capital of Pergamum (today's Bergama) has been an important carpet centre since the 16th century. Contrary to what some commentators claim, the famous Holbein *gul* made up of rows of octagons does *not* have its origins in Ushak but in Bergama, as inspection of the 17th-century carpets housed in local museums clearly demonstrates.

For the most part, these carpets were made in villages in the region by nomadic tribes, hence their customary designation as 'peasant' carpets. Some demonstrate considerable artistry at the populist level and are greatly prized by experts.

Bergama is also the commercial centre for the sale of nomad *Yürük* carpets and kilims.

knots to the square metre. The principal focus is on prayer rugs, distinguished by exceptional expertise and impeccable quality.

The master weavers took their inspiration from ancient models housed in the state collections, but demonstrated their individual talents by creating some original patterns. The *Hereke* logo is frequently woven into the bottom right corner of the carpet. Needless to say, *Hereke* carpets and rugs are *very* expensive.

Key features
- Thick but lustrous wool pile with a warp yarn of mixed wool and goat hair.
- Coarse knots (approx. 800 to 1,200/dm²). Knots are loose and the pile is moderately raised.
- Colours: bold and synthetic, with reds and greens predominating.
- The design shows Caucasian influences with octagonal hooked motifs, multiple lozenges, eight-branch stars, etc. The pattern is blurred due to the thickness of the pile.
- Size: medium, 5 ft × 4 ft 4 in (1.50 m × 1.30 m).

An unusual Kozak carpet from the Bergama region of Turkey, where Caucasian tribes settled several centuries ago. The vivid blues and reds and the geometrical centre medallion are clear indications of the Caucasian influence that permeates the vast ethnic and cultural melting pot that is the Silk Road.

Kozak

Some 12 miles (20 kilometres) from Bergama, the township of Kozak and its surrounding villages house a population that is Caucasian in origin, a fact that has greatly influenced carpet-making in the region. The prevalent motifs and colours are similar to those used by nomadic Kazaks from the central Caucasus.

Innovative knotted prayer rugs made in Kozak aspire to the status of folk art. A distinctive feature is the inverted (mirror-image) 'E' *tamga* (*gul*) woven into the kilim border and attesting to the weaver's ethnic origins.

Key features
– *Good quality wool.*
– *Low knot density (230 Turkish knots per running metre).*
– *High-cut pile.*
– *Bold and vivid colours, predominantly reds, greens and yellows.*
– *Geometrical motifs: hooked lozenges, 'S' motifs, Stars of Solomon.*
– *Small format, 4 ft × 3 ft 8 in (1.20 m × 1.10 m).*

Ghiordes

Ghiordes (Gördes in modern Turkey) is a mountain village best known for giving its name to the traditional Turkish knot. It should not be confused with Gordium, the ancient Phrygian capital of Asia Minor, which is where Alexander the Great is meant to have cut the Gordian Knot.

Ghiordes, completely rebuilt following a massive earthquake at the beginning of the 20th century, is one of the great centres of Anatolian carpet-making. The main village square is a sight to behold: thousands of skeins of wool in every conceivable colour are stretched out to dry in the sun after being removed from the dyeing vats.

Ancient prayer rugs from Ghiordes are recognised by their characteristic seven-row borders known as *sobokli*

(literally, 'rayon borders'), which symbolise the seven steps to Paradise. Patterns are predominantly geometrical.

Ghiordes is also celebrated for its *Kizil-Gördes* marriage rugs that the bride-to-be presented as a gift on her wedding day. The ground was traditionally red (*kizil* in Turkish) and the rugs were originally of a high quality with delicate pastel shades. Production of these marriage rugs was effectively discontinued in the 1920s, however, and the specimens available today are of questionable quality, with coarse knots and garish synthetic colours. They are generally offered for resale by merchants in Izmir (Smyrna).

A fine Ghiordes *prayer rug from the early 19th century, a genuine masterpiece of subtle motifs and colours. The seven-row border symbolises the seven steps of the ascent to Paradise. The olive green used for the mihrab field is typical of* Ghiordes *design. A large central border alternates* boteh *motifs with branches of young peonies in an inverted mirror pattern.*

Koula (Kulah) and surrounding region

The township of Koula lies on the road between Izmir and Ushak. Carpets (and prayer rugs in particular) are produced here on a large scale comparable to that of Ghiordes, though Koula quality is substantially superior, not least because *Ghiordes* carpets use a cotton warp yarn, whereas those from Koula opt for quality wool.

Urban workshops today turn out excellent replicas of 18th- and 19th-century *Koulas*, prayer rugs produced from around the villages of Demirci and typified by a red, very dark maroon and black ground that has earned them the familiar name of *Koula-Kumurju* ('coal-man' or 'charcoal burner' in Turkish). The borders comprise small symmetrical braided motifs known as 'crocodiles'. The central hexagon is woven in red or brown.

Modern-day Koula produces cheap but good quality wool carpets and rugs, whose colours are chemically treated to age and fade them artificially to the pale and delicate pastels of the ancient models used. Tourists snap up these imitation ancient short-pile *Koulas*, often in the mistaken belief that their sheen is due to silk rather than cotton. Also available from this region are so-called *Koula-Yürük* rustic carpets woven in charming and imaginative geometrical patterns.

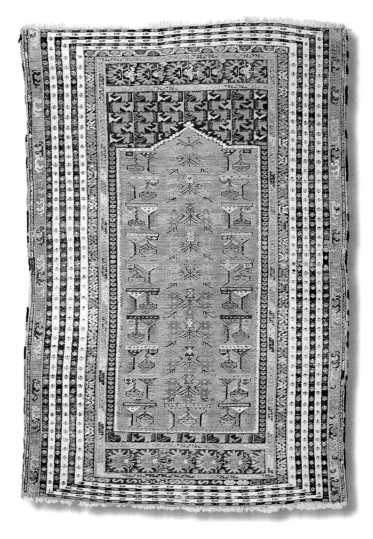

This splendid Mazarlik prayer rug (late 19th century) from Koula achieves a perfect harmony of design and colour. Carpets of this outstanding quality were typically used as a shroud. They are rare since, as a rule, they were kept in the same family for generations or ultimately donated to the mosque. Three symbolic motifs appear: the prayer niche, the weeping willow as a sign of mourning, and the cypress, which connotes immortality. The narrow border with the 'S' motif (a stylised dragon) represents happiness in the afterlife.

Opposite page: A beautifully designed Ushak with a beige-pink field containing a variety of flower motifs in the 'Lotto gul' style. Two small sheep graze above and below the turquoise-blue centre medallion. The carpet reflects both the serenity and the exultation of the weaver. The tamga in the central border belongs in all likelihood to one of the Timur tribes.

Ushak (Usak or Ouchak)

The town of Ushak lies on the road from Izmir to Ankara and is surrounded by unremittingly monotonous steppe. Ushak was famed for its carpets and rugs, all the more so since they appeared frequently in paintings by Renaissance artists, notably the Venetian painter Lorenzo Lotto. Lotto's name came to be associated with the characteristic geometrical motifs that built upon symmetrically repeated arabesques filling the entire central field of the carpet, with no apparent beginning, middle or end. During the Ottoman Empire, Ushak carpets were the first Anatolian carpets to be imported by Venetian merchants of the day. In the main, they were used to decorate stately homes and Christian churches.

The early Ushak weavers turned out *Ushak medallions* and *Ushak stars*, with certain workshops specialising in prayer rugs for use in the mosque; the latter featured geometrical and *saf* motifs. 17th-century *Ushaks* with stylised birds and flowers as their predominant motifs are reproduced in the genre paintings of the French Renaissance artist François Clouet and his circle; magnificent specimens of these exceptional carpets can be seen today only in some major museum collections.

Contemporary *Ushaks* date from the late 19th century. Not many are made and it must be said they are of middling quality at best and, certainly, pale copies of their celebrated predecessors. Warp and weft threads are made of cotton and the pile is loosely knotted. Some of the later designs adopt hybrid motifs found in certain Persian or Anatolian carpets. Today, weavers in Ushak and the surrounding villages work principally for export houses in Izmir that service an undemanding foreign market. That said, semi-nomadic weavers wintering in the mountain villages continue to produce magnificent kilims.

The ancient port of Smyrna (present-day Izmir) was the collection point for carpets woven in south-west Anatolia. There, they were grouped by category, checked and labelled before being shipped in large quantities to major foreign destinations. The Tcolak Zade Company was established in Izmir in 1886 and carpet factories were set up in Koula and Isparta. The generic term *Smyrna* was subsequently applied to output from, among others, Isparta, Koula, Gördes, Bergama, Ushak and Melas. Given their poor quality and low knot density (200 to 500 knots/dm²), these carpets have little or no commercial value.

Today, however, the women from these villages have started to form themselves into co-operatives that can directly access the requisite raw materials and avoid being exploited by the merchant houses of Izmir.

Isparta

Isparta is situated about 60 miles (100 kilometres) from Antalya on the main road to Ankara. Carpet-making is a relatively young industry to the extent that the Isparta Fabrikasi Company, the first major carpet factory, opened its doors in 1925. The plant was modernised in 1982 and in 1989 was taken over by Sümerbank Holdy, as was Hereke production. Mechanical looms were brought in, but hand-weaving continued on metal-post looms installed on the premises. Home-workers wove on their own traditional wooden looms.

A large bazaar (Hali Pazri), housed in a modern building in Isparta, sells carpets and rugs in various qualities and sizes, primarily from Isparta and the villages immediately around it. Prices are extremely competitive but the carpets are not hard-wearing and are often shoddy imitations of carpet types from other regions.

Key features

– *Warp and weft in cotton; pile of coarse and brittle wool poorly pre-treated chemically and artificially faded.*
– *Persian knot, with a density ranging from 500 to 1,000 knots/dm².*
– *Current design templates are those used at the beginning of the 20th century. Output is large-scale, almost to the point of mass production, though personnel continue to knot by hand for both Turkish and export markets. Patterns and motifs draw extensively on ancient Iranian models such as the Kerman.*

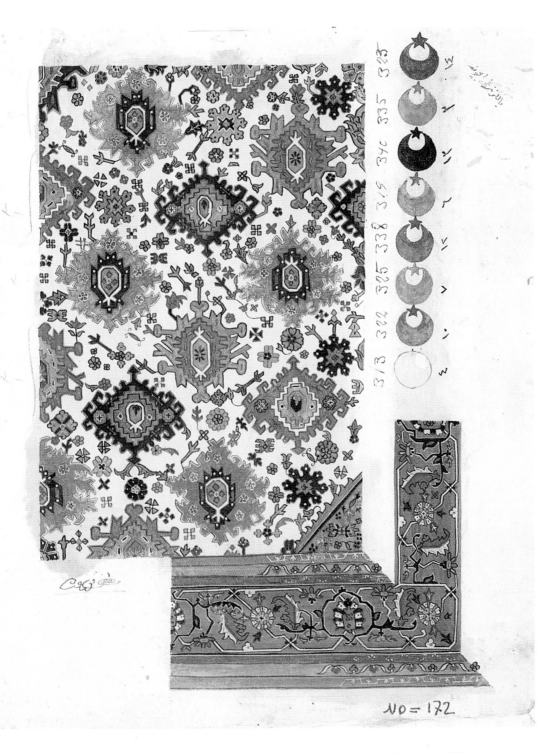

Template and colour chart for an ancient Ushak design carpet woven at the Isparta Fabrikasi factory around 1930.

The Anatolian Central Plateau
Konya and surrounding region

Konya lies 155 miles (250 kilometres) from the Turkish capital of Ankara and is set in the desert steppe of central Anatolia. Since the days of the Seljuq Empire, Konya has been a religious centre and an important pilgrim destination on account of its association with the Mawlawiyah (Mevleviye) order – known in the West as the Whirling Dervishes – founded by the Sufi mystic and poet commonly known as Rumi.

Thanks in great measure to its geographical location, Konya is a city with a long and rich history as a major trading centre. Its carpet museum, housed in a wing of the Rumi Mausoleum, is well worth a visit.

Konya's reputation as a carpet-making city is such that carpets and rugs made in the surrounding region are lumped together under the generic name *Konya*. The specifics of a *Konya* are best exemplified in its prayer rugs, with their red ground and limp texture and motifs representing tulips and larks' feet. *Konya* garden carpets are also produced.

Carpets and kilims from Konya and the neighbouring villages of Derbent and Ladik are on sale in the bazaar in Konya, and carpet merchants from Istanbul regularly visit the region to make contact with individual weavers in other villages.

The kilims from the mountainous region south of Konya have a reputation for excellent quality. Those from the small village of Mut (about 50 miles/80 kilometres from Karaman) are particularly sought after, despite their somewhat thick texture. These *Karamanis*, as they were traditionally known, are woven on a rare white wool ground and have simple geometrical motifs built around a central strip of three to six polychrome hexagons set against the white or (occasionally) indigo ground.

The region centred on the market town of Nigde (between Kayseri and Konya) turns out especially fine kilims known as *Konya-Nigde*. Prayer rugs from here are very similar in composition to the kilims made in Karaman. Like the latter, they are small, made of coarse wool dyed in dark shades, and frequently decorated with three *mihrabs* ranged side by side, culminating in a stepped arch with two sorts of crotchet at its apex.

While the kilim motifs from this area are typically Anatolian, the tonal variations are such as to create different perspectives, as if seen through a distorting mirror. In particular, the colours used for the triangular motifs are never the same as for their symmetrical mirror image. The vegetable dyes are relatively muted and limited to a palette of brick-reds, dark blues and yellows, with shading in black and raw silk tones.

A Mut (Yürük) kilim from the mountainous region south of Konya. The stepped, saw-toothed design recalls that of the prayer rug illustrated on page 66.

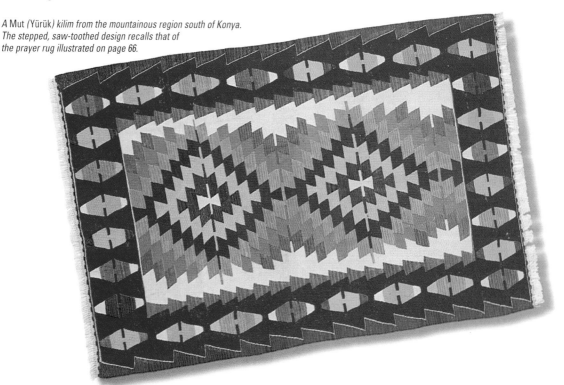

An exceptional Konya-Nigde kilim from the mid-19th century. Lateral borders on a white ground and a frieze of flower motifs (violets) combine to form a powerful visual statement. The field, divided into five sections and with motifs reprised in positive and negative, confers a bold and expressive chromatic harmony on the overall design.

A Konya-Ladik *prayer rug from around
1850, with characteristic red ground and
a stepped and hooked* mihrab. *The lower
part of the field comprises five tulips with
inverted crowns. The tulip was imported
into Turkey by Caucasian tribes.*

Ladik and region

The small town of Ladik, located no more than about 20 miles (35 kilometres) from Konya, has long been reputed throughout Anatolia for the excellent quality of its prayer rugs. There are a large number of extant models, many taking a stylised tulip as their principal motif. The tell-tale feature of *Ladik* carpets is the ivory or purplish-red wool thread which outlines and highlights each motif. The colours are bright, with a blood-red typically predominating in the field. The wool used is finely spun and lustrous. Knot density varies from around 1,000 to 1,500 knot/dm². Because of their similarity to *Konya* carpets and rugs, those from Ladik are generally referred to as *Konya-Ladik*.

Kayseri and region

Kayseri (the former Caesarea) lies about 210 miles (335 kilometres) from Konya and was a leading carpet centre from the days of the Ottoman Empire. Today, Kayseri has re-asserted itself as the principal commercial hub for carpets and rugs made in every province of central Anatolia, including those from Capadocia and Kirsehir in the plateau north of the Taurus, and those brought to the market in Kaseri by nomad Yürüks and Kurds.

The urban factories and workshops, all of recent date, produce carpets and rugs of various generic types destined principally for the export and tourist markets. Privately-owned workshops supply wholesalers who provide them with raw materials and cartoons of carpets that have been commissioned. These wholesalers also have an extensive network of weavers who reside in the outlying villages and work from home on domestic looms. Depending on individual requirements and the price of the finished article, the carpets and rugs they produce can vary from excellent to pedestrian.

Carpet designs and dimensions are specified by the commissioning wholesaler in response to market demand. Typical knot density is between 1,250 and 1,900/dm². Local wool is used to produce a coarse and rather short pile. As a rule, patterns and motifs are along the lines of models from Konya and Persia, the primary source of inspiration being *Tabriz* carpets.

Over the years, Kayseri has always maintained close cultural and commercial links with the Iranian carpet capital; as a *quid pro quo*, silk carpets from Tabriz are often modelled on *Kayseri* patterns.

Certain *Kayseri* prayer rugs, made entirely from silk and interwoven with gold silk thread to achieve a subtle shimmering effect, are of exceptional quality. Finely knotted to a tight pile and with delicate plant motifs worked in subtle pastel dyes, they exhibit a harmony and finesse that is still a jealously guarded secret among the families of Armenian weavers who have worked for centuries in this city of artistic craftsmanship and excellence.

Sadly, there is another side to the coin. Some wholesalers do not think twice about cutting their overheads by mixing genuine or artificial silk waste with mercerised cotton to produce prayer rugs that have a lustre that is identical to that of silk but which has none of its durability. Undaunted, Western buyers acquire these as wall hangings.

Kayseri serves the tourist market by fabricating small (3 ft 3 in × 1 ft 8 in/1 m × 0.50 m) souvenir cushion covers known as *Yastic*. These are woven either in wool or in artificial silk.

Specific mention should also be made of the prayer rugs produced in the town of Kirsehir, the modest output from Muçur, or those from the town of Sivas, where there are two state-owned factories producing copies of *Tabriz* models made with a Persian knot – unlike the original and

splendid *Sivas* models. To these centres should be added the villages around Sivas, such as Kanval, Kavak, Zara and Kangal.

In sum, Kayseri and the region surrounding it constitute a major carpet centre offering a varied and eclectic range of carpets and rugs. Buyer beware is the rule, however: it is for the buyer to choose and choose wisely.

Contemporary fine-silk Kayseri *carpet from* Bursa. *The centre medallion is typical of ancient* Tabriz *models. This carpet rivals a* Hereke *in terms of refined design and quality of execution.*

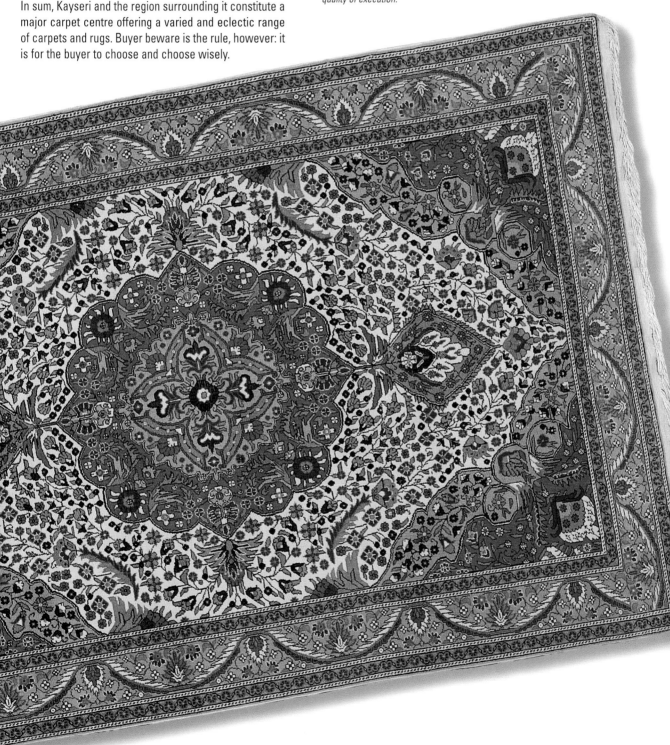

The mountain areas of eastern Anatolia

Kars

The population of eastern Anatolia is a bewildering mix of ethnic groups, including Tartars, Azerbaijani, Circassians, Georgians, Kurds, Armenians, Turkmens and others. Of these, three particular ethnic groups are dominant in terms of carpet-making: the Kurds, the Yürüks and the Armenians.

Carpets made in this region close to the Armenian border draw on Caucasian motifs and feature rough-pile star and cross medallion patterns woven from coarse wool mixed on occasion with goat hair. The finish is perhaps most accurately described as 'rustic'. Armenian weavers work at home on portable high-warp looms. Carpets are typically edged with a kilim strip.

The *Kars*-kilim variety (produced in Kars, a town high up on the austere high plateau of Anatolia) is woven by semi-nomadic Kurdish weavers. These kilims have wool warp yarn with a decidedly dense texture. Kilims woven in the region of Lake Van in eastern Turkey have a more rigid finish and exhibit a limited and rather sombre colour range. Carpet merchants in Van (Cumhuriyet Cad) sell

beautiful carpets and kilims from the region, but the prospective buyer is well advised to buy on the advice of an independent expert.

A late-19th-century kilim distinguished by a highly unusual design featuring a stylised human figure (oddly reminiscent of an 'extra-terrestrial') with a bright-red dagger in place of a heart. In all probability, the kilim belonged to a Sufi sect or was perhaps woven in memory of a famous warrior who died of a stab wound. The overall effect is startlingly powerful and dramatic.

Carpet merchants in all the major towns mentioned here work closely with importers and with private customers. They will take care of customs formalities, notably by furnishing the purchaser with a certificate of authenticity, dating the carpet in question and stipulating where it was made. Should the carpet purchased be more than 100 years old, a designated expert will be called in to determine whether or not it should be permitted to leave the country. The same procedures are followed by carpet specialists in all the grand bazaars or up-market stores in large towns on the Asiatic side of the country.

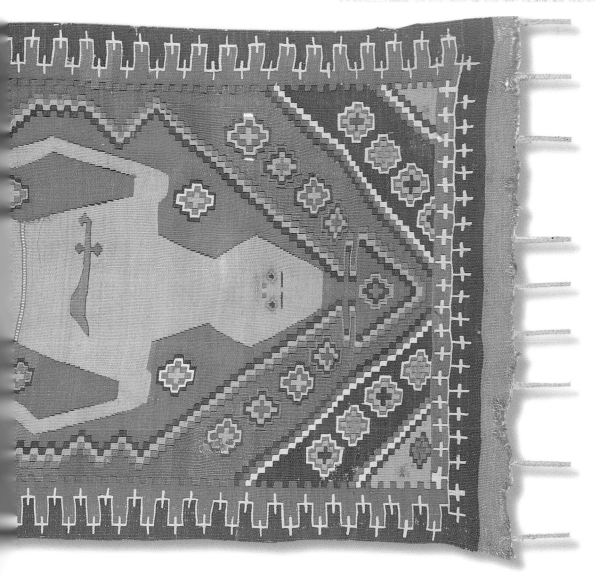

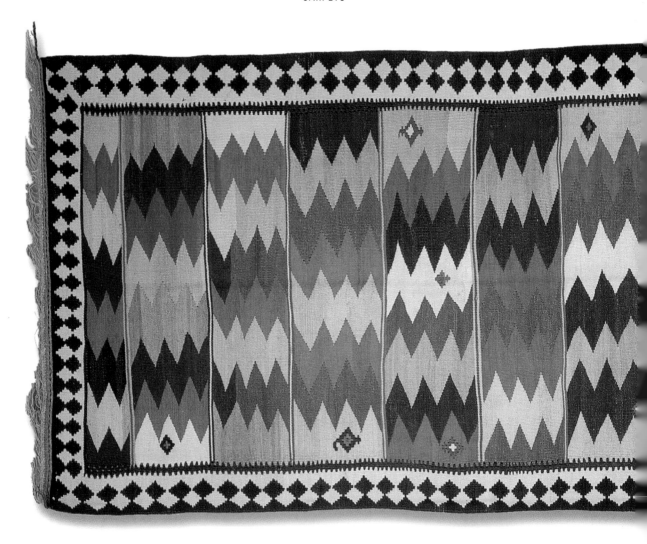

THE NOMADS OF IRAN

Despite recent legislation designed to oblige Iran's nomadic tribes to stay in permanent settlements and integrate with the indigenous population, there are still a large number of isolated mountain regions in the country peopled by the *chador-neshin* ('tent-dwellers'). The women of these nomadic tribes use wool from their livestock to weave soft dense-pile peasant carpets and rugs which often have a charm all of their own. Additionally, they weave kilims for various domestic uses, together with travel bags and horse and camel blankets.

Azerbaijan (north-west Iran)

The Shahsavans (Chahsevans)

The Shahsavans comprise a number of tribes of Turkish-speaking origin that live on the steppes of Central Asia. For the large part, they are now semi-nomadic and live in semi-permanent settlements; that said, those in

use the *soumak* technique that closely approximates to brocading; as a result, geometrical star-cross and animal motifs are usually rendered with remarkable precision. In local bazaars and markets, the collectors may chance upon magnificent travel bags (*khorjin*) or horse and camel blankets decorated in brightly coloured geometrical motifs.

Karadagh (*Karaje*) carpets betraying Persian and Caucasian influences are found in and around the town of Karadagh in the mountainous frontier region north-east of Tabriz.

A Shahsavan kilim from the early 20th century. Small saw-toothed smotifs in different colour permutations are woven into a pattern that is disconcertingly simple and strangely effective (reminiscent of the 'dazzling' designs of Persian Veramins). Note the syncopated border made up of small 'positive/negative' juxtaposed triangles and squares, a pattern frequently found on Neolithic earthenware from Halicar (central Anatolia) dating back to 5000 B.C.

north-west Iran and on the Moghan Plains region still spend summer in their traditional dome-shaped black or white felt *alacigh* tents. They are divided into several sub-groups by reference to the grazing lands they habitually use; thus, there are Shahsavans from Moghan, Hashtrud, Khamseh, Saveh and Veramin.

The women weave carpets commonly (and inaccurately) referred to as 'Caucasian kilims'. The simple motifs exhibit a purity of line and a balanced overall composition, with multiple variants of the star motif tending to predominate. Like their counterparts in the Caucasus, many weavers

Kordestan (Iranian Kurdistan)

By comparison with Kurds living in Turkey, Kurds living in Iran appear to have fewer problems of integration. Iranian Kurds are frequently semi-nomads living in the north-east of the Zagros Mountains in south-western Iran along the border with Iraq. Interesting examples of Kurdish carpets may be found in some urban bazaars, such as that of the Azarbaijan city of Mehabad (formerly Saujbulagh). These are known commercially under the generic heading of *Kordestan* carpets, but it should be cautioned that the many different Kurdish tribes produce carpets and rugs with designs that vary widely, reflecting the particular locality in which they tend to pitch their tents.

The whole spectrum of motifs appears in finely woven kilims from this Senneh region. They boast a wide range of field composition. Delicately worked patterns with floral bouquets, *herati* or *boteh* motifs fill out the entire field and are reminiscent of silk carpets from the Safavid period. Examples from sedentary Kurdish tribes will be discussed in more detail in a later section devoted to output from urban workshops in the region.

Key features

– Long and glossy brown wool, occasionally coarse and mixed with goat or camel hair.
– Turkish-knotted to a density of 700 to 1,500/dm².
– Comparatively long pile.
– Mixture of vegetable and synthetic dyes with dominant dark reds contrasting with camel-hair colour field ranging from light beige to dark brown.
– Geometrical patterns comprising a variety of motifs. The field is often divided into a lozenge grid with star and small rosette inserts. Designs are greatly influenced by those of the local ethnic group.
– Formats are characteristically small, with Sedjadé types usually measuring 3 ft 3 in × 4 ft 3 in (1 m × 1.30 m) or 5 ft × 6 ft (1.50 m × 1.80 m), though Kenare models range up to 6 ft 6 in × 13 ft 2 in (2 m × 4 m). Carpets and rugs are relatively cheap and extremely hard-wearing.

Opposite page: Khorjin *carpet with stylised* Yomut *guls. The sections have been stitched together to form a pannier (saddle-bag) or tent cushion. Right: A Kurdish* namakdan *from west Iran, used as a salt pouch by mountain shepherds. The whole is woven in one piece and using several techniques. The field comprises diagonal bands of colour with superimposed stylised animal motifs (goats, eagles, etc.).*

Luristan (Lorestan) and region

The 'Land of the Lurs' is set in the valleys of the Zagros chain in the south of Turkestan and has been inhabited for centuries by pastoral semi-nomads of Persian stock. The villages of Luristan are peopled by sedentary Kurds and semi-nomadic tribes such as the Bakhtyari. A survey of Lur weavers has revealed that there are more than 20,000 looms in Luristan – about half of all the looms in Kurdish villages as a whole.

The Lurs have settled predominantly in and around the capital Khorramabad, originally a Sasanid Persian settlement. Luristan carpets and rugs sold in the capital's bazaars and in the town of Borujerd (Burujird) are destined mainly for local household use.

Key features

– Silky and thick lamb's-wool, sometimes mixed with goat hair.
– Predominantly dark vegetable and synthetic dyes on a deep blue or brick-red ground.
– Low knot density (between 600 and 1,000 knots/dm²).
– Relatively deep pile.
– Geometrical patterns in a field divided into small hexagons decorated with star, rosette, hooked lozenge and stylised animal motifs.
– Small, 4 ft 7 in × 6 ft 2 in (1.40 m × 1.90 m), rustic, solid and cheap. Luri weavers also produce beautiful kilims.

Fars (Farsistan) and region

For political reasons, various nomadic tribes of different stock have been removed to this remote region far from the major urban centres. The womenfolk continue to weave traditional carpets on primitive low-warp home looms, using wool and hair from their livestock and vegetable dyes – notably madder, indigo plant and henna.

Key features

– Supple and silky wool, with warp and weft in wool mixed with goat hair.
– Medium-density weave with knots at between 1,500 and 2,500/dm².
– Turk-baff (Ghiordes) knots other than in the case of Khamseh carpets and rugs, which feature the Persian Fars-baff knot technique and have a knot density of only 500 to 1,000 knots/dm²
– Vegetable-dyed and predominantly dark tones, especially cobalt blue, red and maroon.
– An unusual feature is that the borders are woven in red and yellow thread, with small tufts of wool protruding from the borders at more or less regular intervals.
– Finely detailed design with principal motifs including the Shiraz rose and boteh, and stylised animals (cockerels, birds, camels and serpents). One major motif specific to the Qashqai (or Kashkai) is a sort of stylised crab. The centre of the field is decorated with medallions made up of lozenges. The ground is sometimes made up of two or three hooked lozenges. Motifs are frequently dispersed haphazardly across the field.

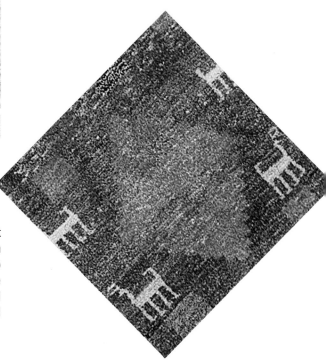

Contemporary Gabbeh woven by a Qashqai weaver. The variegated chequerboard pattern features a diamond shape centred between four stylised goats. This abstract design is strangely reminiscent of experimental colour studies by Paul Klee or Sonia Delaunay. Thousands of women from the semi-nomadic tribes of Fars in the Shiraz region weave these 'rustic' carpets to support their families.

Modern Gabbeh *(1970) with characteristic features such as human silhouettes, lions and peacocks in various colour permutations. The peacock is an essential motif in the repertoire of the Persian weaver. The lion, meanwhile, stands for courage and fortitude and, in association with the dragon, is often regarded as a guardian and protector.*

Carpets and kilims from this region are often referred to by the generic term *Shiraz*, but are in fact made by a range of different nomadic or semi-nomadic weavers such as Afshars, Qashqai (nomads from the high plateaus of the Zargos mountain range north-west of Shiraz), Khamsehs, Luris, Huluku and Mamasani Kugilu. Accordingly, it is often very difficult to identify the exact provenance of carpets and kilims from the Fars province, not least because of reciprocal influences and borrowings before individual nomad groups banded together. In fact, most of the differences are of political rather than of ethnic origin.

Carpets from all over the Fars province are found in the Vakil Bazaar in Shiraz. It is estimated that the 400 or so villages around Shiraz can lay claim to no fewer than 10,000 looms and around 20,000 sedentary weavers, in addition to semi-nomads in the region, such as the Qashqai.

These carpets, even when the weave is coarse, have a peculiar charm that derives from the almost childlike naivety of their stylised animal motifs and from the richness of their vegetable dyes. What is more, they are reasonably priced despite the fact that they are very much in fashion at present. They are often referred to by the generic term *Gabbeh*, a Luri word for 'rustic' carpets for use in the home. The uncommon suppleness of the

Gabbeh style is achieved by the insertion of between five and ten weft threads between every two rows of knots.

George D. Bonneh, a Swiss collector and *Gabbeh* expert, has commented on the loss of traditional weaving techniques and pointed to the pale imitations that exist today. In a preface to an exhibition of his collection in 1992, Bonnet noted that he is in favour of the "promising approach" adopted by a Shiraz wholesaler who is currently encouraging weavers to express themselves freely in the traditional way. "This makes for the creation of fascinating *Gabbeh* carpets and rugs," wrote Bonnet, adding that they "offer traditional artisans an opportunity to come into the 20th century. The *Gabbeh*, when all is said and done, is a woven picture."

Of some 140,000 Qashqai identified in a 1972 census, only about a third are sedentary. During their summer migration, Qashqai weavers throughout the Fars region also weave very beautiful domestic kilims. There is always a low-warp loom set up in front of their black tents, with several women busying themselves at it. Their material of choice is a soft lamb's-wool dyed with madder (mixed with pomegranate in the case of the darker reds). The characteristically geometrical motifs often draw on Caucasian patterns but are woven in a highly individual style and in very bright and cheery colours.

Saw-toothed motifs assembled in a zig-zag pattern reminiscent of that used in 'dazzling' kilims create disconcerting visual effects depending on the perspective from which the carpet is viewed – in much the same way, perhaps, as the paintings of the Hungarian-born French artist Victor Vasarely.

Another type of kilim comprises nothing but parallel lines, whereas others have a field entirely filled out in polychromatic lozenges that form a sort of grid. Others still are made up of simple horizontal bands decorated with very vivid colours. The colours are, to this day, vegetable-dyed, though the overall weave has lost its traditional finesse.

Carpets made by the Afshar (Afchari) community, originally from Azerbaijan, enjoyed a good reputation but are today of only middling to mediocre quality. They exhibit low knot-density (between 600 and 900 knots/dm²) and typically feature 'flower vase' motifs influenced by the major nomadic group of Kermans found to the south of the city.

In addition to carpets, the women also weave practical kilims for use as travel bags and horse blankets. A visit to the market in towns such as Baft and Kerman will often pay dividends in the form of more finely worked and imaginative specimens, such as small bags or saddle-covers, frequently woven with a *soumak* stitch. These are distinguished by their overall harmony and their rich colouring.

Mention should also be made of carpets from Abadeh, a township situated in an arid region between Isfahan and Shiraz. A rough count suggests there are some 15,000 weavers in Abadeh and its immediate surrounding region, all of them former nomads who have now settled permanently. Their sole occupation in these otherwise rather desolate surroundings is to weave rather coarse but hard-wearing carpets with delightfully naïve patterns and motifs that hint at Caucasian influences in their choice of warm and rich vegetable-dye colours. Not surprisingly, perhaps, these carpets are much in demand.

Rustic carpet from the Shiraz region featuring anthropomorphic motifs on a red madder-dyed ground.

A contemporary Bakhtyar *garden carpet* from Chahar Mahall, with typical compartmentalised design of small squares with cypress, Tree of Life, flower and boteh *insets.* As with its 17th-century predecessors, the overall design represents Paradise. Trees are particularly popular symbols from ancient mythology; the cypress is a Zoroastrian symbol of longevity and immortality.

Bakhtyari

The Bakhtyari (Bakhtiars or Baxtyari) spend their winters in the sprawling region of Chahar Mahall that extends all the way to Isfahan and Kurdistan province. A large number of Bakhtyari live in the area south of the Zagros Mountains, effectively cut off from outside influences. Access to their encampments is difficult and only via unmapped routes.

Establishing exactly whether a carpet has been made by the Bakhtyari is, to say the least, problematic. This is because carpets made by the disparate tribal groups in this vast region tend to be lumped together in the market-place as Bakhtieri (Bakhtyar) despite the fact that the individual tribes have clearly marked off their own spe-cific territory – something of a paradox in the case of a 'nomadic' tribe. As a result, Bakhtyari motifs are often diffi-cult to tell apart from those featuring on Luristan carpets. Bakhtyari nomad carpets are known as Kersak (literally, 'bear-like'), no doubt because of their dense pile. The Bakhtyari themselves make a distinction in terms of the specific technique used. Thus, qali-baf is the term used to describe a knotted carpet, sade-baf refers to a kilim, and nasq-gamasisi applied to carpets and rugs woven with the soumak technique.

The huzrin is a shoulder bag used to carry items of clothing. Its peculiarity is that (like some Kurdish shoulder bags) it comprises an amalgam of techniques super-imposed on the warp. The varied effects achieved by the different techniques and their juxtaposition add up to a highly original product whose geometrical patterns are strangely reminiscent of those used in avant-garde carpet design. In effect, they lend themselves to being hung on a wall much as one would hang a painting.

The 'garden motif' Bakhtyar harks back to the ancient garden carpets of the Safavid period (such as the 17th-century example hanging in the Musée des Arts Décoratifs in Paris), though the flower and tree motifs used today are highly stylised. The plethora of motifs and rich colours in each square testify to the weaver's skill and creative originality.

The prices for modern-day Bakhtyar carpets and rugs vary in terms of their technical quality rather than their decorative complexity.

The nomad women also produce kilim tent carpets and travel bags. Exceptionally beautiful kilims oddly similar to those made in the Hamadan region are woven in and around the town of Shustar; they are framed by a broad monochrome border woven in camel hair, and the field seems to 'float' within the vacuum created by this rectangular frame. As a rule, the field features series of small dark-coloured octagonal medallions or boteh motifs.

Key features

– Coarse spindle-spun wool with a shimmering pile attributed by Bakhtyari weavers to the water in which the untreated wool is washed.

– Variable knot density (between 900 and 1,800 knots/dm² other than in carpets made in the town of Shar Koord, where knot densities of between 3,000 and 4,000/dm² are common).

– Raised pile 1¼ in to 2 in (3 cm to 5 cm), irregularly trimmed.

– Dark vegetable dyes, with red madder predominating; grounds in natural off-white. The albumen in sheep droppings acts as a fixative and imparts intensity to the colours. Up to some 50 years ago, weavers ground down and boiled dried cochineal abdomens found in large quantities on the leaves of oak trees.

– A special design feature is the use of 8 in × 8 in (20 cm × 20 cm) compartments which contain a variety of random stylised plant and animal motifs. The chequerboard pattern is framed by a series of up to seven borders decorated with stylised plant motifs such as the cypress that are oriented towards the weaver, the result being that the carpet is 'read' in the direction it is woven, i.e., from top (ĵelow) to bottom (pâyn).

– Formats vary. Sedjadé carpets may range from 4 ft 4 in × 7 ft 10 in (1.30 m × 2.40 m) up to 8 ft 2 in × 11 ft 2 in (2.50 m × 3.40 m). Boldjai (south of Shalamzar) is the only remaining carpet centre that produces large (9 ft 10 in × 13 ft 2 in/3 m × 4 m) models known as bibi-baf (literally 'girls' carpets'). These are of meticulous quality but increasingly scarce.

Sistan and Baluchistan

The area of south-east Iran between the shores of the Persian Gulf and the frontiers with Afghanistan and Pakistan must rank as one of the most inhospitable on earth, what with the torrid heat and the incredibly harsh winters. Baluchistan and, in particular, the region around Khorasan (Khurasan) is home to the Iranian Baluch tribes of Turkmen nomads. The Baluch weave the best carpets sold in the urban markets of Turbat-Haideri, Turbat-e-Jam, Neyshabur and Meshed. Some 9,000 looms and 18,000 Baluchi weavers are thought to live in the 300 or so villages surrounding Turbat-Haideri, despite the fact that these peasant carpets and rugs were habitually looked down upon by Iranian merchants.

Baluchi carpets are more interesting than currently available *Gabbeh* carpets in terms of overall design, colour and variety of motif. The women weave kilims (occasionally interspersed with knots) which are used for every conceivable day-to-day use – as bags, cushions, floor coverings, 'table' coverings and so on. The small prayer rugs known as *akhund* are readily identified by the rectangular *mihrab* that is set off against a light-coloured ground woven in untreated wool or, frequently, camel hair, whose sole decoration is a Tree of Life.

Key features
– Silky Meshed wool and camel hair.
– Medium knot density (between 700 and 1,500 knots/dm^2).
– Medium, irregularly trimmed pile.
– Vegetable dyes (occasionally synthetic) with dark tones fixed with a solution of potassium soda and iron oxide. Grounds are typically executed in natural-shade camel hair.
– Designs vary and often betray influence of Turkmen Tekke or Salor *tribal types* (using the same octagonal gul *across the entire field and over a brick-red ground). Other types employing the* boteh *motif across the entire fields are know as 'almonds'.*
– Small 2 ft 3 in × 5 ft (0.70 m × 1.50 m) or, rarely, medium formats 4 ft 3 in × 8 ft 10 in (1.30 m × 2.70 m).
– Top and bottom borders are often finished with a kilim strip of 2 to 8 in (5 to 20 cm).

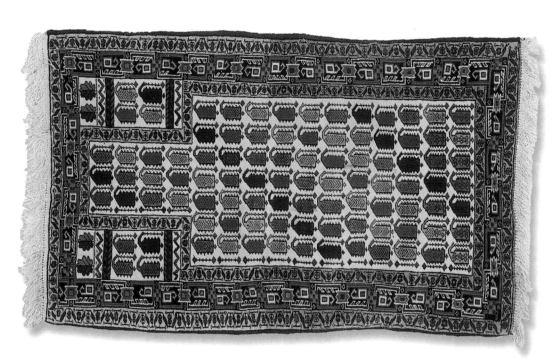

Opposite page: A contemporary Iranian prayer rug woven by a Baluchi weaver. The field contains stylised boteh motifs known to the Baluchi tribe as 'almonds', but which other ethnic groups variously term 'water drops', 'pine cones' or 'tongues of flame'. This boteh motif appears in a wide variety of imaginative forms in contemporary carpets and rugs woven by Baluchi women in Iran and Afghanistan. Baluchi carpets are predicted to become increasingly sought after: they are beautifully woven and are far superior in quality to the rustic Gabbeh style that is very much in vogue at present. Above: An extremely rare late-19th-century sofreh rug woven by a Baluchi weaver from Khorasan. The sofreh is placed directly on the tent floor at mealtimes as a sort of 'tablecloth'. The cross indicates where different dishes are to be placed. The example illustrated here measures some 4 ft 2 in × 4 ft 7 in (1.30 m × 1.40 m). It has a monochrome field woven from camel hair.

Turkmen tribes of the Mazandaran region

The Mazandaran region lies in northern Iran, bordering the Turkmenistan border and the shores of the Caspian Sea. Several Turkmen tribes sought refuge in northern Iran during the war with the former Soviet Union. Today, many of them live as nomads in the traditional *yurt*, a portable home made of skins and felt.

Their carpets and rugs – very similar to those of the Tekke, Salor and Yomut tribes of Central Asia – are sold at country markets usually held each Thursday and in urban markets in carpet production centres such as Gonbad-e-Qabus, where some 8,000 weavers have been identified, mainly from the Turkmen Yomut tribe. The only Turkmen tribe to live exclusively in Iran are the Goklans, who wander along the banks of the river Goklans.

URBAN WORKSHOPS IN IRAN

Persian carpets have always been distinguished by their great variety of design and by the substantial quantities in which they were made. Their reputation rests in part on the unusually fine examples made during the period from the 16th to the end of the 18th century, but also on the fact that Persian carpets have found a world-wide market from the end of the 19th century to the present day – to the point where, for the vast majority of the European and North American markets, 'Persian' has become synonymous with Oriental carpets.

During the reign of Reza Shah Pahlavi (r. 1925–41), carpet manufacture was tightly controlled and many workshops and factories were state-owned. In 1936, the Shah established the Sherkate Farsh Persian carpet association which went on to develop pilot workshops in Kerman, Isfahan and Hamadan, each presided over by the

Turkmen women weaving a Yomut-style carpet on a low-warp loom. They are squatting on the section of the carpet that has already been woven. In their right hands, both women hold small but very sharp knives used to trim the knot ends. The two must work at the same speed in order to ensure that the weft is fed rhythmically across the loom after each row of knots has been completed.

best *ustad* ('master') from the region. The objective was to return carpet-making to its former glory by insisting on the use of hand-spun yarn and specially-adapted vegetable dyes and by reviving and safeguarding traditional designs and motifs which, over the years, had been lost or neglected.

World War II put paid to the export of Persian carpets but, coming up to the 1960s, the Shah reactivated the Sherkate Farsh association to control and supervise output from virtually every urban workshop in Iran. More than 20,000 weavers were employed at one time by this powerful association. In 1976, the Iranian Ministry of Commerce commissioned a nation-wide audit which identified a staggering 545,289 looms and more than a million weavers, 85% of whom were female (and, of those, 44% girls between the ages of five and fifteen). Measures were immediately introduced to bring down the number of under-age children employed in the workshops.

Another audit, this time in 1980, revealed almost the same data (over a million weavers working on more than 600,000 looms and turning out five million square metres of carpet annually). If one adds in all those employed in related occupations (from the shepherd and dyer to the specialist merchant), the carpet industry in Iran today may be said to employ more than two million persons.

It is difficult to arrive at hard data on current output of carpets and rugs. Export markets have re-opened and European merchants have been inundated by Persian produce, some of excellent quality, some distinctly less so. All in all, state involvement has continued to sustain urban workshop quality. At the same time, carpets and rugs produced by semi-nomadic tribes have continued to be original and creative, building to a miraculously vibrant folk art typified by the *Gabbeh* carpets and rugs made in the region around Shiraz.

Sadly, political upheaval has frustrated carpet exports, while persistent international demand has resulted in the most magnificent Persian carpets being slavishly repli-cated in various workshops in China and in Pakistan and passed off as (albeit cheaper) copies of 'original' designs. The technical and artistic decline identified in the case of carpets and rugs produced in Turkey is equally if not more pronounced in the case of Iran. There has been a prolif-eration of synthetic dyes, recourse to inferior grades of wool, increased reliance on the 'double' Jufti knot and, as noted, servile imitation of ancient designs. There are

A Qashqai weaver using two different techniques to produce a blanket. One part of the weft is applied to produce a regular 'tartan' stripe design, while another part is woven using the cicim *technique (a soumak-type weave with additional strands).*

exceptions in the form of remarkable contemporary designs; these will be noted as and where appropriate in the following pages.

In order to chart a course through the bewildering array of different models and styles, this section will adopt the approach used earlier in the section on Turkey, in other words listing the most reputable examples region by region, town by town and, where appropriate, village by village.

Azerbaijan and region

Azerbaijan is a vast mountainous region that extends from Turkey to the Caspian Sea (see also the section on Shahsavan nomads). The sumptuous floral patterns woven into carpets from Tabriz, the capital of the ancient Persian Empire, were inspired by the famous Tabriz miniatures and were among the finest in the Persian tradition.

Tabriz

Current output from Tabriz is uneven, though some private workshops operated by master weavers of the old school continue to turn out carpets and rugs of the finest quality. *Tabriz* carpets are woven to order; some are extremely large – eight metres by five or even larger. These are hard-wearing carpets since the wool pile is highly resilient. As a result, first quality *Tabriz* are correspondingly (and justifiably) expensive.

Some urban weavers have adapted their output to accommodate Western tastes. In an attempt to remain price-competitive, *Tabriz* – although still 'hand-made' – are turned out in large quantities – woven, so to speak, around-the-clock. This mass production approach has clearly had an impact on quality, not least because the weft is knotted by means of a hook rather than directly by hand, the synthetic-dye colours tend to be garish, and the motifs are increasingly banal.

Tabriz workshops also produce all-silk carpets and rugs decorated with figurative scenes – typically, of the hunt. In the better grades, knot densities can be as high as 7,000/dm², with the result that motifs are sharply defined. Alongside these quality *Tabriz* are others destined primarily for local consumption. Designs are highly unusual, to say the least, and it is quite common for these low-grade *Tabriz* to feature reproductions of a postcard or a banknote. In a sense, they represent a marriage between folk art and pop art.

Right: An ancient, delicately coloured Tabriz *prayer rug of a design virtually identical to that of the oldest* Ghiordes *prayer rugs with their two stylised columns on either side of the mihrab niche and a characteristically styled centre lamp. Opposite page: A classic* Tabriz *with a design based on 18th-century models. The complex interlace of flower stalks is most imaginative and beautifully executed. There is a distinct resemblance to certain* Kayseri *models woven in Turkey.*

Key features

– Rich, lustrous wool hand-spun by nomadic weavers who have settled in the various villages around Tabriz.
– Knot density varies with quality, ranging from 900 to 1,000 knots/dm² for poorer grades, and up to 3,000/dm² for the finest quality. (Ancient Tabriz were knotted to a density of between 3,000 and 10,000/dm².)
– The Turkish (Ghiordes) knot (known in Iran as turk-baf) predominates, though some workshops use the Persian (Senneh) knot.
– The traditional flat and dense pile has given way to a slightly raised pile that does not have the same silk-like lustre as that of wool from neighbouring regions. This is primarily because the wool is washed in local Tabriz water, which has a high salt content that negatively affects the dyeing process and subsequent cleaning of the finished product.
– Dyes are chrome-based synthetics, though certain workshops continue to use natural dyes (predominantly red, blue and ivory).
– Designs are inventive, drawing heavily on 17th-century miniatures featuring animals dotted around luxurious landscapes. The herati motif features in centre medallions. The field is either plain-coloured or filled with flower and shrub motifs.

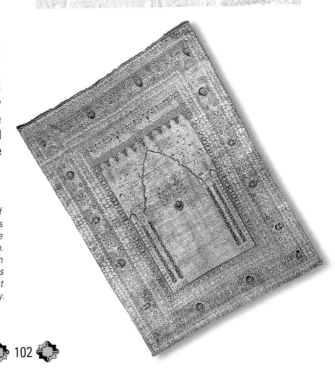

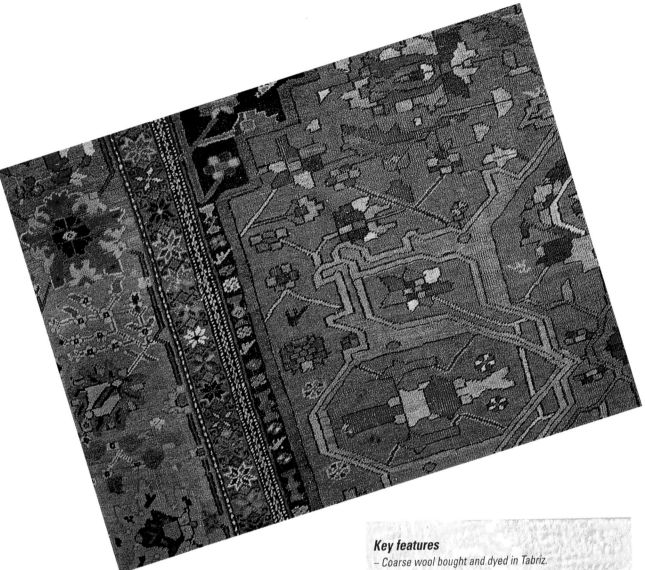

Heriz and region

Heriz and outlying villages such as Yoravan and Sarab lie to the east of Tabriz in the heartland of Azerbaijan. Heriz is famous for its large output of wool and silk carpets that are hard-wearing and comparatively cheap.

The special charm of *Heriz* carpets and rugs derives principally from the unusual colour spectrum used. Newer *Heriz* are readily identified by their relative thickness by comparison with ancient models. That said, many of the 'ancient' *Heriz* available today are of very recent manufacture. They are of good quality, however, and are an excellent buy, provided the price is right.

The designs on silk *Heriz* carpets are specified by the importer. Many are little more than poor copies of classic designs from Safavid Persia and Mughal India.

Key features
– Coarse wool bought and dyed in Tabriz.
– Warp and weft threads in cotton.
– Turkish (Ghiordes) knot density of between 600 and 1,200/dm².
– Comparatively high and irregular pile that is nonetheless hard-wearing.
– Natural madder dye yields both the magnificent pink dugh shades used for plant motifs (flowers, leaves and palm fronds) and the characteristic brick-red field common to traditional Heriz carpets; today, synthetic dyes are frequently substituted.
– The refined and sophisticated medallion and corner motifs typical of traditional Heriz carpets and rugs have been substituted by straight-line 'step motif' stereotypes that extend across the entire field. The (frequently red) border ground is made up of angular herati motifs.

Ardebil and region

Ardebil is located in northern Iran close to the Caspian Sea. Its largest mosque is where the Safavid carpet now on display in London's Victoria and Albert Museum was discovered: a magnificent specimen with lobed medallions alternating with two dragons locked in combat and flying phoenixes.

Ardebil and the neighbouring town of Meshkinshar (on the road towards Tabriz) turn out a large number of *Ardebil* and *Meshkin* carpets and rugs woven mainly by sedentary Shahsavan weavers.

Opposite page: Detail from a large Heriz *carpet (early 20th century), highlighting the skilful deployment of stylised flower motifs.*
Below: A contemporary Heriz *with a highly stylised pattern. The central eight-branch star medallion is framed by four smaller medallions and a border on a white ground that combine to impart a carefully balanced relief effect to the overall design.*

Key features

– Good quality wool, dense pile, coarse but taut weave.
– Knot density from 1,500 to 2,500/dm².
– Bright synthetic-dye colours with blue, red and ivory grounds; vegetable dyes have started to be used again in recent years.
– Gallery carpets are often made up of alternating light and dark lozenge medallions. Motifs draw on geometrical Caucasian models. Designs are fanciful and highly inventive, with field and borders attractively decorated with a wide range of motifs – some traditional (such as the boteh, the comb, the peacock and various star crosses), others innovative (such as the mountain sheep, ducks in flight or small stylised lakes).

Iranian Kurdistan

At present, output from Kurdish weavers is known to us only by reference to the carpets made in the towns and villages of the Kurdistan region, an area that is not readily accessible to foreigners.

Carpets and rugs from this vast area are often – wrongly – known to Europeans under the collective name of *Mosul*. In fact, Mosul (Arabic: Al-Mawsil) lies in north-western Iraq and is that country's third-largest city. The coarsely woven carpets and rugs sold in Mosul, on the other hand, are principally woven in the Hamadan region. It has already been noted in the section on nomadic tribes that Kurdish carpets are essentially woven for domestic use; moreover, that they are frequently difficult to source geographically because of the plethora of styles and techniques that exist side by side (sometimes even in an individual carpet).

Left: A one-off carpet from the Senneh region showing a narrative scene in all probability from the Sasanid period. Four mirror-image lions are in the process of devouring a gazelle while, in the centre, two kings face each other across a ritual chessboard (which symbolises the world). Trees and birds of prey decorate the field.
Opposite page: A magnificent 19th-century Senneh with a field covered in tiny herati *flower motifs. The centre medallion stands out from a white ground and is in the form of a fishbone. Identical* herati *motifs decorate the medallion. The overall visual impact is stunning.*

Below: Contemporary (1920) Senneh with an unusual flower design suggesting a large lily or a mythical bird. The design is clearly the creation of an individual weaver living in a remote region.
Opposite page: A pochti format Bijar rug dating from around 1940. The extremely compact design is centred on a lozenge medallion framed by a rectangle. The sober and attenuated colours are typical of Bijar carpets and rugs.

Key features
– Coarse but lustrous local wool; hard-wearing.
– More refined than rural equivalents, with a knot density of 4,000/dm² or, occasionally, as high as 8,000/dm².
– Flat pile enables individual motifs to emerge clearly.
– Sober and harmonious colours with a large number of pastels: pale yellow, pale pink, ivory, and so on.
– Designs are built up by repetitive boteh motifs, small flowers, and herati that cover the entire field with a fine lattice. The ground is usually blue but sometimes red or ivory.
– Formats are small, e.g., the Sedjadé type, which typically measures some 4 ft 4 in × 5 ft 10 in (1.30 m × 1.80 m).

Senneh (Senna, Sanandaj) and region

Senneh is the town in the heart of Kurdistan that has become synonymous with the Senneh or Persian Knot, although – paradoxically – most Kurdish weavers use the Turkish (Ghiordes) knot technique.

Carpets and rugs from Senneh differ from traditional Kurdish output. To this it should be added that the quality of *Senneh* carpets is highly variable. Today, there are *Senneh* with as few as 2,000 knots/dm². Colours are predominantly dark and in part achieved by chemical dyes that are subsequently washed and artificially faded. Today's designs are also less adventurous and more geometrical than their predecessors.

Senneh is also known for its kilims that are woven with such skill and finesse that it is virtually impossible to distinguish between right side up and reverse. These kilims are known as *Druya* (literally, 'double-sided').

Bijar

The most beautiful *Bijar* carpets and rugs are woven by sedentary Afshar weavers in the villages of Tekab and Tekentepe to the north of the town of Bijar.

The scope of this volume does not permit enumeration of all the other important carpet-weaving centres in Kurdistan. An idea of the potential output from the region can be extrapolated from the most recent (1980) census data covering 3,400 villages in the region; of these, 1,600 were carpet-weaving centres, with no fewer than 40,000 home looms and at least 80,000 weavers.

A splendid Bijar featuring a trellis or grid
design comprising small medallions enclosing
groups of rose blossoms on a blue ground.
The outer border repeats the same rose motif.
The carpet was in all probability
commissioned by a French buyer and is
clearly influenced by 18th-century Aubussons.

Key features

– Use of primitive high-warp looms with
log uprights results in varied warp yarn
tension and causes irregularities in field
and border patterns.
– Both fine and coarse wool, with an
excellent grade of silk-like wool used for
more sophisticated carpets.
– The weaver adds between three and
five tight weft threads (formerly wool,
now cotton) between each row of knots
to add weight and rigidity (Bijar carpets
are said to be 'as hard as leather'). This
makes the carpet difficult to bend
without damaging the warp threads, but
it also makes for a carpet that is very
hard-wearing.
– Medium pile, with a knot density of
around 2,000 to 2,500/dm². Turkish knots
are the most frequent, but Persian knots
are also used.
– Vegetable dyes are used for the main
part, with dark blues and dark reds
contrasting with light colours. Borders
vary from three to eight rows and are
often decorated with arabesques or
rosette motifs.
– The overall design is most frequently
composed of small herati motifs on a
monochrome ivory, camel or dark blue
field. Today's weavers also make
frequent and imaginative use of the boteh
motif. The centre medallion is very finely
worked.
– Bijar carpets and rugs are rare and
much sought after by collectors and
local buyers alike.

Hamadan and region

Hundreds of villages in this mountainous and, in winter, bitterly cold region of east Kurdistan are grouped around the ancient Medes capital of Ecbatana, known today as Hamadan. These villages are peopled by an ethnic mosaic of Turkish, Kurdish and Luri stock.

Hamadan

Hamadan is one of the most important sales outlets for Persian carpets generally and those made in and around the Hamadan region in particular. Recent census data reveal that there are more than 120,000 weavers working some 60,000 looms in the 1,100 or so villages where carpets are made. Carpets and rugs identified as *Hamadan* are, as noted earlier, often mistakenly known by the collective name *Mosul*, the Iraqi city where these carpets and rugs were originally warehoused before being shipped from the port of Trabzon (Trebizond) to Constantinople and, ultimately, to the West.

Hamadan boasts two major state-owned carpet factories – each of which operates 900 looms – together with privately owned workshops which account for thousands of additional looms, not to mention dyeing and yarn-spinning facilities commensurate with intensive export market demand. Generally speaking, Hamadan carpets and rugs are turned out as poor imitations of ancient models with patterns and motifs from different regions arbitrarily lumped together in order to satisfy current demand for low-cost Oriental carpets and rugs. It would seem that every kind of carpet can be imitated at will, including those from Soltanabad (Arak) and Saruk, whose characteristic floral patterns find such favour in the North American market.

It is not practical in the present context to list all the many carpet-weaving centres within a 30-mile (50-kilometre) radius of Hamadan. Most of them output product that is virtually identical with that described above, an exception being made perhaps for the village of Anjellas, where the womenfolk weave unexpectedly charming carpets and rugs. Given the range and variety of carpets available from this region, one may be fortunate enough to chance upon an exceptional specimen with an original and straightforward design woven in natural and delicate colours by an individual or a workshop where quality, tradition and innovation are still respected.

Key features

– Good quality local wool complemented on occasion by silk-like mohair or camel hair is used for the broad monochrome inner borders.
– A single strand of weft wool separates the rows of knots.
– Pile is medium or high; knot density is moderate (900 to 1,800 knots/dm²).
– Typical colours of the region are soft, delicate and muted. Today, the natural camel-hair tint used in the borders and, at times, for the ground now tends to be simulated by using wool dye that includes crushed nuts.
– Designs are as a rule restrained and comparatively simple, with a centre medallion formed by stylised flower motifs. The most striking design feature is the use of a 'frame' formed by a broad monochrome inner border.
– Ancient Hamadans are recognised by their use of camel hair for the ground, their characteristic inner borders, and their weight, which is considerably lighter than that of Hamadans *woven today*.

Contemporary Hamadan (Kelley) carpet made up of three hexagonal medallions. The Caucasian influence is evident in the Chirvan-style hexagons and in the goat figures in red and white placed at each end.

Early-20th-century Hamadan *featuring an unusual design built around a large centre medallion decorated with various flower motifs that are extended across the whole field. Curved lines are used to obtain the pronounced 'bevelled' effect at the four decorative field corners.*

Central Iran: Tehran and central region

This is another vast region, extending from the north of the Zagros Mountains as far as the Iranian provinces of Gilan and Mazandaran and taking in innumerable carpet-making centres. The most recent data available suggest that there are no fewer than 2,334 villages where, when demand is sufficient, more than 200,000 weavers, female and male, can work at any one time on nearly 100,000 home looms.

Tehran

The museums, bazaars and shops of the Iranian capital exhibit Persian carpets from every region and period. The large urban population comprises representatives of all the ethnic groups in the country; weavers from each are employed in private urban workshops both to produce traditional wares and, above all perhaps, to satisfy demand from carpet merchants and exporters.

The Sherkate Farsh association set up in 1936 has encouraged the weaving of what have come to be referred to as 'Tehran-style' carpets and rugs, predominantly with a 'standard' or 'prescribed' floral pattern. These *Tehran* carpets and rugs represent a veritable symbiosis of styles found in centres of carpet production from all over Iran. In effect, their design is cluttered to the point of being baroque: it is so 'overloaded' that next to nothing of the pomegranate red or blue field ground is left unworked.

Tehran prayer rugs – with a knot density of between 2,500 and 4,000 knots/dm² – are of good quality, particularly in terms of their silky wool that produces a lustrous pile. Similar quality goods come from neighbouring centres close to the capital, notably Rayy, Karadagh (Karaje) and Semnan.

Veramin

Veramin, a town about 60 miles (100 kilometres) south of Tehran, is a carpet-producing centre of some considerable standing, whose rigid and densely-knotted carpets and rugs (5,000 to 6,000 knots/dm²) are held to be superior in quality to those made in the capital. While this may be true, it has to be added that, over the years, these

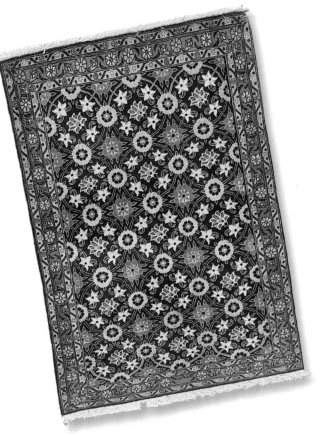

Opposite page: A one-off Veramin *with an imaginative field design on a blue ground. Among the various figurative motifs are a Tree of Life, birds on branches, an oil lamp, tulips, cypress trees, a horse, a saddled goat, a stag, a landscape, butterflies, houses and, not least, a person kneeling in prayer (at top left). The whole scene is highly reminiscent of a Persian miniature.*

Above: A splendid contemporary Veramin *comprising a trelliswork sequence of motifs, each featuring small peonies enclosing tiny narcissus blossoms and a central* fleur-de-lys *(lily). Curved tendrils link these various flower motifs (sometimes known as* mina khano*).* Veramin-*style carpets and rugs are distinguished by their abundance of different flower motifs and are much sought-after collector's items.*

Kashan-style centre medallion carpets have lost much of the originality that derived from sequences of four-flower motifs (*mina khano*) that extend lozenge-like across the entire carpet field.

Veramin is also known for the quality of its kilims that feature unusual patterns and are woven from soft, silky wool. The term *Veramin* is customarily applied to all the kilims woven in the various villages around Veramin itself and the neighbouring town of Gamsar. The chief design feature comprises blocks of small dentate squares in various colours which are set into each other to form geometrical (large lozenge) motifs that effectively 'bleed' to infinity in the absence of left- and right-hand borders.

The town of Veramin represents a catchment area for all the nomadic tribes who have settled in the region – Kurds, Luri, Shahsavans and Afshars.

Kashan (Kachan)

Kashan lies some 130 miles (210 kilometres) south of Tehran in the heart of the Central Iranian Range between Qum and Isfahan and on the fringe of the Dasht-i-Kevir desert. Mulberry bushes are cultivated in Kashan's harsh climate and Kashan is famed for the quality of its silk.

Ancient silk carpets and rugs were produced by the royal factory of Shah Abbas in co-operation with that established in Tabriz. Their weave is extremely delicate, with reds and blues predominating, and the wool is soft and silky, mixed with gold and silver thread. This exceptional quality has not been sustained now that synthetic dyes have started to

An exceptional Kashan dating from 1920. This most unusual design is essentially composed of flowers spilling out from a vase to cover the entire field. In the centre (see detail, this page) there is a narrative scene depicting two Persian men in a pharmacy or dispensary. The Persian text confirms that the scene portrays the celebrated alchemist, physician and philosopher ar-Razi (864–925 A.D.) from the city of Rayy, considered to be one of the greatest thinkers of the Islamic world. The border is remarkable for its rendering of peacocks, horsemen, women picking grapes, and much more besides.

Key features

– Good quality, delicate and lustrous Isfahan wool. After each row of Senneh knots the weaver inserts a very taut weft thread of fine cotton and a further, slacker, thread; the result is a weave that is dense and very solid. The warp is often made from silk.

– Knot density varies from between 2,000 to 3,000/dm². The pile is of medium height and is extremely hard-wearing, lasting for many years without showing signs of wear and tear.

– Dyes are synthetic but of acceptable quality; grounds are red or blue; patterned motifs are very colourful.

– The design invariably features a centre medallion (in rosette or oval form) decorated with flowers and diverse foliage; the ground is usually red.

be used, but the artistry of Kashan carpets is still greatly prized.

Extremely fine all-silk carpets with a knot density of some 8,000/dm² are woven in soft and delicate colours over a pomegranate-red ground. Some knotted silk carpets – known as *suf* – are woven in such a way as to create a relief effect over a kilim-weave base.

Some workshops, anxious to meet European demand and expectations, have copied hunting scenes or other figurative elements inspired by Persian myth. Typical motifs include birds against a leafy ground, and Trees of Life taken from ancient Persian miniatures. The most valuable pieces – in wool or in silk – are expensive, but their price is justified to the extent that an *Aroun-Kashan* produced in a small village close to Kashan is only half as valuable.

Arak (Soltanabad or Seraband)

The city of Arak (formerly Soltanabad or Seraband) is located between Hamadan and Qum. At the end of the 19th century, Arak was a production centre for *Arak* carpets made in the *Tabriz* style.

Ziegler, an export company, originally from Switzerland but headquartered in Manchester, England, opened a trading branch in Arak, complete with its own dyeing plant (which used vegetable dyes only). Carpets and rugs produced by this factory up until the outbreak of World War II are still sold by English carpet merchants under the 'Ziegler' brand name.

Today's workshops are privately owned by Iranian merchants. The carpets and rugs made there are still of good quality but they are imitative, notably reproducing 18th-century patterns which are much in demand locally on account of their sophistication and elegance. In the surrounding villages, weavers work to specification on behalf of Arak merchants who provide them with the requisite raw materials to execute foreign orders. More than 3,500 home looms are active.

The soft, muted designs have found an admiring public among interior designers in Europe, particularly in Switzerland and Germany, where the *Arak* style is frequently used to complement modern furniture. The unusual charm and scarcity of these *Seraband* rugs has led to their being slavishly imitated in other carpet-making countries such as Turkey (at Isparta) and in various places in India.

Key features
– Sturdy wool grades.
– Warp and weft yarn in cotton.
– (Persian) knot density between 800 and 1,300/dm².
– Medium to tight pile.
– Vegetable dyes still used for ground reds and blues.
– The characteristic pattern is generally known as boteh-mir, *i.e. small, complex leaf forms set out in staggered sequence. The main border is quite wide and decorated with arabesques and stylised leaf or flower motifs.*
– Formats up to 13 ft 2 in × 16 ft 4 in (4 m × 5 m).

Opposite page: A Kashan rug with a field decorated with flower arabesques – roses, palmettes and lanceolate leaves – linked by interlacing flower stalks to create a dense, highly decorative and distinctive pattern.
Above: A contemporary Sultanabad carpet with a geometrical design made up of stepped corners that enclose an extended centre medallion inspired by Caucasian models. The muted colours and subtle motifs confirm that less is often more, i.e. that the finest decorative effects can often be attained by restraint rather than excess. This may be one reason why so many collectors show only a passing interest in the typically 'busy' style common to some classic Persian carpets and rugs, notably those from Isfahan and Tabriz.

The village of Saruk (Sarouk or Saruq) lies 25 miles (40 kilometres) or so to the north of Arak and, like every other village in the area, has focused since the beginning of the last century on the large-scale production of full-field, tightly-knotted floral carpets (with *boteh* and *herati* motifs). Their sturdy structure has proved extremely popular in the United States.

Ancient carpets from this region are among the best carpets currently available in Iran and are much sought after on account of being very well-made and delicately decorated in soft and harmonious vegetable-dye colours. Their popularity is such that workshops in the region have reverted to traditional techniques, including very tight knots and a short, extremely hard-wearing pile.

Carpets and rugs from around the town of Malayer are patterned very much along the same lines as those produced in Saruk, but their floral motifs are generally more stylised, tending towards the geometrical. *Malayer* carpets are hard-wearing and can be bought in the bazaar in Hamadan for less than one might expect to pay for a *Saruk*.

A very beautiful and chromatically expressive Saruk with a large centre medallion roughly in the shape of a heavily embellished seven-point star set on a deep red ground. The flower and arabesque decoration is in the style of the 'Lotto gul'.

Qum (Qom)

Carpets have been made in the sacred city of Qum, some 90 miles (145 kilometres) south of the capital Tehran, only since the middle of the 19th century. They are chiefly woven in silk or in fine wool from spring lambs (*kork*) grazed on the Khorasan Plateau. In terms of design and motifs, they derive inspiration principally from classic models of, among others, *Isfahan*, *Tabriz* and *Kashan* carpets and rugs.

Original *Qum* carpets and rugs are a rarity today. There are known to be more than 3,500 home looms in the surrounding villages, however, and very good quality carpets and rugs are to be had from rural and family workshops.

An inferior – decidedly inferior – grade is turned out by certain workshops which use ordinary wool or silk waste, synthetic dyes, and a coarse Jufti knot which makes the field designs – usually vases of flowers – imprecise and fuzzy. With the notable exception of 18th-century replicas, patterns are generally quite uncomplicated. As a rule, the ground is woven in a light colour; *boteh* or small vase motifs are worked into a trellis that covers the entire field, itself made up of tiny plant motifs. Carpet merchants frequently (and wrongly) call this design *Qum boteh* after the Zil-i-Sultan ('shadow of the Sultan') motif found in *Tabriz* carpets and rugs, where small birds are depicted fluttering above a vase of flowers.

Key features

– Fine spring lamb's wool (kork).
– Tightly and neatly knotted, with a density of between 2,000 and 4,000 knots/dm².
– Short pile accentuates the delicacy of design motifs.
– Soft colours obtained through use of vegetable dyes.
– Some floral motifs woven in silk ('silk flower carpets').
– Rural output usually replicates 18th-century models admired by Iranian clients on account of their elegant design and perfect finish.

Opposite page:
A flower-design Qum that effectively 're-interprets' classic flower carpet designs from Kashan or Isfahan. Seven principal design rows reiterate essentially the same motif of a cypress surrounded by two boteh with, beneath it, two peacocks facing each other. The motifs (albeit without the peacocks) are repeated on successive staggered rows and are in each instance linked by stalks and tendrils in alternating red and black. This carefully constructed pattern of repetitive motifs and muted colours generates a wonderful sense of rhythm and continuity.

Left: A contemporary all-silk Qum with a single centre medallion enclosing an elaborate floral bouquet on a green (water) ground. Note the unusual corner zones, where each boteh ends with a sequence of green-red-yellow dentate leaves that create a 'tongue of flame' effect.

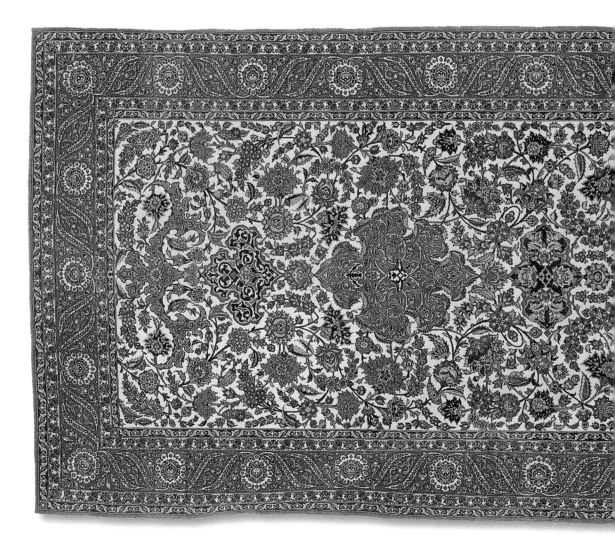

Isfahan and region

Isfahan silk carpets

Isfahan was the former capital of Safavid Persia during the rule of Shah Abbas I (r. 1588–1629). It boasts some of the most prestigious monuments to this great period in the history of the Persian Empire.

During this period, the Shah's workshops produced lavish carpets using subjects inspired by Persian miniatures. Other major centres such as Tabriz, Herat, Kashan and Kerman turned out carpets in the same prestigious style but with local thematic variations – garden carpets, hunting scenes, medallion carpets, prayer rugs and so on.

In each instance, these were 'one-off' carpets destined for the imperial court or presented as gifts to ambassadors from all over the world. The collapse of the Shah Abbas dynasty effectively put paid to the production of these magnificent specimens, and it was not until near the end of the 19th century that, with the intervention of foreign trading firms such as Ziegler, Persian carpets started to be exported to England and to Germany. With this new wave of commercialisation came – inevitably, perhaps – a drop in both technical and aesthetic standards. The Carpet Association set up in Iran in 1936 made a valiant effort to prompt a return to earlier high standards of carpet-making, advocating the use of

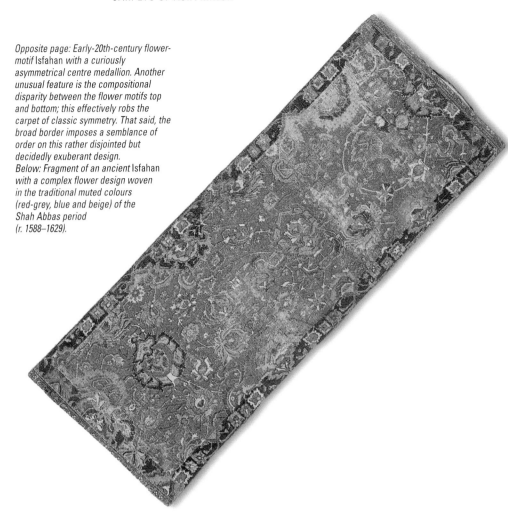

Opposite page: Early-20th-century flower-motif Isfahan *with a curiously asymmetrical centre medallion. Another unusual feature is the compositional disparity between the flower motifs top and bottom; this effectively robs the carpet of classic symmetry. That said, the broad border imposes a semblance of order on this rather disjointed but decidedly exuberant design.*
Below: Fragment of an ancient Isfahan *with a complex flower design woven in the traditional muted colours (red-grey, blue and beige) of the Shah Abbas period (r. 1588–1629).*

vegetable dyes and placing a renewed emphasis on the quality and stylistic tradition that once characterised the individual centres.

In Isfahan, contemporary carpets continue to draw on traditional 'Persian' themes. On the whole, current output is noteworthy in terms of technical expertise and artistry. A recent census revealed that there are now more than 13,000 looms installed in small private household work-shops operated by weavers and their families. Isfahan dealers also sell product manufactured by nomadic Bakhtyars and Lurs.

All-silk carpets and rugs (warp, weft and pile) tend to be figurative, portraying hunting scenes or mythological

Key features
– Fine, supple and lustrous hard-wearing wool.
– High knot density (6,000 to 8,000 knots/dm²).
– Very close-cropped pile.
– Vegetable dyes in a range of 15 shades with harmonious colour contrasts.
– Traditional motifs include floral patterns with medallions and the Tree of Life; the field is framed by large borders. The exceptionally intricate designs were imposed after World War II by merchants in Tabriz and Kashan who were anxious to service the international export market. Today, Isfahans are extremely popular with native Iranians, who greatly appreciate their overall finesse, classic designs and durability.

events. The colour palette is extremely rich and varied and the knotting technique is exceptionally sophisticated. The quality of Isfahan silks is at least the equal of some of the finest carpets and rugs produced in Tabriz and Kashan. Several shahs have been more than willing to

have their portrait rendered inside the centre medallion – and skilled Isfahan weavers have duly obliged.

Signed *Isfahans* are known as *Isfahan-Sarafi*. The signature is normally found outside the field proper, typically in the centre of the upper border.

Nain

The town of Nain lies 100 miles (160 kilometres) from Isfahan on the road leading to Yezd and Kerman. Since production started in 1930, Nain has built an immense reputation by virtue of the uncommonly beautiful and exceptionally densely knotted carpets and rugs it produces. These are widely regarded as the finest knotted carpets in all of Iran, as well they might be, considering that they are knotted at the incredible rate of 93,000 knots per square foot (1,000,000 per m²).

Patterns are in the classic flower style typical of their *Qum* counterparts, but the contours and motifs are invariably more pronounced as a consequence of the brilliant contrasts achieved by the silk-knot known as *gharty*.

The use of similar colours results in a 'standard' appearance, but this is immaterial to merchants and downstream buyers alike. The finely knotted weave imparts an incomparable suppleness.

Opposite page: A richly decorated early-20th-century Isfahan. The field has a cream ground that accentuates the overall flower motif pattern. The corner zones are woven on a black ground that highlights the contours of the centre medallion, which effectively fills out the entire field. A particular feature of this example is the absolute symmetry exhibited between upper and lower motifs.

A contemporary Nain carpet typifying the soft tones and incomparable lustre of woven silk. The design is harmonious and inventive – note, in particular, the grazing deer. This example fully illustrates the typical freedom enjoyed by the solitary weaver in her choice and interpretation of classical designs. The (albeit somewhat monotonous) repetition and deployment of identical floral themes can often result in a superb and highly personal thematic restatement that never fails to fascinate.

Feridan

Following the bloodbaths of 1917, major groups of Armenians were scattered across regions of the former Soviet Union and Azerbaijan, Turkey and Iran. Mention has already been made of those who found themselves in Koula and elsewhere in Turkey.

Back in the 17th century, Shah Abbas I had already banished around 300,000 Armenians from around Yerevan to the region of Chahar Mahall in western Iran. A minority settled in Feridan, a town lying to the south of Isfahan in the heart of the Chahar Mahall, a region peopled by semi-nomadic Bakhtyari and Qashqai.

The exceptional skill of Armenians and the quality of their geometrical designs have already been stressed, as has their influence on all the ethnic groups living in the vast region known as Asia Minor. Perhaps the most salient feature of Armenian carpets and rugs is the cross motif.

Today, Feridan weavers turn out garden carpets with compartments decorated with highly stylised flower, bird and tree motifs that are highly reminiscent of carpets and rugs made by Bakhtyari in the city of Shahr Kord, the capital of the Chahar Mahall, or in Chale Sotor.

A contemporary geometrical Shiraz carpet with a dark red ground and a large stepped centre medallion. Inset into the four corner zones are arrowhead crosses that indicate the four cardinal points of the compass and so represent infinity.

A magnificent Shiraz from the late 19th or early 20th century, made by Qashqai weavers in an urban workshop. The design draws inspiration from the classic mille-fleurs patterns of 17th- and 18th-century Mughal carpets. The chieftain of a Qashqai tribe is alleged to have accompanied the Persian Emperor Nadir Shah on his conquest of India and to have brought back a Mughal carpet that has since served as the prototype for several designs.

Fars and region

Fars (Farsistan, formerly Persis) lies in south-western Iran in the very heart of ancient Persia. As the earlier section on nomad tribes indicated, various nomadic groups gravitated towards Shiraz and the region around it, not least the Qashqai (Kashgai), whose carpets are habitually known as *Gabbeh* or *Shiraz.*

Abadeh

Abadeh, a town located between Shiraz and Isfahan, boasts 15,000 weavers among the formerly nomadic population that has settled there. They produce magnificent carpets and rugs on high-warp looms. Weaving is the sole activity and source of revenue in this particularly arid desert region. *Abadeh* carpets are much sought after because they are hard-wearing, reasonably priced, vegetable-dyed and with a multitude of attractive stylised motifs – resembling those of output from Quashqai – which are set against a brown ground.

Late-19th-century Kerman *inspired by ancient models made in this major carpet-production region. The centre medallion is in the form of an eight-branch star whose composition is echoed in the four corner panels. The field is covered with flower motifs that are intertwined via inverted 'S'-shaped tendrils. Each of the borders comprises identical flower motif composites. The term* mâhi *is used to describe this design and variations on it.*

Kerman (Kirman) and region

The city of Kerman lies in southern Iran at close on 6,000 ft (183 m) above sea level and is surrounded by expanses of desert peopled by Afshar and Baluchi nomads. Most of the small villages in the vicinity of Kerman specialise in weaving: in 1960, it was estimated that there were some 60,000 looms in the region. Immediately following World War II, the Sherkate Farsh Persian carpet association responded to growing demand on the US market for carpets modelled along the lines of 18th-century *Aubusson* and *Savonnerie* carpets, typically with a monochrome cream ground and bouquets of roses. These hard-wearing and exquisitely designed carpets find favour with Iranian collectors. Lower grades produced here use synthetic dyes and have recourse to the Jufti knot and lower-grade *tabbaki* wool (from dead sheep).

Output from the city of Yezd (Yazd) 250 miles (400 kilometres) north-west of Kerman, replicates Kerman motifs, though knotting techniques are less refined and the pile is much higher. In the 19th century, Yezd was particularly famous for its imitation cashmere wool scarves, the patterns of which are hinted at in some carpets and rugs that feature the *boteh* motif.

Key features

– Very fine-grade wool with silk-like lustre.
– (Persian) knot density varying from 2,000 to 5,000/dm².
– Superior-grade vegetable dyes. Local dyers are particularly skilled in that a typical Kerman will use up to 30 different colours in order to impart a high degree of sophistication and complexity to the floral designs woven to a lustrous silk-like pile finish.
– Complex, essentially flower-based motifs fill the entire field (which is almost invariably woven in ivory, although sometimes in pastel blue). Some carpets and rugs have a high figurative content, with representations of animals and other subjects against a luxuriant plant background.
– The most striking feature of the Kerman carpet is the free-flowing border that does not 'frame' the individual motifs but extends them through to the monochrome ground of the field. Some specimens have 'closed' borders.
– Formats are frequently large-scale, ranging from 6 ft 6 in × 9 ft 10 in (2 m × 3 m) to 13 ft 2 in × 16 ft 4 in (4 m × 5 m).

The Khorasan region

The Khorasan (Khurasan) region of north-eastern Iran encompasses the immense land mass bounded by Turkistan, Afghanistan and Baluchistan. The capital – Meshed – is an important religious and commercial centre. Some 3,700 villages lie within the Khorasan province, with an estimated 70,000 looms and a weaver population approaching 140,000.

Meshed

Meshed (Mashhad) is the generic name for Khorasan carpets sold in the city's bazaars where a large range of ethnic groups are represented, including Iranians, Turks, Afghans, Arabs, Turkmens and Baluchi. Upwards of 20,000 weavers work on an estimated 10,800 looms located in the small workshops found in the 500 or so villages in the vicinity of Meshed. Some workshops work under the supervision of a recognised master weaver (ustad) and employ anything from between 20 to 60 weavers.

As in most of the major carpet-producing centres of the country, there are considerable variations in quality. In some instances, particularly where the Jufti knot is used to speed up production, the carpet will be excessively limp and will, as a result, wear badly. Carpets authenticated and stamped by the Sherkate Farsh and sold through the association's official sales outlets carry a quality seal; they are comparatively cheap by comparison with carpets of similar quality made elsewhere.

The most beautiful – and most expensive – Meshed carpets are often signed with the name of the workshop or even the individual ustad. The signature will generally be found in a 'cartouche' or scroll at top centre. It should be noted that this is not a watertight guarantee of quality, since some workshops are perfectly willing to append their signature to poor quality carpets.

Moud carpets and rugs from the Meshed region are of the highest quality, beautifully woven to a high knot density (between 5,000 and 7,000 knots/dm²) and vegetable-dyed. Thanks to their flat pile, they are more supple than the standard Meshed range.

Moud carpets and rugs are produced in limited quantities and most examples are quickly snapped up by Iranian collectors directly from the workshop.

Meshed carpets and rugs are very similar indeed to those produced in other towns and villages in the immediate vicinity, such as Moudjour, Kashmar, Birjand or Sabzevar. These differ only by reference to local variants, such as pile height, knot density, colour palette or the use of synthetic as opposed to natural dyes. Most of their output is destined for export.

Key features

– Fine and silky hand-spun and tightly-woven Khorasan wool.
– Knot density ranging between 4,000 and 5,000 knots/dm² results in solid and heavy-pile carpet.
– Vivid colour palette with dominant red (cochineal and madder-based) ground and yellows extracted from pomegranate skins and vine leaves.
– Large rounded centre medallion decorated with flower and leaf wreaths and scrolls. The field is frequently woven in ivory, crimson or light blue and is decorated with the herati or mâhi motifs in yellow and ochre. The border comprises 6 to 12 rows of decorative flowers.
– Formats vary considerably from small (Namasse) rugs measuring 4 ft 7 in × 2 ft 7 in (1.40 m × 0.80 m) to medium-sized examples (Sedjadé: 8 ft 10 in × 4 ft 4 in/ 2.70 m × 1.30 m) and large (Kelley: up to 16 ft 4 in × 6 ft 6 in (5 m × 2 m).

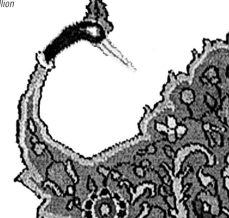

A Khorasan decorated with representations of animals and birds (lions, rabbits, doves and parrots) set against a red ground. Upper and lower medallions depict a 'mirror-image' bird (peacock or duck) with outspread wings and a head at both extremities. This is a highly imaginative carpet woven in all probability in an urban workshop in Meshed. 'Standard' Khorasan models feature a large centre medallion woven in crimson.

Carpets, kilims and *soumaks* from the Caucasus

Political and ethnic upheaval in this immense region of the former Soviet Union (which included Georgia, Armenia, Azerbaijan and Dagestan) means it is at present well-nigh impossible to draw up an inventory of current production.

NOMADIC AND SEMI-NOMADIC TRIBES

Nomadic tribes across the region have only recently gained their independence and, to a large degree, become sedentary. This has triggered a re-emergence of cultural identities suppressed under Soviet control.

As mentioned earlier, it was here in the Altai Mountains in the Caucasus that the most ancient of all knotted carpets was discovered intact. The animals, real and imaginary, which appear in the celebrated Pazyryk Carpet, which is of Scythian inspiration, also feature on typical Caucasian models, above all in the so-called 'dragon carpets' woven in the 16th and 17th centuries.

To the north, in Georgia, the term *Kazak* is commonly used to describe nomads and semi-nomads from a variety of ethnic groupings, including Circassians (*Cherkes*), Turkmens, Tartars and Mongols. Carpet merchants tend to use the generic term *Kazak* to designate these characteristically long- and lustrous-pile Caucasian carpets and rugs with their sweeping geometrical motifs, predominantly of

vividly coloured stars and crotchets, irrespective of whether they were woven by rural or urban populations. A degree of terminological confusion is thus unavoidable. This holds true at even of carpet merchants themselves, who often have difficulty distinguishing between carpets and rugs made by nomadic and sedentary populations. Regardless of the cultural and artistic heterogeneity of each individual region, however, semi-nomadic weavers typically produce kilims and *soumaks* that have various points in common. In the final analysis, it is usual to assign kilims made by semi-nomadic tribes to two main centres of production: Shirvan and Kuba.

Shirvan

Shirvan in Azerbaijan produces knotted carpets and rugs and, until very recently, almost all Caucasian carpets and kilims from neighbouring provinces were known as *Shirvans*. Typical patterns are very close to those featuring on Kuba kilims, though the motifs of hooked lozenges, steps or zig-zags tend to be more abstract and arranged in sequences of horizontal rows in a sumptuous interplay of reds, yellows, blues and maroons.

A late-19th-century Shirvan *prayer rug with field consisting of trelliswork stylised flowers on a cream ground. Tiny animal motifs are set into the top of the mihrab, together with various symbols, e.g. combs and magic 'good luck' numbers. Some carpets from this Dagestan region – such as those from Maresah – have the same compartmentalised grid design, but the stylised flowers are replaced by variegated boteh motifs.*

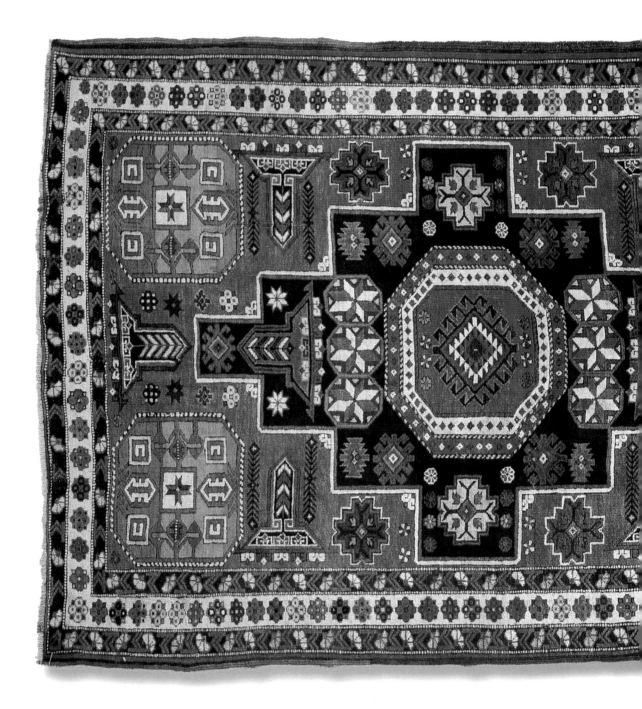

A carpet from the Kongkend village in the Kuba region. The large midnight-blue medallion is in the form of a stepped cross. Smaller medallions on a grey-blue ground are set into the corners and are reminiscent of Egyptian hieroglyph cartouche. These may be sun-related symbols that formed part of an ancient tamga. Mention should be made of the lateral borders with their four 'sabre' motifs characteristic of Kazak carpets.

Kuba

Kuba is a town in Azerbaijan close to Dagestan. The kilims that are conveniently known as *Kuba* are woven very fine, with an overall design comprising large abstract patterns. These patterns are essentially dentate medallions placed vertically in a field framed by a border that frequently features the hourglass motif – which is not the case in kilims from Shirvan. Kuba kilims also exhibit variations on the *kotchak* cross used by Armenian weavers. Some designs feature a mixture of stepped and hooked lozenges or lancet leaves.

Care should be taken not to confuse kilims with flat-pile carpets woven by the original *soumak* technique that some experts claim to have originated in Kuba. Other experts believe that the term *soumak* comes from the dominant reds produced from the juice of berries from a shrub of that same name.

This type of rug is produced by all semi-nomadic or sedentary tribes throughout the Caucasus, but is particularly common to southern Dagestan and to central and north-west Azerbaijan. Meanwhile, flat-pile carpets known as *Silé* and *Verné* originate in the region around Karabagh (Karaje) and are woven in a highly similar fashion. *Silé* models are distinguished by their use of a large geometrical 'Z' motif which, for some, symbolises a dragon but which to Armenians represents (when reversed to form an 'S') the first letter of the Armenian word for 'God'.

At times, various weaving techniques – kilim, *soumak*, *cicim* (*zili*) – are combined, as in the case of Kurdish travel bags. That said, the principal characteristic of rural output lies in the heterogeneous geometrical motifs that mirror the ethnic diversity of the region.

Key features
– *Good quality warp and weft yarns.*
– *Relais (slit) technique commonly used.*
– *Colours are bright and contrasting; a preference for synthetic dyes is attributed to the more vivid colour contrasts achieved than with their tradition vegetable-dye counterparts.*
– *Motifs are essentially geometrical – polygons, hexagons and lozenges.*

URBAN WORKSHOPS BY REGION

The recent political division of the Caucasus into sovereign states does not make for ready classification, all the more so since there is an overarching and unifying 'Caucasian' style despite the diversity and richness of output from various parts of the region. As a rule, this 'Caucasian' style is characterised by the use of vivid and contrasting colours and a preference for highly abstract geometrical motifs, such as the ubiquitous eight-branch star.

Under Soviet rule, carpet and rug production was organised into *kolkhoze* co-operatives in a bid to standardise designs. This notwithstanding, some village weavers continued to produce carpets and rugs to their own design; these are genuine and rare examples of folk art.

Georgia

Georgia is a mountainous country that extends from the Black Sea to the Caucasus range, sharing frontiers with Turkey, Armenia and Azerbaijan. The port of Batumi lies directly opposite the Turkish port of Trabzon (Trebizond), from where Caucasian carpets and kilims are shipped to the West.

The provenance of the various types of carpets and rugs from this vast region is difficult to establish, and they are frequently referred to instead in terms of their dominant motif, for example 'star' carpet, 'medallion' carpet, 'swastika' carpet, and so on. Additionally, towns like Karachop, Shulaver and Borcialu have lent their names to carpets and rugs produced there.

Armenia

Today's Armenia is a modest territory flanked by Iran to the south, Georgia to the north, Turkey to the west and Azerbaijan to the east. The country and its renowned carpet-weaving traditions have already been referred to on several occasions in this book. Armenian merchants have played a key role in marketing Caucasian carpets and rugs in the Middle East and in the West, and innumerable Armenian-born Europeans have set up large and diversified commercial distribution networks.

Before the swingeing political changes of recent years, Armenia produced traditional carpets and rugs under the auspices of a state-owned organisation called Aikork. Current Armenian output does not reach Europe. The capital Yerevan (Ereran or Erivan) has given its name to a type of carpet manufactured in the region. The principal distinguishing feature is the use of several star medallions set against a strong red ground. Typical knot density ranges between 1,400 and 1,600/dm^2.

Contemporary Kazak carpet from the Karabagh region. This type – known as a Chelaberd – generally features three or four medallions that run vertically down from the top of the field. These are often called 'sunburst' or 'winged' Kazaks on account of the rays that radiate from the centre of each. German dealers and collectors sometimes refer to these as Kazak-Adler, interpreting the branches as 'eagle wings'. The pattern is sometimes referred to as a 'sabre' or 'armour' motif. In this instance, however, the sun symbol clearly predominates.

Dagestan

Dagestan (literally, 'mountain country') lies to the north of Azerbaijan on the edge of the Caspian Sea. Derbent, one of Dagestan's major cities, is the main collection point for carpets and rugs woven in this region of the central Caucasus. The entire region is an ethnic mixed bag of nomadic tribes such as the Lezgin and the Avars, who have now settled in the hill villages and for whose women weaving is both a main occupation and an almost sole source of income. It goes without saying that output from each ethnic group has its own distinguishing traits.

Key features
– Cotton warp, weft and pile in fine and lustrous wool sometimes mixed with goat hair.
– Medium pile, with tight Ghiordes knots to a density of between 800 and 1,400/dm².
– Vegetable dyes, typically reds and dark blues for the ground; vividly coloured motifs.
– Basic design features one- to three-stepped medallions in star form, each with a smaller star insert. Each star is coloured differently. The ground comprises a variety of motifs scattered across the field: tiny flowers, rosettes, hooked squares, stars inset into octagons, boteh, etc.
– Formats vary from 3 ft 3 in × 5 ft 3 in (1 m × 1.60 m) to (infrequently) 6 ft × 12 ft 10 in (1.80 m × 3.90 m).

A beautiful Kazak-type medallion carpet from Soumak-Seychur (Dagestan). The upper and lower contours of the three medallions set on an indigo-blue ground are separated by four arrowhead hook motifs on a white ground (top) or red ground (bottom). This specimen literally 'runs out of warp', only a part of the fourth medallion having been woven. The centre border on a white ground features a 'running dog' motif. Overall, there is a remarkable harmony and balance achieved between design and colour.

Azerbaijan

Azerbaijan lies on the southern flanks of the Caucasus between the Caspian Sea to the east and frontiers with Iran to the south and Armenia to the west. As a result, Azerbaijan has been greatly influenced by the Persian tradition. The women of the region weave knotted carpets and rugs, together with kilims and *soumaks*. Azerbaijan carpets and rugs are commonly classified by reference to the principal town or area from which they are distributed: Shirvan, Kuba, Karabagh and Ganja (Kirovabad).

Shirvan

Shirvan is the name applied both to a village and to its surrounding region. The name also connotes the renowned carpets and rugs produced here ever since Shah Abbas I (r. 1588–1629) established the imperial carpet factory.

Shirvan carpets and rugs come from outlying villages but also from urban workshops such as those in the city of Baku (Shemakha), once the region's capital and formerly

known as Soumak, the name now given to a particular technique. Output from the region can best be described as heterogeneous – a clear reflection of its ethnic mix. The commercial success enjoyed by *Shirvan* carpets and rugs has been such that it has they have been imitated not only by Armenian workshops but also by centres in Iran and, in particular, in the Ardebil region.

Kuba

Mention has already been made of the kilims woven in the region of the city of Kuba located in south-east Dagestan. Knotted carpets made in neighbouring villages such Seikhour – to the north of Kuba – exhibit common characteristics.

Opposite page (top): An attractive contemporary Shirvan featuring a large central medallion with three octagons set on a red ground, framed above and below by a classic Caucasian Wurma or 'ram's head' motif known as Perepedil. It is flanked by another traditional motif – the 'sabre' – whose hilt design represents a variant on the ram's horns. The indigo-blue ground of the field is littered with tiny motifs that symbolise the Sun, the Moon, the cross, etc., or represent mythical animals.
Opposite page (below): A Kuba-inspired Yalame carpet with three hexagonal saw-toothed medallions joined to each other by an 'umbilical cord'. A mille-fleurs design is woven over a crimson ground. The main border is in the style of a frieze depicting a succession of mythical dragons. The permutation of muted colours and dominant reds induces a subtle and skilful harmony typical of all great art.

Key features

– *Relatively coarse but good-quality warp wool; weft in wool or cotton.*
– *Medium pile, comparatively close-cropped.*
– *Good knot density (1,200 to 2,500/dm².).*
– *Vegetable dyes in bright but never garish colours; progressively substituted by synthetic dyes that are harmonious and full but lack the traditional vegetable-dye richness. The ground is generally in blue or light ivory and (occasionally) in red.*
– *Patterns often comprise motifs set into a lattice of stylised plants or into hexagonal medallions that are sometimes starred and always geometrical. The ground is decorated with various small animal motifs (lions, ducks, ostriches, swans, antelopes, eagles, cats, chickens, etc.) – a veritable Noah's Ark. Tiny stylised human figures also appear, sometimes on foot and sometimes mounted on horseback. The various motifs dispersed across the field lend a particular charm to this carpet style. One particularly characteristic feature is a motif called Perepedil, named after a small village in the Kuba region. This is essentially a schematic 'ram's head' motif that is frequently associated with a 'sabre' motif.*
– *Borders are made up of two to six rows and decorated with faux Kufic script or dentate leaves.*
– *Formats vary from around 2 ft 6 in × 3 ft 6 in (0.75 m × 1.10 m) and 5 ft × 11 ft 6 in (1.50 m × 3.50 m).*
– *Prices are higher than those for Kazak carpets and rugs.*

Key features

– *Warp frequently in cotton but sometimes in good-grade wool; weft in fine-spun and lustrous wool.*
– *Medium-high pile with distinctive sheen.*
– *Low (Ghiordes) knot density (1,000 to 1,500/dm².).*
– *Balanced colour palette predominantly in blues, reds, yellows and beiges.*
– *The design comprises large abstract patterns, generally in the form of dentate geometrical medallions. Motifs are assembled by bringing together various multi-coloured sub-motifs.*
– *Formats are modest – 3 ft 3 in × 6 ft (1 m × 1.80 m) – or medium (4 ft 8 in × 8 ft 2 in /1.20 m × 2.50 m).*

Ganja

Ganja (Kirovabad) is located on the main trunk road that links Tbilisi and Baku, which is to say, at the crossroads of Russia, Turkey and Iran. Carpets made here are often confused with those made in Kazak some 60 miles (100 kilometres) away.

The region around Kazak is mountainous and, as has been noted, peopled by numerous semi-nomadic or sedentary tribes, whose output of carpets and rugs is frequently lumped together under the generic term *Kazak*. These examples represent a synthesis of characteristic Caucasian elements and, in a sense, serve as templates. The various influences range from Mongol China to Sasanid Persia, and the carpets may justifiably claim to be expressions of genuine folk art. This is particularly true of those examples that have a ground composed of small

and scattered floral and stylised animal motifs and, at times, even human figures. All these motifs, woven in bright and even crude colours, are set off against a ground that is frequently off-white or ivory. The influence of so-called 'dragon carpets' is also discernible.

A typical *Kazak* is the variety known as the 'eagle and sword' design. Here, the ground is framed by decorative rosettes and comprises one or two multiple-branch star-shaped medallions that radiate out from the centre. Some experts identify these as the talons of an eagle, others see them as 'swords' or 'sabres'. In any event, this carpet type is much sought after on account of its aesthetic properties and – despite a comparatively low knot density – its durability. The high pile flattens under foot and the patterns gradually emerge more distinctly as a result of repeated use. These are carpets that can be readily integrated into a modern décor.

A splendid late-19th-century Kazak-Adler *('eagle Kazak'), known also as a* Chelaberd, *from the village of that name in Dagestan. The medallion designs are variants on those seen earlier on the* Kazak *model illustrated on page 138 and are derived from the* khatai *('rosette') motifs seen in ancient dragon carpets. The medallions are thrown into relief against a light-coloured ground, notably as regards the stylised branches of blossom that connote the rays of the sun. Note also that the 'third' medallion is only partially woven.*

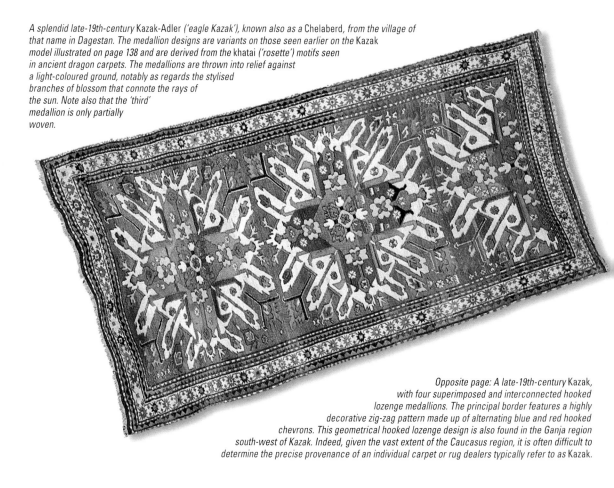

Opposite page: A late-19th-century Kazak, *with four superimposed and interconnected hooked lozenge medallions. The principal border features a highly decorative zig-zag pattern made up of alternating blue and red hooked chevrons. This geometrical hooked lozenge design is also found in the Ganja region south-west of Kazak. Indeed, given the vast extent of the Caucasus region, it is often difficult to determine the precise provenance of an individual carpet or rug dealers typically refer to as Kazak.*

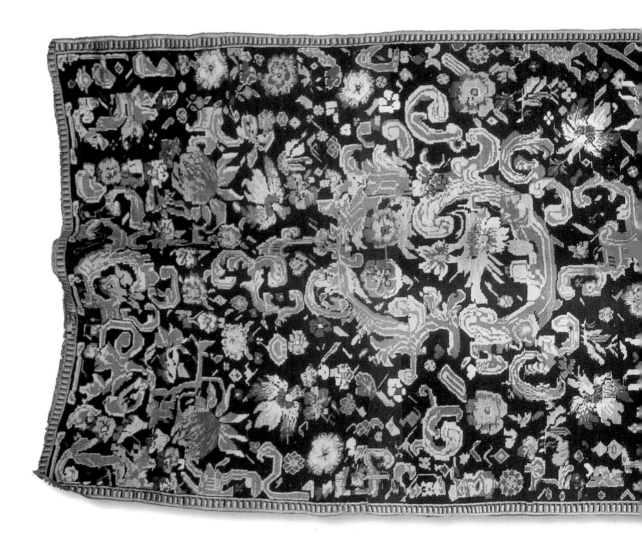

Karabagh (Karaje)

Karabagh (literally, 'black garden') is an autonomous mountain region inhabited by Tartars and Armenians. Carpets and rugs made in the Karabagh region generally betray Persian design influences: one or two centre medallions on a monochrome blue or red ground, with classic Persian motifs such as the *herati*, the *boteh* or palmettes linked by a profusion of plant stalks. Karabagh weavers nevertheless succeed in imparting considerable originality to their designs.

The sprawling region of Azerbaijan boasts other production centres too numerous to be listed exhaustively in the present context. Carpet types are frequently referred to by the name of the nearest town, for example *Konagend* and *Perepedil* varieties that approximate to carpets and rugs made in Shirvan. This brief inventory may be sufficient, however, to hint at the complex task of classifying 'Caucasian' carpets and rugs with any degree of precision.

Above: A magnificent 19th-century Karabagh with an extremely intricate design essentially patterned after the style of ancient dragon carpets but with overtones of Savonnerie flower motifs of the 18th century. A bold and beautifully executed composition underpins the swirl of tendril-linked flower motifs and undulating dragon shapes picked out in browns or on a black ground. The term Karabagh ('black garden') succinctly encapsulates the overall atmosphere of this surviving fragment from what was originally a substantially larger carpet (the fragment has no 'real' borders).
Left: A Karabagh rug, dated 1330 in the Islamic calendar (i.e. 1912 A.D.), featuring three star-cross cruciform medallions on an indigo-blue field. Note the pronounced sobriety of motif and colour.

Carpets, kilims and *soumaks* of Central Asia

The term 'Central Asia' encompasses an immense land mass that includes a number of independent republics formerly attached to the Soviet Union, such as Kazakstan, Uzbekistan, Turkmenistan, Tajikistan, Kyrgyzstan, the autonomous region of 'Chinese' Turkestan (Sinkiang) and, not least, the war-torn country of Afghanistan.

Since time immemorial, Central Asia has been repeatedly traversed by conquering hordes and, less dramatically but just as importantly, by caravans of merchants and pilgrims travelling the Silk Road back and forth from West to East. Not surprisingly, the Central Asian region is a melting pot of cultural and artistic influences. Nevertheless, it seems useful to attempt a broad classification of the principal centres of carpet production in Afghanistan and in eastern and western Turkestan.

NOMADIC AND SEMI-NOMADIC TRIBES

The Turkmen of western Turkestan

Western Turkestan extends from the shores of the Caspian Sea to the Chinese frontier, taking in along the way five republics of the former Soviet Union that are today virtually autonomous. Pronounced differences in altitude between the valleys and the high plateaus have proved conducive to an essentially pastoral way of life. The nomadic tribes of this vast region have a long tradition of weaving, producing carpets, kilims and travel bags, the last-named particularly useful during the long journeys in search of fresh pasture.

Carpets are used principally as floor coverings for the nomad *yurt* or tent. A central carpet known as a *Duyup-Ghali* is laid on an underfelt to protect it from damp; the *Dip-Ghali*, meanwhile, is a smaller carpet or rug placed across the tent entrance. Prayer rugs, unrolled at appointed hours only, are known as *Aiatlik-Nemazlik*.

The nomadic tribes make other items for day-to-day use, including *salatchak* ('cradle') carpets that are slung like hammocks; *khorjin* double kilim or knotted travel bags; *joval* bags to carry horse blankets; and *chetlik* to transport camel blankets. The women of the tribe weave on low-warp mobile looms and use the Persian knot technique.

Turkmen carpets are habitually known as *Bukhara*, in other words by the name of the junction town where they are generally warehoused and sold. Carpets are distinguished by a specific *gul*, and overall design is effectively constant across the various regions where Turkmen carpets are made. Originally, the *gul* – a sort of emblem or tribal totem known as a *tamga* – was transferred on marriage from one tribe to another, with the *gul* of the weaker tribe being discarded. Alternatively, the victors would acquire the *gul* of the vanquished as part of the spoils of war.

The four main Turkmen tribes divide into groups known as the Tekke, Yomut, Salor and Ersari, together with sub-groups known as the Bachir, Dalys, Unichs and Kanitchs.

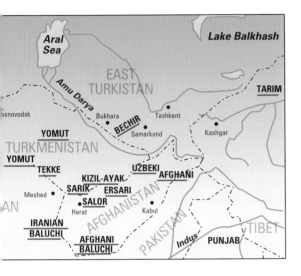

A splendidly worked contemporary Turkmen *woven in identical format to a much larger* Joval Saryk *model. It features an elongated and dentate* Salor *gul.* Joval *rugs are cushions or tent bags woven crossways rather than lengthways.*

Key features

– *Very soft* carci *wool, often taken from the silk-like belly wool of young lambs.*

– *Tight (Senneh) knots to a density of between 1,800 and 3,600/dm². Although carpets are typically large (8 ft 2 in × 9 ft 10 in/2.50 m × 3 m), the weave remains supple and the carpet can be easily rolled or folded.*

– *The pile is lustrous and flat (to the point where some buyers are deceived into thinking the carpet to be ancient or heavily worn).*

– *The geometrical design features rows of primary gul motifs separated by secondary guls in the interstices, thus enabling numerous permutations on the same theme.*

– *A feature of genuine* Tekke *carpets and rugs is the strip of kilim border known as an alam, which is designed to protect the leading edge of a knotted rug when it is used as a tent doormat in winter.*

– *Floral inner field designs are exceptionally fine and highly stylised. Animal motifs are frequent on* Arabatchi-type *carpets.*

– *Formats vary between 5 ft × 7 ft 10 in (1.50 m × 2.40 m) for smaller rugs and 7 ft 6 in × 11 ft 6 in (2.30 m × 3.50 m).*

– *Prices vary considerably depending on the quality of the item in question. Carpets and rugs are usually sold in marketplaces and bazaars under the generic term* Bukhara.

Tekkes

In the 19th century, the dominant Turkmen tribe was still the Tekke. After the Russian annexation in 1873, however, the re-drawing of administrative borders broke up the regions and pasturelands formerly occupied, obliging individual tribes either to remain on conquered territory or to disperse and find refuge elsewhere, as a rule in Iran or in Afghanistan.

Despite political pressures on them to settle permanently in one location, the traditional home of the Tekke nomads continues to be their *yurt*, the circular tent that is perfectly adapted to the nomadic way of life. The felt-covered *yurt*, with its large number of carpets and rugs and its array of woven bags and pouches for household paraphernalia, offers a fascinating glimpse into the world of textiles.

Ancient carpets of the Tekke tribe are known as 'royal' *Bukhara*. There are two principal centres of production, one in the region around Merv (Mary or Mouru), a major marketplace on a par with Samarkand and Bukhara, and the other in the Akhal region along the Kara-Kum river. The two regions turn out very similar products, the one substantive difference being the reds used to dye the ground. Madder roots employed by Tekkes in the Merv region are less rich and intense than those found in the Akhal region. That said, the colour red – ranging from dark brick to cochineal-based reddish purple – is the characteristic ground colour of Turkmen carpets as a whole. This is an interesting example of how a specific geographical location can impact on carpet production.

The rounded octagonal 'lobed' *gul* employed in the two regions is the same as that found among other Turkmen tribes. It is differentiated, however, by the motif placed inside the medallion – a motif divided into a cross shape by means of fine black lines which divide the whole into four different 'mirror' compartments, whereby each inverts the position of the one facing it. The centre is filled by a small (often eight-branch) star motif that the weavers refer to as the *gorbaghe* ('frog') *gul*. This motif is coloured alternately red and black, with a small area picked out in yellow.

This small variant apart, *Tekke* carpets and rugs are virtually identical in design and motif, although it should be noted that those used today are so stylised and abstract that any interpretation of the *gul* would be unwise.

Depending on the angle from which the carpet or rug is viewed, the colours appear to change and the pile acquires a different luminosity. Looked at *against* the light, the pile colours seem more intense inasmuch as the lighter red deepens into claret; looking at the pile *with* the light, on the other hand, makes it seems less intense as the red softens into a gentler pink. This visual effect is a feature of every good quality Turkmen carpet.

Tekke carpets are rare and, unfortunately, it has to be said that there are often vulgar replicas produced elsewhere, notably in Iran and Pakistan. Some of these imitation *Tekke* products are of acceptable quality but, in the main, they are mediocre copies that devalue the style. As ever, when buying a *Tekke* carpet or rug, it is essential to deal with a reputable merchant.

Variants on the *Tekke* theme appear in *Kizil-Tekke* examples, where the *gul* is not divided into four compartments and where the small crosses which link the *guls* are substituted by small stepped polygons. Another variant is the *Yasti-Tekke*, a small knotted carpet that is folded and stitched together to form a bag or pouch. These bags are in demand in the West, where they are used as cushions (from the Turkish term for a cushion, *yastik*).

Yomuts

The majority of Turkmen Yomut (Yomud) tribesmen living in the Gorgan and Atrak regions are now sedentary, though some from the Khiva (Chiva) region still cling to their traditional nomadic ways and continue to live in *yurts*.

Yomut weavers are very skilful and capable of weaving almost any fabric needed in their nomadic habitat. *Yomut* carpets and rugs are identified by various *gul* motifs. The weave is solid and silky, with the same overall sober design as the *Tekke*. *Yomuts* are generally more expensive.

A contemporary Yomut *carpet* comprising a sequence of Dyrnak guls, *i.e. elongated lozenge motifs set into smaller four-part lozenge patterns. Outlining the sides of the lozenge in off-white imparts a new decorative element to the* gul *and to the overall design, which is visually very effective. The upper and lower borders (alam) are finished with arrowhead or spear-point motifs.*

Salors

This Turkmen tribe produces carpets and rugs that are akin to those of other Turkmen groups as far as overall decoration is concerned, though certain differences exist with respect to how the *gul* is designed and applied. Additionally, *Salor* carpets tend to be more densely knotted (2,000 to 6,000/dm²) than other Turkmen types.
The *gul* habitually employed by the Salors is also divided up into four compartments, but the interior of each features delicate plant stems used to link assorted floral motifs – typically in clover-leaf format. The quarters are set off one against the other: two are woven in light red

and black on a white ground, and the opposing two are woven in red and black but on a lighter brick-red ground. In recent years, *Salor* carpets and rugs have come to be known in the market as *Penteh* carpets, the name being derived from a steppe region. In fact, these carpets and rugs are made by the Turkmen Sariq (Saryk) tribe which has settled south of Merv. They insert star-cross motifs between each row of *guls*, whereas *Salor* models tend to use a smaller *gul* motif for this purpose. Further, these *Penteh* types are substantially less densely knotted (1,700 to 2,500/dm²) than their *Salor* counterparts. Their market value is correspondingly lower than other tightly and delicately woven Turkmen carpets.

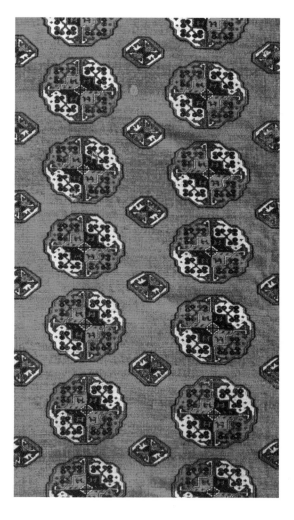

Ersaris

The majority of this Turkmen tribe now live in Afghanistan and the carpets and rugs they produce are often classed as *Afghan*. Some of the tribe continue to live in villages in the Bukhara region; their carpets and rugs are commonly – and wrongly – known as *Bechir*. Ersari output is highly diversified, though certain common features prevail.

Quite a number of Turkmen tribes lend their name to the carpets and rugs they produce: *Chaudar* (Chador, a Yomut sub-group), *Sariq* (from the Penteh steppe), or *Imereli* (from the Amu-Darya delta). In each instance, the overall design, despite some variants, is essentially similar to the basic Turkmen model.

In addition to the Turkmens, there are of course other ethnic groups in Central Asia who produce carpets and kilims. The principal features are noted here, although the persistent climate of political uncertainty throughout the region unfortunately precludes a detailed inventory of current output by Uzbek, Kirgiz, Kazak and Kara-Kalpak (Qaraqalpaq) groups.

Key features

– *Warp in delicate and lustrous wool mixed with goat hair; weft and raised pile in soft and silky wool, with individual motifs frequently highlighted in real silk.*
– *Lower (Persian) knot density than usual in the case of other Turkmen models (900 to 1,200/dm².).*
– *Dense pile.*
– *Predominant colour is red (light to dark claret) with a persistent orange tinge.*
– *A superabundance of vivid multi-coloured motifs in blues, yellows and greens, picked out and thrown into relief by black and maroon thread.*
– *Large octagonal* guls *similar to the* gulli gul *and other Turkmen motifs in the case of Afghan Ersaris. Bukhara Ersaris draw inspiration from Persian* boteh *and* herati *flower motifs, as do inventive* Bechir *designs.*
– *Formats are small, ranging from 3 ft 8 in × 4 ft (1.10 m × 1.25 m) to a maximum of 4 ft 8 in × 5 ft 3 in (1.40 m × 1.60 m). Models are used primarily as door flaps or as prayer rugs and only rarely as floor coverings.*
– *Prices tend to vary with knot density.*

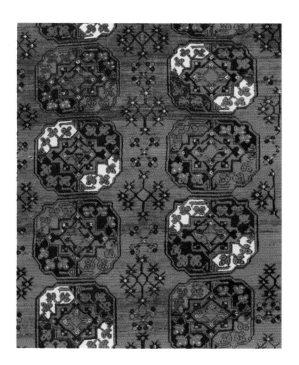

Afghanistan

Most of the ethnic groups enumerated in the preceding section (Uzbek, Baluchi, Tekke Turkmen and Ersari) are found in Afghanistan since many nomadic tribes sought refuge there following Soviet annexation. Carpets and rugs made by these tribes are frequently grouped under the general heading of *Afghani*, although each individual tribe outputs carpets and rugs in accordance with its own traditions (and with a view to prevailing demand in the West). Synthetic dyes are used and designs are simplified versions of ancient models. *Afghani* carpets and rugs are available in most marketplaces and bazaars throughout Afghanistan.

Uzbek weavers are scattered throughout Uzbekistan and Afghanistan. In northern Afghanistan in particular, they weave copies of Turkmen carpet styles. Their multi-coloured geometrical kilims, however, are nothing short of magnificent. Weavers here also produce vividly coloured felt carpets.

The Afghan Ersaris turn out a great variety of carpets and rugs, either in traditional formats with their individual *gul* set against a rust-red or orange-red ground and highlighted in black, or in 'borrowed' formats which reprise motifs used by other ethnic groups. Bright synthetic dyes are used and are often artificially faded.

Baluchi *Afghans* are almost identical to those made by the Baluchi in Khorasan (Iran), which has already been singled out for special mention in these pages. In an article in the review *Aura*, Italian painter Piero Dorazio (who has designed carpet cartoons on behalf of the Artcurial Gallery) described these carpets and rugs as follows: "In Baluchistan, the Baluchi tribe inhabits a yellow desert, their eyes dazzled by the light. As a result, their carpets tend to be dark, with minute flecks of red and green and beautiful permutations of black and grey. The eye is instinctively cast down against the glare and our imagination is captivated by this peripheral vision of beauty."

Patterns are predominantly geometrical and may feature a large and stylised Tree of Life embellished with numerous imaginative motifs of flowers, birds, camels and other creatures. Carpets are woven in delicate and lustrous wool. Knot density is a modest 1,500 to 3,000/dm². Camel blankets are especially ornate and decorated with variegated pom-poms.

Throughout the region of Herat and Andraskand, urban and village workshops turn out carpets and rugs that betray a range of influences, though they are all designated by the vague term *Afghan*. They are destined for Western markets. Items available in the bazaar at Herat, for example, are purely commercial, as indeed are the scarcer peasant-type carpets and rugs made by nomads of the region.

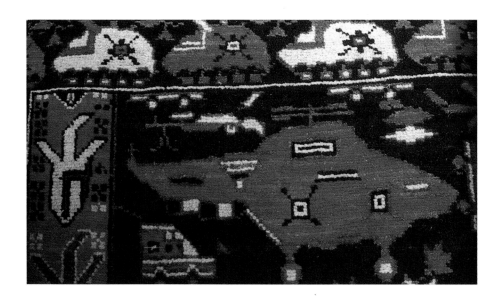

Left: Close-up of a recent Afghan Baluchi with border elements consisting of tank motifs and a field decorated with helicopters. Opposite page: A Baluchi Santeh design features on this long and narrow model with pouches used to hold kitchen utensils. The pouch has a crocheted bottom edge decorated with pom-poms.

Eastern Turkestan

Eastern – 'Chinese' – Turkestan lies in the autonomous region of Sinkiang and is inhabited mainly by Uighurs but also by a variety of other ethnic groups from Central Asia who migrated along the Silk Road, including Tartars, Mongols, Kirgiz, Uzbeks, and Hans.

Carpets and rugs woven here generally take the name of the eastern Turkestan city where they originate, namely Samarkand. The most ancient examples are rare and much in demand on account of their exotic designs and their rich natural colours.

Today, *Samarkand* carpets are woven in state-owned factories in the principal oasis towns along the Silk Road, including Khotan, Yarkant, Kashgar, Turfan and Urumchi. The Chinese authorities recently conducted a census of this predominantly desert region that revealed that it currently boasts some 10,000 looms. Knots are thick and knot density on the low side (400 to 800/dm^2), though Urumchi carpets and rugs frequently run to between 1,400 and 2,000 knots/dm^2. Vegetable dyes have been substituted by rather garish synthetic colours that are artificially faded by various means. Designs mirror the ethnic diversity of the region.

A Central Asian Pendeh *model woven by Turkmen immigrants to eastern Turkestan. The* gul *shows Tekke and Yomut influences. The border effect (alternating bands of white and red) is particularly attractive. The two ends are finished in kilim weave.*

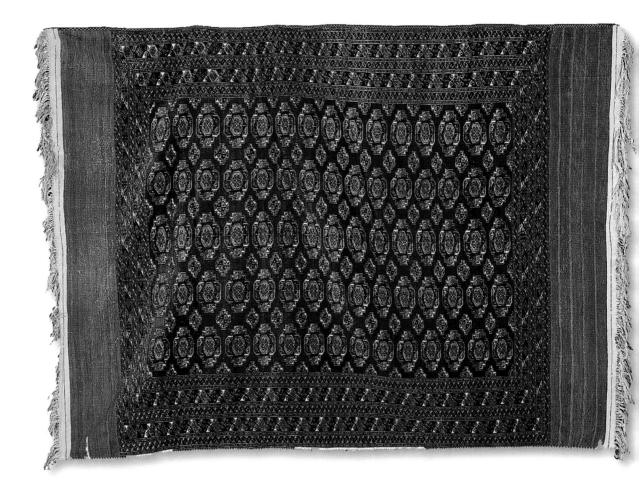

A carpet sold as a Samarkand *on the grounds that this and similar models are commonly available in the marketplace and bazaars of that city in western Turkestan. In fact, the carpet in question was woven in eastern Turkestan. This particular model – in large format (some 12 ft 10 in × 7 ft/ 3.90 m × 2.10 m) and dating from the late 19th century – is characteristic of those woven in the Yarkan Oasis. The field is covered in a stylised 'pomegranate' motif, with large vases located at the outer edges. Each tree branch has pomegranate flowers, buds and blossoms in light-red madder. In Iran, the pomegranate tree is a Tree of Life symbol; in Buddhism, it connotes happiness and fertility. Note the diagonal 'Grecian' frieze of the inner border, which introduces an innovative 'classical' motif.*

Chinese carpets

Ever since the Han Dynasty (206 B.C.–A.D. 220), Chinese silks have enjoyed great prestige, especially when later exported to the West along the Silk Road. By contrast, China was never held in esteem for its knotted carpets. Examples were rare and generally destined for the domestic market. From the end of the 19th century, however, European demand greatly encouraged the production of knotted carpets in China.

No attempt will be made to catalogue all the carpets that come from this vast region. It should nonetheless be pointed out that Chinese exports to Europe and beyond stem without exception from state-owned factories and workshops situated in the major cities such as Beijing (Peking), Tientsin or Shanghai. Output has been standardised to the point of mass production (the pile is often shaved using an electric mower!). These production centres often exploit underpaid female labour to turn out carpets in all shapes and sizes, including round and oval rugs.

Order specifications and templates supplied by the client enable carpets of any kind whatsoever to be faithfully copied. Accordingly, there are Chinese 'Persian' carpets, Chinese 'Turkish' carpets, Chinese '*Aubussons*' and Chinese '*Savonneries*'. Needless to say, countless 'Peking-style' carpets and rugs manufactured in these large industrial complexes are machine-made.

As distinct from these commercial ventures, carpet-weaving is practised at the local level at locations from central China to the Mongolian steppe.

A contemporary Beijing-made carpet in the French Aubusson *style. Note the characteristically Chinese turquoise-blue ground.*

An early-20th-century carpet made in Beijing. The field holds a large medallion (of sorts) where the weaver has scattered countless small motifs over a red ground. The motifs are essentially ideograms and 'good luck' charms. Note the unusual 'Chinese-Greek' border pattern.

Key features

– Warp and weft in cotton.

– Pile in lustrous long-fibre wool from a breed of sheep raised on the Tibetan plains. Although silk is intensely cultivated, all-silk carpets are comparatively rare.

– Knot (Senneh) density is low (600 to 1,000/dm²), but the dense raised pile is resilient. A characteristic Chinese technique is to crop the pile to different heights in order to throw design features into relief (an effect not dissimilar to that obtained in older 'carved' Venetian carpets).

– Synthetic colour palette with 'typical' Chinese blues and golds and finely nuanced apricot, ivory and beige tones.

– Patterns are extremely varied and distinguished by symbolic motifs with a mythological bias (dragons, phoenixes, etc.) or by ideograms associated with religious ritual (notably the shou motif in the form of a hooked 'H', the symbol for longevity). Colours also have symbolic value: red for fire and the phoenix; black for evil; white for mourning; blue for the sky and the way of the dragon; yellow for the earth and fertility; and so on.

– The ground is for the most part monochrome, with no ornamentation inserted between the field motifs. The overall design is delicately rendered.

– Formats vary as a function of Western expectations and tastes.

A Ningsia workshop carpet that reprises classical motifs from ancient Peking. The field has a golden-yellow ground with cameo-like Chinese characters and several small medallions whose form is suggestive of lotus blossom (the symbol for longevity) or peonies (which stand for friendship and love). Elsewhere, the field contains stylised bats symbolising happiness. The border takes the form of a classical 'Greek' frieze.

The Inner Mongolian city of Batu is a centre that currently turns out 'Peking-style' copies of ancient carpets and rugs earmarked for export and tagged with a commendably honest (if somewhat confusing) label: 'antique finished'. In other words, the items in question have been subjected to chemical treatment to impart a patina that the occasional less-than-scrupulous Western merchant will potentially market as a sign of authenticity and 'age'. In Beijing, a range known as *Hankung* finds inspiration in Persian motifs (for example the large centre medallion) that appeal to Western buyers. Predictably, perhaps, these models are marketed as 'Persian Chinese'. As Erwin Gans-Ruedin notes in his book on Chinese carpets, these products illustrate the "innate ability of Chinese artisans to produce to order any given design and to imbue it with the requisite refinement of touch".

All these copies and replicas can cause the uninformed collector serious headaches, particularly since Chinese carpet-makers are at pains to match the technical skills of their counterparts in Iran. What is more, they have demonstrated their ability to do precisely that – thanks in part to the help of master-weavers from Iran.

Round carpets and rugs are often assembled by 'injecting' individual wool tufts into a stretch cotton canvas base by means of an electrically powered 'gun'. The reverse is then coated with a latex adhesive to secure the tufts, and then covered by a canvas sheet. This technique, developed to cut production costs, is marketed in the West as 'hand-tufted', and the dense and soft pile that ensues can easily be mistaken for that of a genuine hand-knotted carpet. At the same time, however, Chinese craftsmen are fully capable of producing knotted round carpets, a skill that testifies to their remarkable technical prowess.

Tientsin carpets exhibit good quality and technique, notably as regards knot density (which can be as high as 9,000/dm^2). These are sold as 'superior Chinese' goods. Tientsin factories also turn out all-silk carpets with in excess of one million knots to the square metre. The latter are generally copies of Persian models such as *Shiraz* or *Tabriz*, but some are based on classic Chinese designs featuring peonies, lotus blossom, peach flowers or mythical creatures such as dragons and the like.

Since Tibet was annexed by China, regional carpet production has declined, with many Tibetan weavers having decamped to Nepal (where they weave 'Tibetan' carpets for the export market).

Carpets from the Ningsia to the north-east of Lan-chou are reputed to be the finest in all China, due in no small part to the exceptional wool grade employed and the delicate colour palette achieved by the use of vegetable dyes. The flower patterns feature peonies and lotus blossoms. A *shou* symbol of longevity, shrouded in cloud, is often inserted into the centre medallion.

All in all, both classic and derivative Chinese carpets and rugs can be said to be of good technical quality despite their poor knot density. The particularly soft and lustrous local wool used is often mistaken for silk. To accommodate rising export demand, a superior wool grade is now imported from New Zealand. Output from the state-owned factories and workshops is phenomenal – and confusing, for it makes it difficult to determine the exact provenance of an individual Chinese carpet, since they are *all* produced by every single manufacturer (other than items from Tientsin and Tibet).

The Chinese produce good quality imitation Oriental carpets that should never fool an expert. On the other hand, if a 'Persian-style' Chinese carpet is attractive and relatively low-priced, there is nothing to be said against purchasing it – in the full knowledge, however, that one is acquiring a copy and not the genuine article.

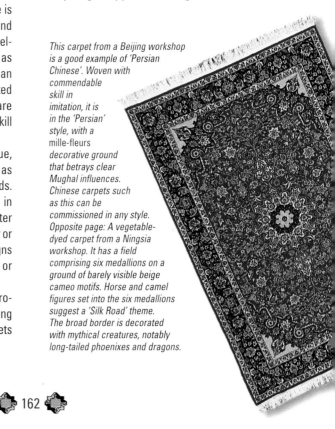

This carpet from a Beijing workshop is a good example of 'Persian Chinese'. Woven with commendable skill in imitation, it is in the 'Persian' style, with a mille-fleurs decorative ground that betrays clear Mughal influences. Chinese carpets such as this can be commissioned in any style. Opposite page: A vegetable-dyed carpet from a Ningsia workshop. It has a field comprising six medallions on a ground of barely visible beige cameo motifs. Horse and camel figures set into the six medallions suggest a 'Silk Road' theme. The broad border is decorated with mythical creatures, notably long-tailed phoenixes and dragons.

Carpets of India, Pakistan and Nepal

Carpet-making in India goes back only as far as the Mughal emperors of the 16th and 17th centuries. Reminiscent of Mughal miniatures, the few surviving examples hint at great splendour and artistry. Such carpets were woven by Persian craftsmen who travelled to India at the invitation of the Mughal Emperor Akbar (r. 1556–1605).

During the 19th century, English merchants from the East India Company set up carpet factories in the principal Indian cities and towns, 'sweat-shops' that exploited low-cost child labour. As elsewhere, the merchants specified designs that were in line with and adapted to Western tastes, the result being a synthesis of Indian and Persian motifs. At the same time, quality standards were lowered in order to secure an optimum return on investment.

When India achieved independence, carpet and rug production was taken under the wing of the state and traditional respect for quality and regional cultural identity were stressed. That said, there is still considerable export demand for copies of foreign designs. By contrast, in both northern and southern India there still flourishes a rural textile industry – producing decorative fabrics, notably for saris – that displays a genuine folk tradition of great originality.

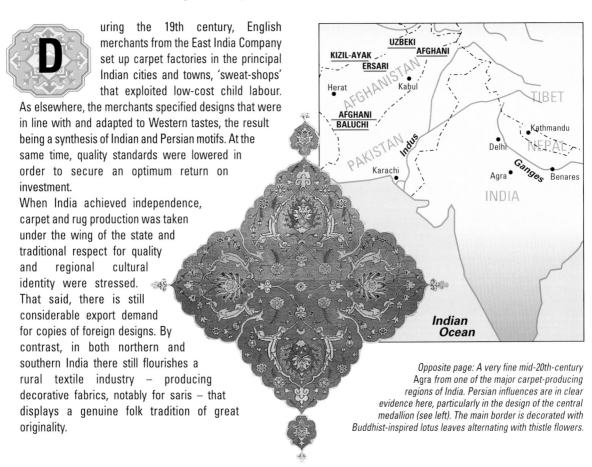

Opposite page: A very fine mid-20th-century Agra from one of the major carpet-producing regions of India. Persian influences are in clear evidence here, particularly in the design of the central medallion (see left). The main border is decorated with Buddhist-inspired lotus leaves alternating with thistle flowers.

India: Kashmir

The most beautiful *Kashmir* specimens come from the famous workshops at Srinagar in the Vale of Kashmir. Output is on a large scale, fuelled by tourist and Western export market demand.

Key features

– *Fine and silky cashmere wool taken from the down of certain species of goat and similar to that used to produce cashmere scarves and shawls. Chinese silk thread is also used.*
– *Extremely dense and very short-cropped pile comprising a mixture of wool and silk.*
– *The (Persian) knots exhibit a high density (between 4,000 and 7,000 knots/dm². In the case of silk-knotted carpets, however, knot density can attain an unprecedented 42,000 knots/dm² (420/cm²) in order to render as faithfully as possible the various Hindu deities depicted in the design.*
– *Soft and extremely delicate colours, predominantly light pinks, light beige, ivory, yellow and sky blue.*
– *Designs for top-of-the-range silk carpets are frequently taken from ancient scarves or shawls, sometimes with no field motif other than the boteh extending over regular interconnecting rows that exhibit a high degree of compositional originality. Others feature a centre medallion on a background of flower motifs and set into arabesques with stylised antelope and tiger designs. The entire ground is covered, worked like a piece of ornamented gold. One classic theme is that of a vase holding all manner of flowers – tulips, roses, violets, iris, lotus blossom, etc. Some motifs and patterns are drawn in part from Buddhist mythology and feature gods and goddesses and border texts in Sanskrit. Wool carpet formats are large (approximately 6 ft 8 in × 9 ft 10 in/2 m × 3 m), whereas silk rugs with Buddhist themes tend to be smaller (1 ft 8 in × 2 ft/ 0.50 m × 0.60 m) and are usually wall-mounted; other types are generally in the region of 6 ft × 4 ft (1.85 m × 1.20 m).*

Kashmiri weavers are exceptionally creative and particularly adept at tackling large-scale themes with all the originality and intricacy of ancient shawl designs. The gentle colour harmonies, the finesse brought to individual motifs, and the overall compositional balance achieved have combined to make these carpets and rugs an extremely attractive complement to classical and modern interior design. It must be admitted, on the other hand, that some carpets are of poor quality, notably where the fine wool is substituted by coarser grades and knot densities are lowered to the point where the carpet or rug is neither firm nor hard-wearing.

Elsewhere in India, state-owned workshops and factories are the general rule; these are found in cities such as Jaipur or Agra where, as in China or Pakistan, the bulk of the output is mass-produced on the basis of foreign designs. Regions such as in and around Benares, Bahadolhi, Mirzapur and Masulipatam tend to turn out coarse carpets and rugs with Persian-inspired flower motifs. Indian kilims are woven in cotton (*darri*); designs are simple geometrical forms with some flower elements. Some, notably those woven for wedding ceremonies, are made of silk.

A contemporary silk Kashmir with medallions using the boteh motif, recalling cashmere shawls fashionable in 19th-century Europe. Cashmere workshops also produce very beautiful all-silk garden carpets in the compartmentalised Bakhtiar style, together with tableaux featuring scenes drawn from local mythology.

*An imitation 'Caucasian' carpet produced in one of the many
workshops in Karachi and throughout the surrounding region.
Carpets and rugs are woven in all conceivable styles and formats.*

Pakistan

Pakistan was established in 1947 by the union of several Moslem provinces of northern India, including the Punjab, Baluchistan and a part of Kashmir. When the Mughals still reigned in Lahore, the Punjab was a major carpet-weaving region. On the formation of the new state of Pakistan, Moslem refugees streamed into the Punjab and, particularly, into Lahore and Karachi. Among them were many weavers, on whose skills the government immediately capitalised to develop an export market for cheaper carpets using synthetic dyes and industrial yarn. These mediocre carpets duly flooded European markets, where they were known by the catch-all term 'Pakistani'.

The carpets and rugs in question use coarser-grade wool, chemical dyes and the Jufti knot. They are often patterned with rows of Tekke or Salor *guls.* These Turkmen-inspired products exhibit a different colour palette, however, with the traditional brick-red ground being substituted by blues, yellows or greens – colours which, allegedly, are more in line with Western tastes. A few years ago, factories and workshops in Lahore identified growing demand for carpets and rugs that imitate Persian *Kashan* and *Kerman* models, and started using better-grade wool to produce a flat and lustrous pile. As a rule, these are low-priced carpets, though prices will naturally vary according to wool grade and knot density.

Pakistani copies of the Turkmen Bukhara *style. Carpet output in Pakistan is substantial, with no less than 32.3 million square feet (3 million square metres) produced in 1993 alone. Quality varies considerably from one workshop to the next.*

A modern design created by Marcel Zelmanovich and produced by an urban workshop in Kathmandu, Nepal.

In the 19th century, the city of Amritsar boasted a great number of carpet factories that today still exist, primarily to produce copies of *Bukhara* models. These outlets also make beautiful carpets which draw on genuinely 'Indian' motifs; typically, they feature flower arabesques with inset variegated bird motifs or a bewildering array of animal (stag and tiger) designs. Once again, however, they draw inspiration from Persian or Caucasian carpet and rug designs.

Baluchi weavers in Pakistan weave very attractive low-pile carpets and kilims, together with bags decorated with pom-poms and embroidery.

Nepal

Since Tibet was overrun and occupied by China, Nepal has inherited skilled Tibetan weaver immigrants. Traditional religious-motif carpets and rugs are still made in Nepal.

On a visit to Nepal, the painter Marcel Zelmanovich was captivated not only by the quality of the (habitually still hand-spun) silk-like wool from the chill regions of the Kathmandu Valley, but also by the expertise of Tibetan weavers and Indian dyers, and by the traditional rinsing techniques used. As of 1982, Zelmanovich has been working closely with a workshop in Kathmandu, providing contemporary designs to be woven using the traditional Tibetan knot (which boasts a density of between 60,000 and 80,000 knots to the square metre (5,555 to 7,410 per square foot). Local wool is used, and the *in situ* chemical dyeing processes result in excellent colour fastness. Zelmanovich regularly exhibits at the Diurne Gallery in Paris and makes limited edition carpets and rugs available to selected outlets.

This is a fine example of co-operative enterprise with a pronounced social content, providing as it does employment for more than 100 people. Artistically, it represents a means of encouraging contemporary design in a traditional artisanal context. The carpets and rugs are marketed at reasonable cost per square metre, and various formats are available. The Zelmanovich initiative has attracted the interest of many European interior designers by calling attention to the decorative potential of modern carpets.

Nepalese workshops also produce Tibetan-style carpets and rugs made by refugees, together with replicas of virtually every carpet type under the sun – in much the same way as the mass-production facilities operating in today's Pakistan.

Carpets and *hanbels* from North Africa, Egypt and Arabia

This section covers three countries in North Africa – Morocco, Algeria and Tunisia – as well as Egypt and Arabia.

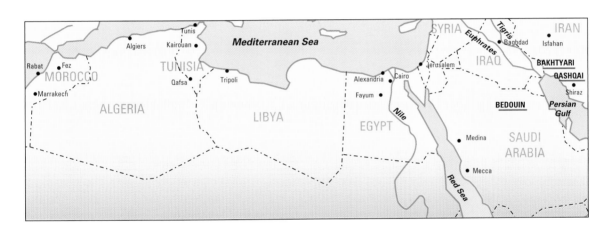

MOROCCO

Carpet production is today an important sector of the Moroccan economy, with each region and large city producing its own particular range. In 1930, Morocco exported a total of 597,860 square feet (55,544 square metres) of rugs and carpets. As of 1947, the launch of a new quality label made it easier to identify ancient and modern carpets made in the traditional way by reference to weave quality, overall colour-fastness and originality of design. This quality label, coupled with affordable prices, has resulted in production rising substantially: by 1974, the country was turning out some 10,742,370 square feet (998,000 square metres) annually. This figure had doubled by 1979. Output from Rabat-Salé (Rabat Shella) alone accounts for over half of the entire national output.

In 1988, Morocco's Ministry for Crafts and Social Affairs reached an agreement with the Konrad Adenauer Foundation to launch an inventory programme known as 'Coopart', which built on an earlier programme in place since 1927 under the auspices of France's Prosper Ricard. No attempt is made in the following to list all the production centres identified in the 'Coopart' census. Instead, we shall restrict our focus to those whose products are distinguished by their quality and originality.

Rural regions from the Middle Atlas to the Atlantic Ocean

Carpet-weaving is the principal occupation of one person in three of the active population in the north-western town of Khemisset. The weavers (exclusively female) work on a high-warp loom. Carpets and rugs are sold either to bazaar-stall owners who regularly visit individual villages, or directly to the public at weekly *souks* such as that in Khemisset (Tuesdays) or Tiflet (Wednesdays).

The wool comes from sheep grazed on the Middle Atlas and is purchased ready-spun at local village markets. For the most part, the dyes used are of vegetable origin – madder (*taroubia*) for reds, crushed pomegranate leaves, turnips, figs and a dash of henna for black. Sulphur is added to hanks of natural wool to bleach it white. 'Berber' knots are used, in other words one knot to every two warp yarns.

Basic motifs are in the main geometrical patterns similar to those found in Oriental carpets (lozenges, triangles, crosses, stars and squares). In some carpets and rugs, one also finds flower motifs or 'mythical' designs that the weaver has taken from her immediate physical surroundings or simply extemporised. The dominant colour is red. Patterns are woven in white and black on a red ground (the three traditional colours of the region) with, more recently, touches of orange, yellow and green. The motifs are arranged in horizontal or vertical rows or in chequerboard or lozenge grid patterns. To cite one example, Zemmour weavers in Khemisset make carpets and rugs with motifs arranged in a primarily red and orange chequerboard pattern; examples of these are available in the markets at Khemisset and Tiflet.

One carpet type from Douar Sheikh is particularly interesting on account of its 'dislocated' lozenge design, where the points of the lozenges are offset to create an unusual visual effect. Also of interest is the recurrent 'spider' motif (*taaoullite*) similar to that which often appears also in carpets and kilims made by many semi-nomadic tribes in Asia Minor.

The prototype raised-pile Berber carpet is the simple maroon-check lozenge design (*takhamt* or 'little tent') on an off-white ground, a feature of which is the use of the 'Rabat' knot tied over four warp yarns (like the Jufti knot).

Left: A hanbel *from the Khemisset region of the Middle Atlas, with an unusual design featuring stylised minarets.*
Above: A Berber rug in red madder-dyed wool from Tazenakt in the High Atlas (courtesy of the Paris-based Moroccan Crafts Delegation).

*A High Atlas Berber carpet with white ground and
various motifs in relief.*

Hanbel rugs, which have a close-cropped pile, are typical of this region. Dimensions vary according to use: some are long and narrow, used to close off the ground flaps of the tent; larger *hanbels* are used as blankets, while smaller ones are woven as saddle blankets, pouches or cushions. They are woven using a canvas stitch across alternating threads with an 'embroidered' colour thread interposed on the weft.

The *hanbel* has remained true to its Berber origins. Motifs are essentially geometric and woven in reds, white and black. Designs vary according to the tribe in question. The field pattern in a *hanbel* woven at Sidi Allah-Lamsaddar is typical: broad and narrow alternating rows, each with its own different motif, assembled in a rhythmic, quasi-musical pattern. The truncated lines intersect to form concentric lozenge patterns – a motif known as *kan-rzem* (literally, 'open and close').

Every motif has its own evocative Berber name: the comb, the frog, the chequerboard, the saw, the dog's ear, the tea-urn, the shears, the tailor's scissors, the snake-bone, the mirror, the arabesque, the spider, the turtle shell, the rose petal, the snake's tongue, and so on. Each tribe draws on this design reservoir to create its own compositions. Carpets and *hanbels* are often identified by their individual tribal name. *Hanbels* made by the *Zemmour*, for example, are woven by women reputed to be the most accomplished weavers in Morocco. Irrespective of the individual tribe, however, each *hanbel* draws on virtually the same design vocabulary. On the other hand, the motifs and technical expertise selected are often dictated or (at least) tempered by faith and superstition. The Berber tribes are deeply superstitious, each having its own mythology and its own array of guardian spirits and protectors.

The indigenous population of the mountainous Boulemane region is of Berber stock. In most instances, carpets and *hanbels* are woven for day-to-day use. The hand-spun wool generally comes from domestic livestock. Individual tribes are so diversified, however, that it is well-nigh impossible to classify carpet and *hanbel* types. All the variants and permutations noted elsewhere are also present here.

The Beni-Mguild, Zagan and Beni-Mtir tribes live in a mountainous region on whose plateaus some sedentary semi-nomadic groups still live. The principal towns are Meknès, Ifrane and Khenifra. *Hanbels* are woven throughout this region for use as tent decoration or as floor coverings in the home of tribal officials. Red is the dominant colour and white is used to outline and highlight the classic geometrical patterns typically used to make up the design.

Beni-Mguild tribes in the town of Azrou have formed themselves into a weaver co-operative. This is one of the most important Berber production centres. Markets are held each Tuesday. *Hanbels* from this region are distinguished by their bright colours and the use of innumerable spangles or sequins (*mouzon*). The overall design comprises a very broad lozenge grid. The pile is unusually long and thick. As a rule, the ground is white and decorated with dark maroon lozenges.

Mention should also be made of carpets and rugs from Beni Sadden to the east of Fès, and those woven by the Marmouchas to the south of Ahermoumou; the latter are displayed in the Imouzzer *souk* every Tuesday alongside the very sober deep-pile wool *hanbels* with their maroon, red and orange lozenge motifs woven by the Beni-Booyahi tribe.

The rural High Atlas

This mountainous region overlooks the Plain of Marrakech and the Sous Oued ('river'). The bulk of the population is centred on Ouarzazate and on two other towns, Tazenakt and Amerzgane. The latter two localities produce an estimated 90% of all carpets known as 'High Atlas' (better known to *souk* carpet merchants as *Glaoui*).

The weavers are from many different tribes and classification is by style rather than provenance; thus, there are monochrome, horizontal band, centre medallion field types, and so on. Although there are many different styles, certain elements are common to most if not all High Atlas carpets and rugs. The vegetable-dye *hanbels* of the Ait Ouaousguide tribes, typically stitched together at the edges to form travel pouches, are a combination of flat-pile and knotted-pile techniques, with designs that closely resemble those of High Atlas *Glaoui*. They are sold in the weekly market at Ouarzazate.

In the plains and mountains around Marrakech, carpet and *hanbel* weaving for domestic purposes was always highly developed. Today, output has been increasingly oriented towards commercialisation – for self-evident economic reasons. The *souk* at Marrakech sells every type of carpet and *hanbel* produced in the region.

Haouz carpets are known as *Chichaoua* after the name of a village some 45 miles (72 kilometres) south-west of Marrakech, where there is a co-operative operated by the women of the Ouled Bou Sbâa tribe of Arab stock, who weave very dense, flat-pile rugs with a black border of mixed wool and goat hair.

The most strikingly original feature of these rural carpets and rugs lies in their naïve design. The weavers do not work from templates and are thus free to design at will, giving free rein to their imagination. Strange, at times even crude, motifs scattered about the light- or dark-red field are often no more and no less than stylised representations of everyday objects, such as a tea-urn, shears, a comb, brooch or clasp, domestic or wild animals, and so forth. These motifs commingle with flower and star patterns and build to a rhythmic

A hanbel *featuring a stripe design on red ground.*

Key features
– *Warp and weft in very fine wool from mills in Marrakech.*
– *Pile wool is lustrous and often hand-spun from local herds to yield a silk-like texture.*
– *A ⅜-in to ⅝-in (1 cm to 1.5 cm) Turkish knot used; knot density varies between 8,000 and 20,000 knots/m².*
– *Dyeing is done in situ, with locally purchased chemical dyes (aniline) predominating. The colour palette is more varied and much brighter than in the past, with violet, green and orange used extensively.*
– *Motifs have different names from one duar (encampment or tented village) to the next, but are common throughout the region: window, butterfly, necklace, ancient engraving, house, lion, turtle, porcelain plate, tile, chequerboard, clasp, etc.*
– *Formats are medium, ranging from 5 ft 10 in × 4 ft (1.80 m × 1.20 m) to 9 ft 6 in × 5 ft 3 in (2.90 m × 1.60 m) for the largest.*

Berber weaving ritual

With the Berber, the top roller on a high-warp loom is known as 'Heaven', the bottom one as 'Earth', thereby establishing the link between the visible and the invisible world. When weavers complete a carpet and before they cut it from the frame, they recite a special prayer of thanks for a successful 'delivery', effectively equating the warp threads to the umbilical cord. They are careful only to cut part of the warp yarn and leave enough space for a young girl to pass through, symbolically safeguarding her virginity until marriage.

The carpet is removed from the loom and spread on the ground, where it is covered with dates which are eaten in ritual celebration by the whole family, participating in what is a shared experience. During the process, the young girls have to refrain from stepping on the warp yarns.

Any man passing within striking distance is symbolically beaten with a bobbin of warp wool and is obliged to pay a token amount in coin to the weavers to ensure that no evil subsequently befalls him.

Looms are set up on Mondays and Thursdays only (weddings are held exclusively on those days) and are oriented towards Mecca. The weavers claim that the repeated striking of the warp threads to tighten the weave breathes life (roh) into the carpet.

composition which is invariably innovative. Among the most commonly used colours are yellow (from pomegranate peel), orange (from henna dye) and blue from the indigo plant. A 'scorpion' motif is frequently fashioned out of several small interlocking lozenges, with one end representing the claws; another common motif is made up of broken lines that connote 'rivers'.

The urban tradition

Urban carpets differ from their rural counterparts to the extent that they are invariably much more elaborate. The influence of Ottoman Empire carpets and rugs from Asia Minor is evident. There are two major centres of production: Rabat-Salé and Casablanca.

Some commentators take the view that carpet weaving in Rabat goes back to the end of the 16th century and was spearheaded by Arab weavers who settled there after leaving Andalusia. Others argue that the carpet motifs are consistent with Turkish models from 17th century Anatolia, notably as regards the centre medallions.

Today, traditional designs are complemented by the free expression of highly personal motifs introduced by rural weavers who have come to work in urban workshops. The generic name *Rabat* has, in fact, come to be applied not only to output from *ateliers* in Rabat and Salé but also to carpets and rugs woven elsewhere, such as in Fès, Chaouen, Teouan and Casablanca itself. *Rabat* is also used to describe output from the Mediouna tribe from the Casablanca region.

Carpets and rugs are destined for local and tourist markets but also for the vitally important export market. Colours, designs and knot densities vary appreciably.

A red 'modern carpet' label of quality may be affixed to modern monochrome carpets or 'modern design' specimens, provided however that they are of recognised technical merit.

It is clear from what has been said that traditional Berber carpets, rugs and *hanbels* from the Middle and High Atlas exhibit the most appealing and original designs. In addition to items made in regional centres affiliated to the Ministry for Crafts, a number of craft co-operatives also produce carpets and *hanbels* to order.

Key features

– Wool or (occasionally) cotton weft.
– Warp and pile in Middle Atlas wool or in imported New Zealand wool (for the higher grades).
– Ghiordes-knotted. Knot density varies according to quality label requirements: 50,000/m² for standard output (grey label); 70,000/m² for medium-grade (yellow label); 90,000/m² for superior grade (light blue label) and 160,000/m² for superior-plus grades (pink label). The label is a piece of canvas mounted on a brown background and sewn onto a carpet or rug.
– Basic colours are red, blue, green-yellow, orange, black and white. The ground is generally in madder red. Labelled carpets are required to be certified grand teint ('colour-fast') if the dyes used are not of vegetable origin.
– Rabat carpets and rugs must use motifs drawn from the formal repertoire in order to uphold traditional standards. According to one venerable ma'allem (carpet-master), the design of a Rabat carpet or rug should follow a prescribed pattern and comprise "the outline of a house, with the carpet field surrounded by a garden border and rows of flowerbeds and paths at different levels around a centre medallion representing a pool or basin in the middle of the garden. Two arches should be woven to symbolise the two sculpted stone niches that decorate each end of the main reception area." To some, this garden carpet is an abstract and highly poetical evocation of the Garden of Eden which contains all that is most beautiful in Creation – flowers, fruit, peacocks, gazelles, stars, etc. Thus, the classic Rabat carpet will have a centre medallion (koubba) highlighted by a red ground, decorated with tiny motifs, and set into a field that is closed off at either end by two arches described by pairs of stepped 'bird-wing' triangles. The frame is formed by between three and seven borders decorated with flower and star motifs.
– Rabat formats vary, the largest being some 16 ft 4 in × 9 ft 10 in (5 m × 3 m); generally speaking, they are more modest, typically 2 ft 4 in × 3 ft 3 in (0.70 m × 1 m) or 4 ft × 3 ft 8 in (1.20 m × 1.10 m).
– 19th-century examples often come as 'twinned' or 'serial' carpets, with two, three or even five individual carpets and rugs of similar colour and design intended for use in a large reception area.

A contemporary 'Royal Rabat' on a magnificent blue ground and with a weave density of 14,865 knots per square foot (160,000 per square metre).

A beautifully woven 'Royal Rabat' featuring traditional motifs on a pink ground, with a weave density of 45,520 knots per square foot (490,000 per square metre).

ALGERIA

Algeria has always occupied an important place in North African carpet production. In the 1930s, the carpet firm Myrbor, under the artistic direction of Marie Cuttoli, set up workshops in Algiers and in Setif (Sétif) to weave designs produced by artists such as Jean Lurçat, Fernand Léger, Jean (Hans) Arp, and Pablo Picasso. These were the first carpets ever to be designed by prominent painters.

Political events in Algeria have undoubtedly led to a substantial decline in carpet production, but major factories still operate in Algiers, Oran and Tlemcen and turn out Berber carpets and rugs, together with replicas of ancient Anatolian and Persian designs earmarked for domestic consumption and export markets. For original designs, however, one must look to the tribes of the high plateau.

In the Amour-Djebel mountain region – an area inhabited by the ancient Ouled Sidi Cheikh confederation of tribes – carpet and rug production is increasingly scarce today, but such examples as do exist have attractively symmetrical motifs, muted colours (predominantly carob and indigo plant dyes, frequently with added green) and a pronounced deep pile.

Until quite recently, fine-quality closely woven carpets were produced in the region south of M'zab. These were distinguished by their complex geometrical designs arranged, almost *hanbel*-like, in parallel rows woven predominantly in reds and oranges interspersed with black and gentler shades of lichen green. Examples rarely become available for purchase. The same holds true for *el-Kala* carpets made by the Ben Rached tribe in the region of Oran, where flat-pile carpets and rugs with clear-cut design contours are essentially hybrids which betray both Berber and Middle Eastern influences. Up until only a few years ago, the dominant reddish-brown colour was obtained from a mixture of henna and green oak bark; today, it is produced by chemical means.

The arts and crafts market in Algiers offers a full range of Algerian-made carpets and rugs – some excellent, some decidedly less so.

Opposite page: A Berber grain pouch (aures) with one side decorated in geometrical motifs and the other side left plain.
Above: A carpet market in southern Tunisia.

TUNISIA

Carpet production in Tunisia is known above all for models woven in the city of Kairouan (al-Qayrawan): soft, smooth carpets and rugs in a limited range of colours, with designs that are clearly influenced by Middle Eastern models. The carpets and rugs are woven in state-owned factories, in privately owned workshops and in individual homes; it is said that almost every woman in Kairouan is an experienced weaver.

The *souk* and the crafts shops in Kairouan offer a selection of deep-pile red and brown carpets and rugs known as *Zerbia*. Another Kairouan carpet type known as an *Alloucha* features a natural colour palette made up of whites, beige, maroon and black. Meanwhile, the Tunis suburb of Den-Den (not far from the Bardo Museum) is now a dedicated carpet manufacturing centre supervised by the ONAT (Office National d'Artisanat), which also monitors carpet-making in other centres such as Safaqis (Sfax), Bizerte (Banzart) and Gabès (Qabis). The ONAT quality label (like its counterpart in Morocco) is a warranty of quality and price. Unfortunately, in a bid to boost production, the ONAT has imposed a set of norms that effectively discourage some traditional motifs and prescribe a narrower range of synthetic dyes. That said, recent years have seen a fresh impetus imparted to contemporary design in both carpets and tapestry work; what is more, production has passed increasingly into private hands.

Particular mention should be made of kilims from Qafsah (Gafsa) known as *Ferrachia* or *Haouli*. These are used as blankets and/or floor coverings, and are decorated with small geometrical and figurative motifs of sub-Saharan influence set into chequerboard compartments that often cover the entire – typically blue – field. (Incidentally, these motifs provided inspiration for some of Paul Klee's work during his sojourn in Tunisia.)

The Qafsah repertoire of motifs is considerable: fish, camels, caravans, tents, squares, chequerboards and lozenges are perhaps the most common symbols, though Qafsah weavers have not shied away from substituting the traditional mode of transport towards Mecca – the camel – by a more up-to-date motif: the aeroplane. This folk art form is under threat from one quarter in particular – the excessive demands of the tourist trade.

Carpets woven from designs by contemporary artists (such as Nja Mahdaoui or Hmida Ouahada) clearly demonstrate that the kilim tradition in Qafsah is experiencing something of a renaissance, with mass-produced chemically dyed models being replaced by vegetable-dye carpets designed by avant-garde Tunisian artists. The excellent calligraphy of Nja Mahdaoui exemplifies this, insisting on the "autonomy of the woven text that develops its own infinite space to create its own texture and context" – in other words, a modern re-affirmation of the age-old principle of inscribed carpets.

Carpet and rugs produced on the island of Djerba (Jarbah) are also worthy of mention. A ground of vivid colour underpins strange dark motifs that emerge as a kind of braid calligraphy. Examples of these are on view at the ONAT exhibition centre in Houmet es-Souk (Hawmat as-Suq), the island's capital.

Opposite page: Traditional Qafsah *(Gafsa) hanging with variegated motifs.*
Right: A modern (1992) Qafsah *from the ONA workshops in that city; based on a cartoon design by the painter Hmida Ouahada, one of the prime movers behind modern Tunisian carpet design based on the study of ancient models.*
Below: A vegetable-dye rug woven in natural wool to a design by Hmida Ouahada.

EGYPT

Before concluding this section on North Africa, a few words on Egyptian carpet and rug production is in order. Egyptian models made in Cairo during the Mameluk and Ottoman periods were magnificent; by contrast, today's output is at best mediocre.

Output on a large scale did not recommence until 1950 and was designed to halt the massive influx of Iranian carpets and rugs. As with China, India and Pakistan, Egypt works principally through major co-operatives, producing to order commercial replicas of any and all Persian models in wool or in silk, including *Nain*, *Kashan*, *Tabriz* and *Hamadan* types. In actual fact, the technical quality is relatively good (with a knot density of between 1,800 and 6,000/dm^2) and, admittedly, prices are competitive.

New carpet designs draw their inspiration from frescoes and reliefs in the tombs of Ancient Egypt and – somewhat embarrassingly – are known as 'Pharaonic'. It is difficult to believe that there is anything other than local demand for such kitsch.

By contrast, kilims made in Harania are comparable to tapestry rather than to carpets. The Egyptian architect Ramses Wissa Wassef used to run a workshop school where he instructed young children in the art and technique of kilim weaving. Simple (not to say, primitive) high-warp looms were used, and there was no recourse whatsoever to cartoons or classic Coptic templates. Those children are now adults who weave for a living. The most beautiful tapestries of all are woven in the art centre run by Wassef's wife, Sophia, but kilim tapestries produced elsewhere, notably in the villages of Harania and Kerdassa, feature naïve scenes of village life at the foot of the Giza Pyramids. The Upper Egypt village of Garagos (near Luxor) also manufactures kilims like those woven in Harania. Father Philippe Ackermann is the driving force behind this initiative, which has enabled genuine folk art to continue to flourish despite the crass commercialisation of the carpet sector in the wake of rising tourist demand.

A fish-motif kilim woven by a former Harania village pupil of Ramses Wassef.

Above: Detail from a kilim from the Nile Delta.
Opposite page: 'Earthly Paradise' ('The Garden of Eden'), a kilim woven in the workshop of Sophia Wassef, who continued the creative carpet design tradition of her late husband.

ARABIA:
BEDOUIN NOMADS

The seemingly endless stretch of desert that lies between Africa and Asia Minor is still the province of wandering Bedouin tribes. Itinerant Bedouin weavers in

Opposite page (top): Detail from a type of fringed camel saddle-bag woven to this day by Bedouin nomads in Saudi Arabia.
(Below): Vegetable-dyed camel saddle-bag with lozenge motifs woven by Bedouin women for domestic use.

Saudi Arabia, Syria, Jordan and the former Palestine continue to work on primitive looms to weave the textiles that are essential to their nomadic existence. The low-warp looms used are identical to those pictured on ancient Mesopotamian seals: four stakes driven into the sand support two uprights that hold the warp. The weft thread is coiled on a wooden bobbin and fed into the weave by means of a long wooden knife or spatula that serves to part the warp threads and, at the same time, to press the weft threads firmly down into place.

With only this rudimentary equipment at their disposal, the Bedouin womenfolk create tent coverings, blankets used to separate the male and female quarters inside the tent, floor coverings, sacks for grain, travel pouches which double as cushions, horse and camel saddle-bags blankets, harness straps and trimmings. These prodigious weavers use only wool from their own sheep and hair from their own goats and camels. The colours are vegetable-dyed, primarily by using plants and insects found in the desert.

Colour is an important factor in Bedouin weaving and one that the Bedouin takes very seriously in terms of its symbolic value. White symbolises purity and also fecundity, wealth, happiness and light. Golden yellow corresponds to power, and red to festivities and pleasure. Red is also the colour of blood and, by extension, of life; black connotes the night, rebellion and destruction, whereas green stands for re-awakening – for resurrection. Green is the Moslem colour *par excellence*. By contrast, throughout the Middle East, blue is the colour associated with bereavement and mourning.

Today, the Bedouin have changed profoundly as more and more abandon the nomadic way of life. In particular, encroaching civilisation threatens their centuries-old oral traditions and, not least, the uniquely Bedouin approach to the weaver's art, where time is *not* of the essence. It is difficult to imagine how the Bedouin and their traditions can be integrated into today's increasingly industrialised cultures.

In Kuwait City, an association of sedentary Bedouin weavers has been established in an effort to ensure continuity of Bedouin carpet-making expertise. Whether this or other initiatives will be sufficient to preserve their genuine and unique folk traditions is a moot point indeed.

Contemporary carpets

Industrialisation popularised carpets, bringing oriental style rugs within the reach of a newly affluent, upwardly aspiring social class. But almost immediately there was a backlash as manufacturing techniques were criticised for having a detrimental effect on aesthetic qualities and standards of production.

One of the key figures to influence 20th-century carpet design was William Morris, who founded the British Arts & Crafts movement. He described his aims as follows: 'for the future, we people of the West must make our own hand-made carpets... and... these, while they should equal the Eastern ones as nearly as may be in materials and durability, should by no means imitate them in design, but show themselves obviously to be the outcome of modern and Western ideas, guided by those principles that underlie all architectural art in common.' These guidelines remain relevant to carpets designed by artists in the 21st century.

Morris's fellow carpet designers included Charles Francis Annesley Voysey, Walter Crane and Lewis Foreman Day. The view of such designers was that the design of floor furnishings should depend on linear design, with no deliberate attempt to create an illusion of depth. Voysey's designs, for example, are typified by simplified, large-format floral and vegetal repeat motifs. Within a short space of time, a thriving production line of Arts & Crafts carpets following Morris's dictates, some incorporating Celtic and Scandinavian design elements, was established in Scotland and Ireland, notably by John Templeton & Company of Glasgow, and in Kildare, Donegal, Kilkenny, Abbeyleix and Durrow in Ireland. The most famous designer of the Glasgow School was Charles Rennie Mackintosh.

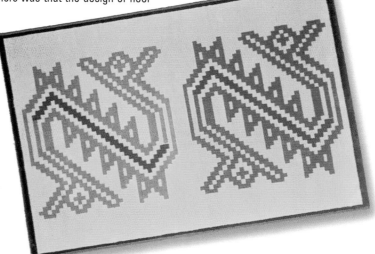

'Quetzal', a carpet designed by Manuel Canovas and produced by Flipo.

'Labyrinth', a hand-tufted carpet designed by Sonia Delaunay and released by Artcurial.

Liberty of London, founded in 1875 by Arthur Lasenby Liberty, initially concentrated on the sale of imported Eastern goods and occasional exhibitions of historic textiles. By the late 1880s, however, it had become one of the most fashionable shops in London, selling carpet and rugs from the Arts & Crafts Movement and Indian *druggets* (flat-woven cotton rugs) and Oriental rugs, silks, muslins, 'tapestries' and other furnishings. Liberty also sold rugs from the influential London Silver Studio atelier, whose mainly abstract designs were softened by naturalistic colours and features.

Otto Wagner, one of the foremost Viennese proponents of the curvilinear, nature-inspired Art Nouveau style, directed the architecture department of the Academie der Bildenden Künste, where his students included such influential artists as Josef Hoffman, Josef Maria Olbrich, and Koloman Moser. These three were all founding members of the Wiener Sezession (Vienna Secession), a radical art and design movement formed in 1897. All three designed carpets that employed the Viennese 'look' (rich, intense colours and patterns) in designs in both the Art Nouveau style and also early transitional expressions of the emerging International Modern style. Hoffman was keenly aware of the work of the British Arts & Crafts Movement, and maintained a close association with Mackintosh and the Glasgow School of Art, as well as with the Modern Movement developing throughout Europe.

Meanwhile in Munich, where Art Nouveau was known as Jugendstil, rugs were designed at the Deutscher Werkstätte (German Workshops) and then the Deutscher Werkbund (German Art Union), the founding members of which had also been influenced by the British Arts & Crafts movement and by the work of Mackintosh and Baillie Scott of the Glasgow School. In Dresden, Gertrude Kleinhempel, who taught and designed textiles, expanded her repertoire to include carpets, and around 1909 her elegant geometric patterns were put into production by the Werkstätten für Deutschen Hausrat (Workshops for German Household Interiors).

Although the carpets of Morris and his colleagues enjoyed a certain success in the USA, and inspired a flurry of popular American imitations, the carpet industry there was more conservative than its British counterpart. The highest-profile carpet designer was the architect Frank Lloyd Wright, who incorporated rugs into his

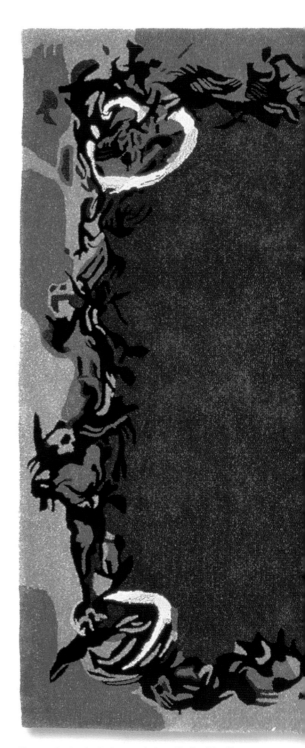

'Nocturne', a hand-tufted carpet designed by Zao Wou-Ki and released by Artcurial in a limited edition of 100.

all-over plans both as practical and decorative elements, and also as a means of defining living spaces within his open-plan interiors, for example in his 'prairie houses'. Wright's textiles – which typically have a plain ground and no borders, or simple linear patterns – influenced rug design throughout the USA and Europe.

Also in the USA, Gustav Stickley used the label 'Craftsman' for all the products he sold, whether made in his workshop or bought in from elsewhere – India, the Middle East or Donegal, or from Morris, Voysey and other designers. His annual catalogue, *The Craftsman*, described his carpets as 'Good Rugs that are within the Reach of People with Moderate Means'. American taste in carpets was further influenced by two brothers, Charles Summer Green and Henry Mather Green, architects and interior designers, much of whose work was done in California.

As the 19th century gave way to the 20th, Paris emerged as the centre of a thriving avant-garde art scene and luxury goods market. The city was a melting-pot of design trends, and its Exposition Universelle of 1900 attracted designers and artists from Europe, the USA and Japan, all avidly seeking new and inspirational designs to mark the start of the new century. Many French artists and fashion designers allied themselves with interior decorators, and hungrily seized on the brilliant colours and concepts introduced by Diaghilev's Ballet Russes.

Opportunities were broadening, and as well as private clients there were now important corporate commissions to design complete interior schemes for shops, offices, banks, exhibition pavilions, grand luxury hotels, and, most sumptuous of all, the new ocean-going liners. The Exposition Internationale des Arts Décoratifs et Industriels Modernes, held in Paris in 1925, allowed Europe to parade its achievements in the fine and applied arts. Among the most prominent interior-design studios was Süe et Mare, the partnership of Louis Süe and André Mare. Their traditional/transitional carpets often contained period references, as well as classical motifs such as garlands and shells, inspired by the Louis-Philippe style but with a contemporary slant. Long-established carpet and tapestry weaving factories such as Savonnerie, Aubusson, Felletin, Cogolin and St. Cyr collaborated with firms of decorators and new galleries such as Galerie Myrbor, run by Marie Cuttoli, an energetic promoter of daring designs by new artists.

When the Ballet Russes initially burst on to the Paris scene, the fashion designer Paul Poiret was strongly affected by their fresh, bold concepts. In 1911 he set up a design and production studio, Atelier Martine, and the rugs, furniture and other wares produced there were marketed through his own outlet, Maison Martine. As Atelier Martine designers progressively incorporated changing artistic styles such as Cubism and Surrealism, they took a firm hold on public attention, and the clear colours and naïve motifs they employed dominated all aspects of French interior design until the Atelier's closure in 1934.

During this period, one of the most successful carpet designers working in Paris was Edouard Benedictus, an artist strongly influenced by Fauvism. His designs – light-coloured geometric forms arranged with orderly precision – contrast dramatically with those of, for instance, the Russian-born Sonia Delaunay, who, with her husband Robert Delaunay, worked as a set designer for Diaghilev's Ballets Russes de Monte Carlo. The syncopated shapes she employed in her rug designs, in colours influenced by the vibrant palette of the Ballets Russes, have a pronounced sense of rhythmic movement not unlike that suggested by a chorus line. Another artist working for Diaghilev at the same time and also designing carpets was Pablo Picasso, then in his Cubist period. Picasso's carpets were sold through Galerie Myrbor.

Meanwhile in Britain, from approximately 1910 to the end of the 1930s, there was a new wave of innovative design. Some of the most progressive designs emerged from the Omega Workshops, formed in 1913 by Roger Fry. Fry gathered together a group of young avant-garde artists, including Duncan Grant, Frederick Etchells and Vanessa Bell, with the aim of fusing art and interior design. They were heavily influenced by the art and design scene in Paris, particularly by avant-garde movements such as Cubism and Fauvism, and workshop precedents such as Paul Poiret's Atelier Martine, which had opened two years earlier. Omega's work was too radical for contemporary British taste, and so it failed to develop a wide enough clientele to survive, closing in 1919. Shortly afterwards, Ambrose Heal set up business, specialising in carpets whose Modernist designs were less visually challenging, their orderly grids revealing Scandinavian influences. His company, Heal & Son, in London's Tottenham Court Road, was at the forefront of contemporary design and in fact continues to promote modern rugs to the present time.

Leading figures in British rug design in the 1930s were the American-born husband and wife team, Marion Dorn and Edward McKnight Kauffer. Their flamboyant Modernist rugs, woven by the Wilton Royal Carpet Company, were exhibited at the Arthur Tooth & Sons Gallery in London. Dorn created her own signature look, employing delineated rectangles of plain colour, usually in tones of brown and cream with lines in contrasting shades. She created an all-white patterned carpet for one of the most famous rooms of the 1930s, the white drawing room of decorator Syrie Maugham, which used white on white, relying on contrasting textures rather than colour for effect.

To return to France, any account of French modern carpet

Left: A circular Cogolin carpet designed by Leleu. Opposite page: A contemporary carpet designed by Oliver Debré and woven by Tisca-France.

Carpet designed by Sylvain Dubuisson and woven by Tisca-France.

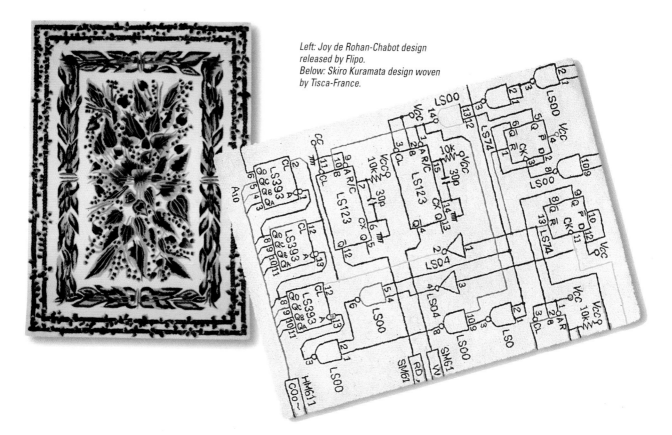

*Left: Joy de Rohan-Chabot design released by Flipo.
Below: Skiro Kuramata design woven by Tisca-France.*

designs must also include Valdemar Bobermann and the Leleu family. Bobermann's work used abstract forms and naturalist motifs, such as boats and human figures, and his famous composition of naked figures, published in *Tapis Modernes* in 1929, provided a clear contrast to the abstract works dominating French carpets of the period. Jules-Emile Leleu set up a family company after World War I and was joined in the venture by his brother Marcel, daughter Paule, and son André. Paule Leleu trained under Ivan Da Silva Bruhns and for several decades from 1932 designed the family's rugs. Ivan Da Silva Bruhns, born in Brazil, trained as a painter and, unlike most artists turned designers, focused solely on carpet design. His main sources of inspiration were the Berber weavings he saw at the exhibitions of Moroccan art held in Paris in 1917 and 1918. Commissions came from as far afield as India, where he designed rugs for the palace of the Maharajah of Indore. Indian royal families patronised several leading modern architects and were avid purchasers of Art Deco jewellery and interiors so effectively show-cased by

luxury ocean liners and hotels. As a consequence, weavers in India began to produce carpets and *dhurries* in this modern Western style for local consumption, and China followed suit, exporting Deco carpets to the West. Another important movement in carpet weaving was the textile workshop of Germany's Bauhaus school of architecture, art and design, which opened in the year the Omega workshops closed, flourishing between 1919 and 1933. Initiated by Walter Gropius in Weimar, the Bauhaus sought to bridge the gap between craft and industry through the creation of commercially successful products that retained their artistic merit. Carpet design was influenced by the artists who taught at the Bauhaus, who included such luminaries as Paul Klee, Josef Albers, Wassily Kandinsky, Laszlo Moholy-Nagy and Gunta Stölzl, who headed the department.

Further north, in Scandinavia, the newly emerging style became known as Scandinavian Modern. It combined the more restrained architectural forms of International Modernism and Art Deco with simple lines and clean, muted colours. A leading figure among Scandinavian carpet and textile designers was Märta Måås-Fjetterström, who applied the stylised floral motifs of Turkish and Persian rugs to her soft, pale designs.

Art Deco spread from Europe to the USA, and in 1929 an exhibition of European applied arts in New York, which included contemporary rugs from France, Germany, Sweden, Britain, Austria and Belgium, introduced these new ideas to the American public. The American designer Donald Deskey trained in Paris in the 1920s, and was one of the first designers to experiment with abstract-geometric patterns in the USA. People loved this 'jazzy' look, and in 1937 New York's Museum of Modern Art hosted an exhibition entitled 'Rugs from the Crawford Shops Designed by American Artists'. These were traditionally made hooked rugs, but with contemporary designs, and the exhibition was so successful that work by many of the same artists appeared in an exhibition held in the same year at the Metropolitan Museum of Art. Emboldened by public response, the museum purchased from the

Modern design woven in a workshop in Konya (Turkey).

Myrbor Galerie in Paris several carpets designed by modern artists.

The bright exuberant designs of 1930s Europe ended with the outbreak of World War II. Nevertheless, many artists and designers in France continued to work despite the rationing of materials, and, making a virtue out of necessity, relied on a play of patterns and contrasting textures rather than colour effects. In the USA, however, the situation was different. The resounding success of its 1937 exhibitions encouraged the Metropolitan Museum of Art to continue in this vein, and in 1941 they showed 'Rugs by Modern Artists', which displayed 'imported' works by the main Art Deco designers working in France, who included Fernand Léger, Louis Marcoussis, Joan Miró, and Jean Arp. The influence of these exhibitions inspired artists and manufacturers in the USA, culminating in another show a year later, 'New Rugs by American Artists'.

In 1946 the Victoria and Albert Museum held an exhibition, 'Britain Can Make It', which provided the first post-war opportunity for British companies to display their newest wares. This included carpets, and by the late 1940s and 1950s Scandinavian design had become the height of fashion, with a fresh new look using pale wood, blocks of bright colour juxtaposed with neutral shades, and traditional *rya*, shaggy long-pile technique, so that pattern was achieved by exploiting different textures. Sweden was not alone in producing modern rugs of this type, for similar fabrics were being made in Norway, Finland, and Denmark.

The restrained palette and patterns of the 1940s and 1950s were suddenly overthrown in the 1960s and 1970s as the bright primary colours of Abstract Expressionism, Pop Art and Op Art styles burst on the scene. Highly designed fashionable interiors resulted in a situation similar to that of the 1920s and 1930s, whereby renowned artists of the day once again designed rugs and carpets. In London, Heal & Son produced rugs in brilliant shades, and in Italy the geometric compositions of Op Art found particular favour. The designer Gaetano Pesce, who had trained as a film-maker, applied his interest in visual movement to rugs, using a variety of textures to achieve Op Art designs. In 1962, the World House Galleries in New York hosted an exhibition of 26 rugs that juxtaposed the work of earlier artists such as Léger, Miró and Picasso, with that of contemporary designer Miriam Leefe. The exhibition 'American Tapestries', held in 1968 at the Charles E. Slatkin Galleries, New York, sought to demonstrate that textiles were the bridge between fine art and decorative design. The exhibition displayed woven textiles based on paintings by 22 Pop Art and Abstract Expressionist artists, and the show was so popular that a second was held in 1970, 'Modern Master Tapestries'. Andy Warhol's *Marilyn* was translated into textile in 1966, in a limited edition of four, and the Pop Art 'anti-sensibility' images of Roy Lichtenstein, with their witty observations on modern life, were woven as hand-knotted rugs in 1979.

One of the most important figures in contemporary carpet design and promotion has been the American Jack Lenor Larsen; in 1980 the Musée des Arts Décoratifs in Paris held a retrospective exhibition of his work. More recently Christopher Farr and Matthew Bourne achieved success with a London gallery dedicated to commissioning and exhibiting hand-made rugs woven in Turkey but designed by leading artists such as Gillian Ayres. They also included designs by names better known in the fashion world, such as Rifat Ozbek, Georgina von Etzdorf, and Romeo Gigli.

The 1980s saw a huge expansion in the market for one-off and multiple-edition handmade rugs and carpets, as well as for designer-and-artist-designed rugs, a trend that continued to grow throughout the 1990s and into the 21st century. Fashion decreed polished or bleached wooden floors, which are enhanced to perfection by beautiful rugs.

Despite well-founded initial concerns about industrialisation, the strong reaction of artists and designers culminated in improved quality of production and materials, combined with bold and innovative designs. Today's finest carpets are both works of great beauty and also sound investments for the future.

A vegetable-dyed modern Gabbeh *with a stripe design and scattered small motifs filling the entire ground. The* abrach *(variation in hue) is clearly visible.*

Choosing a carpet

BUYING A CARPET OR KILIM LESS THAN 100 YEARS OLD

This section offers some general guidelines on purchasing, caring for and selling a carpet. Irrespective of whether you are buying a quality 'Oriental' carpet in its country of origin or in your own country, the best advice is to deal with a carpet merchant of international repute, or, failing that, with a merchant who has been specifically recommended to you. Failing to do either can end in tears.

General observations

What to look for

If you are not already a specialist in the field, you should read this section carefully before moving on to more in-depth studies on the subject. Visit as many museums as possible in order to learn to appreciate the intrinsic beauty of carpets and the craftsmanship that goes into making them. Then pay a visit to as many established carpet merchants and public auction houses as you can. In both cases, you will be able to look at specific details more closely and, above all, you will be able to touch the carpet in order to develop an intimate 'feel' for its softness and sheen, the firmness of the fabric, and the subtle sophistication or otherwise of the weave.

Once you have made *physical* contact with a range of carpets – which may take some considerable time – you will start to appreciate almost blindfold their various key elements: quality, origin, technique, age.

Buying as an investment

Your sole motivation in purchasing a carpet should *never* be that it promises to be a 'good investment', that it can subsequently be re-sold at a profit. Carpet experts who regularly evaluate carpets for insurance claims or litigation will confirm that there is no way the value of a carpet can be guaranteed over a period of, say, twenty years. Fashions change, as do prices. At present, for instance, carpet buyers are attracted to 'rustic' carpets made by semi-nomadic tribes, most likely because their motifs and colours are more in tune with current trends in interior design. Complex and 'fussy' Persian carpets are not fashionable – at least, not for the time being...

As far as carpet prices are concerned, it must be pointed out that they taper off sharply in the case of a carpet or rug that is not of exceptional quality. This is particularly true of carpets made since World War II – in other words, some 90% of those on the market.

In the rustic carpet category – those made between 1890 and the present – prices vary as a function of quality, age, condition and format. Older carpets tend to hold their value because, quite simply, they become progressively rarer and so liable to attract museums, galleries and private collectors. Absolute top-quality specimens rarely come on the market. These are fully-fledged works of art and, as such, unique (and vulnerable). What is more, they become scarcer and more fragile as time goes by.

An 'ancient' carpet is generally taken to mean one that is over 100 years old. It follows that today's carpets will be 'ancient' and 'desirable' in a matter of decades, by which time – it is fervently hoped – those who weave them will no longer be exploited as they have been in the past. What this also implies, of course, is that labour costs will escalate appreciably – as will the cost of the finished product. With international investment markets at almost unprecedented but (one dares to hope) temporary lows, now is perhaps as good a time as ever to buy a quality carpet and to start a collection that can only appreciate in value.

Always remember, however, that a carpet is not only a financial investment – it is an investment in pure pleasure, an investment in emotional and intellectual gratification.

Condition

Never let your enthusiasm for a particular carpet blind you to its condition. Restoring an ancient carpet is an expensive business. The rule of thumb is that any damage to the carpet in question should not extend beyond 20 to 30% of its surface area. If it does, the carpet as a whole will swiftly lose its value. In other words, if the pile is worn, if there are a number of holes, or if the borders are frayed the carpet will have effectively no market value. Its sole value will be sentimental (in the case of a dedicated collector) or as a museum piece. Above all, look out for traces of damp that can damage the carpet weave.

Other technical considerations

Knot density may be an important factor in assessing the strength and durability of a carpet, but it is by no means the principal determinant in terms of price. Be careful to question the seller on specific technical data in his or her possession: knot density, whether vegetable or chemical dye, and so on. When a sales certificate is issued, it should carry as much pertinent detail as possible, including the date of manufacture and – note well – the country, region, town or village of origin. Some regions are more sought after than others – and for a variety of reasons, notably with regard to rarity and craftsmanship – and these factors will have a direct bearing on the purchase price.

In this guide, I have repeatedly stressed the desirability of vegetable dyes; to a large degree, these began to be supplanted, from the 1870s, by aniline-based dyes that were subsequently treated to age and fade the original harsh colours. No serious-minded carpet dealer would consider selling you a carpet without guaranteeing its authenticity. Such a guarantee will safeguard you against fakes. Serious-minded merchants will also tell you without much prompting whether the dyes used are vegetable or synthetic, or whether the silk is genuine or mixed with silk waste, rayon or mercerised cotton. They will also inform you whether the wear-and-tear and ageing are genuine or induced by acid bath or other processes. Not least, they will guarantee that the carpet is hand-knotted: make no mistake, some so-called 'hand-knotted' carpets have 'knots' that are simply strands looped round the warp yarn.

All in all, a reputable merchant will protect you against all manner of traps and pitfalls that a less-than-honest seller will go out of his way to conceal.

Buying ancient carpets abroad

The market

When in a carpet-producing country, never expect to chance upon a 'bargain' in the guise of a rare and valuable carpet that is going for a song in a city or town bazaar or in a specialist gallery in a popular tourist district. This simply does not happen. Carpet merchants in every country know their market and their product inside out. They keep a watchful eye on what is being bought and sold and, quite frequently, they have relatives in Europe or the United States who monitor trends in those markets on virtually a day-to-day basis.

There are specialist publications such as *Hali* that track prices at recent auctions. The prospective buyer would do well to consult these to gain some insight into world market prices for late-19th-century and early-20th-century carpets; those from before 1870 are now incredibly rare in the marketplace and the asking price is typically far beyond the financial resources of the private individual.

It should never be forgotten that it is not the age of a carpet or the fact that it was woven in pure silk that imparts value. What counts is its beauty, its rarity, and the particular patina and aura that come with age and use, the subtleties of design and natural colours being enhanced by the passage of time.

Pitfalls and ploys

As has been pointed out elsewhere in this book, some carpet merchants are not averse to selling 'ancient' carpets that have been artificially faded and aged by being treated in a variety of fraudulent ways. It is not unknown for some merchants to drag a new carpet behind their car for a couple of weeks to give it the appearance of age. One sometimes comes across villages or districts in larger towns where carpets are spread out in the middle of the road or street at the mercy of every passing car, truck, cart or camel. The usual explanation is that this helps 'beat the dust out of the pile'. This is patent nonsense, since exposure to dust, rain, sunlight and passing vehicles is simply intended to age the carpet or rug in question. In 99 cases out of 100 the carpet will have come off the loom only a short time before and will have already been subjected to a variety of 'processes' that will ostensibly age it by 50 or even 100 years – all in a matter of days or weeks.

There are always fakes in any branch of the arts and the Orient, despite its cheap labour and traditional craftsmanship, is no exception. As noted in earlier chapters, many workshops in various countries are perfectly capable of churning out excellent replicas of 'old' carpets from any or all of the most important centres. Needless to say, an honest merchant will tell you so up front and will sell you a replica carpet at a fair price – in which case no fraud is intended. By contrast, some urban workshops will go to any lengths to deceive the buyer, even by artificially simulating the discrepancies and imperfections that result from the use of vegetable dyes in order to demonstrate the carpet's 'genuine' nomad origins.

Another pitfall to be avoided is being waylaid by a highly personable 'merchant' who welcomes you to his shop and plies you with coffee or tea while passionately singing the praises of his wares, more for his own delectation, he will assure you, than for that of the would-be purchaser. Typically, he will unveil 'prize' items in his collection which – he will insist – are *not* for sale on the grounds that they are 'irreplaceable'. After the inevitable invitation to his home for dinner and the opportunity to view other 'priceless' items in his private collection (which have been treasured by his family for countless generations), the buyer is often persuaded that he has found a friend who would *never* think of pressuring him into buying. When, finally and reluctantly, the merchant does agree to part with an item, the buyer is often tempted to leap at the opportunity, if for no other reason than to demonstrate goodwill, not to mention a shared appreciation and new-found expertise.

Some of these 'merchants' are genuinely amusing and have a wealth of seemingly credible anecdotes. What is more, they appear to be willing – in the long run, and with some reluctance – to part with a rare carpet at a 'special' price. It is important not to be taken in by this show of affability and frankness. The harsh reality comes later, when the purchased item is subsequently examined and valued by an expert. A final word of caution: this experience is by no means confined to foreign parts: merchants in the buyer's home country are perfectly capable of the same 'sincere' deception. As ever, it is the buyer who must beware.

Export formalities

If you purchase a carpet from a specialist dealer in a foreign country, the merchant will assume responsibility for all the formalities and procedures associated with packing, shipping and customs clearance. Where the carpet to be exported is more than 100 years old, many countries require it to be submitted to a carpet expert (typically, someone seconded from a museum).

This person is mandated by the customs authority to approve or reject the export of the carpet, in the latter case primarily on the grounds that the item in question is a unique and very valuable part of the country's heritage. The message here is that you should never pay in advance for a carpet without having first received export authorisation and being in possession of the requisite documentation.

Upon arrival in your own country, you will usually be required to present your purchase for inspection at customs. The receipt and an exact description of the carpet should be kept. In some instances, an import or added value tax will be payable. Reciprocal agreements with some countries may result in these charges being waived. However, if the amount indicated on the receipt seems at odds with the putative value of the carpet in question, the carpet may be retained at customs pending investigation. In practice, however, customs officials tend increasingly to be lenient, particularly in the case of newer carpets.

Buying at home or abroad

Buying from a carpet merchant

When buying a carpet, a reputable dealer will invite you to select from items that fall within your price range. They will give you ample time for reflection. Use this time wisely, not least to compare the price proposed with that of carpets or rugs from the same period and from the same country or region. Above all, take your time – you will have to live with your selection for many years, and your children and grandchildren will be grateful for the care you take.

At present, top-quality carpets and rugs are often cheaper in Europe than in the East; what is more, major European merchants are able to offer a selection that compares favourably with their counterparts in the country or region of origin. This certainly holds true for

Great Britain, Germany and France (in the last-named, interest in buying and selling carpets and kilims is relatively recent). If the merchant you are dealing with knows you or knows of you through other clients, he may propose that you take the carpet home with you for a few days to try it out 'in situ'. If your initial impulse to buy is still as strong, then – and only then – should you proceed. In this respect, it is important to remember that the tonalities of the carpet will effectively 'change' at different hours throughout the day as the light varies in intensity and direction. This holds true not only for natural but also for artificial light.

Buying at auction

If you decide to purchase an old or contemporary carpet at auction, you will have prior opportunity to unearth a bargain provided you know the expert who acts as advisor to the auction house. On the eve of the auction, he or she may be persuaded to explain the pros and cons of the carpet or rug that has caught your eye.

It is important to note that the reserve price indicated in the catalogue is the minimum price established between the expert and the vendor, in other words the price below which the carpet will be withdrawn from sale. The estimated price, by contrast, is the price the expert has established as the value of the item for insurance purposes. If the expert knows the reserve price, he or she will be in a position to tell you how high you should bid without too much risk.

That said, exceptionally rare items can be bid up substantially once a museum or private collectors show interest. The latter may be prepared to go to exceptional financial lengths to acquire a specific item. Be careful not to get carried away: when the hammer falls on your final bid, the carpet is yours at that price. On the other hand, a carpet or rug that does not attract professional bidders can, in your mind, represent good quality and substantial charm for a given outlay. In other words, bargains are still possible.

Note that the acquisition price will be net of statutory sales tax and auctioneer's commission, both of which have usually to be paid in cash and on the spot. As a rule, goods will only become yours after your cheque has cleared.

Price range

Price guidelines are notoriously difficult to establish, since the cost of a carpet or rug can vary almost monthly depending on market conditions. The best counsel is to track developments at the major international sales – these are listed in the *Hali* review. The following examples are by way of illustration only.

A 19th-century Turkmen *Salor* carpet measuring 8 ft 4 in by 10 ft (2.54 m by 3.04 m) was recently sold for some £6,000 in London, whereas a smaller Caucasian carpet from the end of the 18th century (2 ft 8 in × 8 ft 4 in/ 0.81 × 2.54 m) went for around £10,000, despite being badly worn and having a number of holes. The key was rarity value rather than condition. Equally, a mid-19th-century *Kachan Mille-Fleurs* measuring 8 ft by 10 ft (2.40 × 3.04 m) was recently sold in Zürich for 120,000 Swiss Francs; whereas an early-20th-century *Tabriz* – only slightly larger, at 9 ft 2 in by 11 ft 10 in (2.80 x 3.60 m) – fetched 200,000 Swiss Francs. Meanwhile, at a recent sale at Druot in Paris, a large early-20th-century Iranian *Ardekan* with a characteristic floral medallion failed to make its reserve price of 15,000 French Francs, as did a similarly priced *Mesched* of roughly the same size.

The long and the short of it is that no single, authoritative price scale can be said to exist.

PURCHASING A MODERN CARPET OR KILIM THAT IS NEW OR LESS THAN 50 YEARS OLD

The market

A vast number of new carpets have flooded the market in recent years, with the result that there is a substantially greater range to choose from. It follows, however, that there is a correspondingly greater potential for duplicity and deceit – though the financial consequences are considerably less onerous in the case of newer carpets and rugs. An attempt has been made in this guide to point out possible pitfalls by country and region, bearing in mind that many carpets made today are simply poor imitations of ancient models. Rather than waste money on those, it is far better to look out for genuine rustic carpets made by semi-nomad weavers, such as the currently highly popular *Gabbeh* types from the Shiraz region or *Baluchi* carpets and rugs from Iran and Afghanistan, which are set to become fashionable.

Reputable merchants who specialise in 'new' carpets are highly unlikely to be the same merchants who deal in old carpets (and who refuse as a matter of principle to trade in any specimens less than 50 years old). It should be added that some merchants deal exclusively with kilims.

Traps for the unwary

On no account allow yourself to be tempted by the prospect of a 'massive public sale of up to 1,000 oriental rugs and carpets' scheduled for 'a limited period only' and 'at greatly reduced prices'. All the more so if this 'everything-must-go' type of sale is hyped by a 'guarantee' that 'all our stocks are hand-made and come complete with a certificate of origin'. More likely than not, a 'team of experts' will be on hand to counsel you in your choice from among 'hundreds of different carpets'.

It need only be repeated that there is a world of difference between a carpet 'made by hand' and a carpet that is '*knotted* by hand'. The difference is plain for all to see. And, if the carpet or rug in question does turn out to be hand-knotted, it is easy to imagine the sweatshop where it was made and the child labour that is cruelly exploited to make it. It would be far better to spend the same money on a new hand-tufted carpet or even on one that has been mechanically woven.

These warehouse sales of oriental carpets offer at knock-down prices 'authentic Shiraz' carpets measuring two metres by three, small *Hamadan* rugs (4 ft 7 in × 7 ft 3 in / 1.40 m × 2.20 m), as well as 6 ft 8 in × 4 ft 7 in (2.03 m × 1.40 m) collector's items such as ancient silk and cashmere carpets at 'incredible bargain prices' of less than £1,000. You need only pause to consider how many months it takes to weave and hand-knot a carpet like that to realise how questionable these warehouse discount sales must be.

As an added inducement, some so-called carpet merchants offer an ostensibly generous 'five-year same price' buy-back guarantee. This is not worth the paper it is written on, since the company or dealer will have folded within a year.

None of this should be taken to imply that there are no competent and honest wholesale importers in New York, London, Paris, Milan or Hamburg. But those merchants do not as a rule deal directly with the private buyer, preferring to earmark their carpets for sale to reputable retailers and/or to buyers from large department stores who come by regularly to stock up their carpet department. When these wholesale importers do announce a stock liquidation sale, you can be sure it is to get rid of carpets which have not attracted the interest of trade buyers. In that case, picking up a bargain *is* a distinct possibility.

Machine-woven carpets

Bear in mind that machine-woven 'oriental' carpets – such as wool or synthetic *Shiraz* and *Bukhara* varieties – are made to this day in Belgium and Germany and sold at ridiculously low prices. A 6 ft 6 in by 9 ft 10 in (2 × 3 m) imitation *Bukhara*, for instance, might cost about £150, whereas the hand-made real thing would cost anything between five and fifty times as much, depending on the quality of the individual carpet.

You must also be wary of the lead customs seal affixed to a carpet. This is no guarantee whatsoever of a carpet's authenticity or quality (carpets machine-woven on Jacquard looms also come with a lead import seal). In fact, some dealers in Western Europe ship machine-woven carpets to their agents in the East in order that these can be re-imported into Europe with a bogus 'customs import certificate' from Turkey or Iran or wherever. Needless to say, many people are taken in by this.

If in doubt, check the knots. A machine woven carpet will have none and the pile will be easily detached by pulling on the weft threads – something that is not possible with a knotted carpet or rug.

Other traps

Impulse buying – at private auctions held in a hotel or town hall, or at 'clearout', 'tax-free' or 'discount' sales and, not least, from door-to-door salesmen – is gradually coming to be recognised for what it is: foolish.

Nevertheless, all manner of ingenious approaches continue to be employed. Among the classic scenarios is a 'recommendation from a friend' whose name rings a faint bell and who has recently been 'privileged' to purchase a carpet or rug like the one being offered to you. This 'mutual friend' has been kind enough to pass on your name so that you too can benefit from this extraordinary opportunity to purchase directly (without going through an intermediary) a carpet or rug of rare and exceptional quality. The doorstep salesman will then go on to present a business card that identifies him as an expert who has 'personally' visited some remote village or other in, say, Iran and has acquired this magnificent carpet that, to his deep regret, he is obliged to part with at a derisory price.

It is sad to think how many elderly people in particular have fallen for this patter and parted with their hard-earned cash in order to purchase a carpet that turns out to be of inferior quality and with no re-sale value.

Another trap to be avoided is the phone call that informs you that you have been 'selected' to purchase a carpet or rug at a most advantageous price. More often than not, this is simply a variant of the door-to-door approach designed to fix an 'appointment to view' that can on no account be cancelled.

Prudence is also the watchword when it comes to buying anything from sales premises rented on a short-term basis in order to clear 'exceptional' carpet stocks. Typically, these 'businesses' close down after a few months, at which point it is usually announced that carpets and rugs are to be remaindered at 'sacrifice' prices. Incredibly, some would-be purchasers are taken in by this sort of thing.

Little wonder then, that the term 'carpet salesman' often has a pejorative ring to it. Happily, internationally reputable carpet merchants represent the other side of the coin: a listing in *Hali* magazine, for example, constitutes a guarantee against shabby practices such as those described here.

Department stores

In addition to some specialist sales outlets that offer authentic and honestly priced new oriental carpets, many department stores now provide a range of carpets and rugs. Among these, one might cite Harrods in London or Au Bon Marché in Paris. Aristide Boucicaut, who founded the latter store in 1874, was the first French businessman to offer a choice of oriental carpets and rugs and capitalise on the then current French vogue for all things Eastern. One clear advantage of dealing with a major department store is that home deliveries and favourable credit facilities can be negotiated.

New hand-knotted oriental carpets and rugs are currently available at a price which, when one considers the months of work that has gone into weaving them, is very reasonable. That said, be wary of extensive mark-downs: a 10 to 20% discount is often standard, whereas a 50% discount should be viewed with some suspicion. In effect, prices have already been hiked by between 30 and 40% in order to accord a so-called '10% discount'. This practice is to be deplored, for customers are misled into thinking that they have acquired a carpet or rug at something approaching half its original price.

Buying locally

It is generally possible to negotiate – haggle – on a one-to-one basis with the owners of local outlets selling carpets and rugs. Common and acceptable as this process may be, however, there are certain unwritten rules that must be respected. The merchant in question will be pleased to demonstrate and discuss with you the particular properties of a carpet or rug and, provided you have done some background research, you will be in a position to show that you know what he is talking about. When they realise that you know a thing or two about the subject, they will generally ask you to select from among the better items in their collection. Meanwhile, you will have taken the precaution of asking around to establish their credentials and discover whether they are regarded as reputable.

Under no circumstances, however, should you buy solely on the basis of a 'good deal'. Quite the contrary; you should purchase a carpet or rug because its beauty appeals to you. If you feel you 'must' have the carpet in question, then don't hesitate, providing his best offer is acceptable to you. At all events, you will have made a better buy than had you purchased a similarly priced machine-made carpet.

Experience has shown that carpets produced in recent years in countries where state quality controls apply (for example in Morocco, where an official stamp of quality is affixed) tend increasingly to be vegetable-dyed. This was certainly not the case with many carpets produced at the end of the 19th century and the beginning of the 20th, when output from urban workshops increased a hundred-fold.

If it is your intention to purchase a new hand or machine-made carpet designed by a contemporary artist and sold by a specialist gallery, please refer to the preceding section of this guide.

CARING FOR CARPETS

A first consideration is to establish whether a brand new carpet will 'shed' – in other words, whether small balls of loose wool will gather on the carpet surface. If this happens, they can be removed by brushing lightly once a month or so. On no account should the carpet be beaten or cleaned with a heavy-duty vacuum cleaner.

Cleaning

Irrespective of the age of the carpet, accumulated dust should be removed from time to time and the carpet or rug should be carefully washed and dried at least once every four years or so by a specialist cleaning firm.

Over time, using a heavy-duty vacuum cleaner or carpet beater will damage the pile, fringes and borders; instead, a hand-held vacuum cleaner should be used or, better still, a simple straw brush. It is also important to remove any dust that has accumulated beneath the carpet. A useful piece of advice is to turn the carpet face-down for a week or so from time to time in order to dislodge any accumulated dust, particularly around the knots. Grit and sand are particularly aggressive since, over time, they can cause serious damage to the weft threads.

The carpet should not be shaken roughly, draped over a window ledge, or beaten with a brush or carpet beater (as our grandmothers were in the habit of doing), since this too carries the risk of damaging the yarn.

Unless the carpet or rug is colourfast, never attempt to remove a stain by dabbing water on it; you will simply smudge the stain and make it even bigger. Accordingly, it is important to determine whether your carpet or kilim is colourfast, in which case it can be washed with cold water and a special, commercially available carpet detergent foam.

To find out if the colours are fast, take a section of damp white cloth and rub it vigorously over different colour sections. If a colour leaves traces on the cloth, you can be certain that the dyes used are synthetic. If the carpet or rug is old, however, it is always advisable to have a specialist test the dyes for fastness. At the same time, it is recommended that, if this has not already been done, the carpet be professionally treated to protect it against carpet moths.

A carpet's enemies

A carpet has several enemies, including:
– Moths, mice, high-heeled shoes, and heavy furniture that can crush the pile and eventually tear it. If your carpet or rug has not been treated against carpet moths, cover it at the end of spring with naphtha-impregnated paper.

– Damp, which can cause the yarn to rot. Damage is often caused by standing a vase of flowers on a carpet without using a watertight protective saucer.

– Excessive exposure to sunlight, which will lead to fading and discoloration.

– Dog and cat urine, whose acidic content will damage the yarn.

– Burning cigarette ash or hot cinders from an open fireplace. Always use a fire-guard if your carpet is placed in front of or close to an open fire.

– Dust (and, especially, sand or grit), which becomes lodged between the knots and causes excessive wear by friction. Turn the carpet or rug face-down from time to time to release ingrained particles of dust, sand and grit.

– Stains from spilt liquids such as coffee, tea or wine. In every instance, use a desert spoon to scoop up as much of the surface liquid as possible before taking a sponge to the affected area, rinsing it in cold water, then patting the area dry with a piece of absorbent paper.

Repairs

Professional advice and technical expertise are essential when a carpet or rug is in need of major repair. By contrast, you yourself can undertake some small or stop-gap repairs; for example, in the case of a kilim where a tiny section of weft thread has unravelled, in which case you will need wool as close to the same colour as possible and a canvas needle to effect repairs. You can also tie off an end which appears to be frayed or in danger of becoming detached, using strong thread (ideally, braided linen) and a classic 'scallop' stitch. The same applies to mending a damaged border, though this is a much more delicate operation that presupposes more intimate knowledge of how carpets are best repaired.

When it comes to mending holes or tears, you must always seek professional advice. Re-weaving and re-knotting are highly technical procedures requiring special expertise and access to the appropriate raw materials and colours – not to mention total familiarity with different knotting techniques and other specialist knowledge needed to repair a *soumak* or kilim.

Finally, before sending your carpet or rug to a specialist to repair it and prevent further damage, it is helpful to secure the damaged area by applying a provisional overcast stitch.

Additional hints to avoid damage and undue wear-and-tear:

To the extent that old carpets are usually fragile, it is never advisable to place them in busy areas of the house such as entrance halls, living rooms, or very bright, sunlit rooms. Strong light – even artificial light – can ruin delicate colours, so pay particular attention to spotlights and halogens.

A carpet or rug may be so delicate or fragile that it is best hung against a wall. This must be done carefully, since there is a risk of distending the carpet or rug and causing it to lose shape. On no account should you nail or tack the carpet directly to the wall or otherwise suspend it by the corners.

All manner of techniques are used to hang carpets. The simplest procedure is probably to sew a two-inch (5-cm) wide strip across the full width of the reverse side and affix tiny rings at intervals of three inches (8 cm) or so, taking care to attach these so that they will be hidden once the carpet is suspended. The rings are then simply slipped over small hooks set into the wall at three-inch intervals.

If the carpet or rug is comparatively lightweight, it is frequently enough to attach it by using self-adhesive (Velcro) tape. An adhesive Velcro strip sewn across the full width of the reverse side engages with a similar Velcro strip affixed to a narrow strip of wood fixed to the wall.

When a carpet or rug is placed on the floor, it should be done so directly, in other words without an intermediate or backing layer of protective canvas. To avoid wear-

and-tear by rubbing on tiles or on fitted carpet, simply apply strips of double-sided adhesive tape length-wise and crosswise about two inches (5 cm) in from each border. This will stop the carpet slipping or developing 'waves' that, over time, can damage the warp and weft yarns.

SELLING A CARPET OR RUG

Who to talk to

It is always easier to buy a carpet than it is to sell it, since the potential buyer will almost invariably find some reason or other to talk down its value. That said, the bottom-line advice as regards selling a carpet is essentially the same as that which applies to purchasing it: talk to a reputable professional.

The ideal solution, of course, is to sell the carpet back to the merchant from whom it was purchased several years previously. If the carpet was bought at fair value, the merchant should show little hesitation about buying it back – even at a slightly higher price. Rare carpets and rugs *always* find a buyer and their value increases year on year (other than during a recession). If the carpet or rug was originally purchased at an inflated price, however, the merchant will more than likely find some pretext to avoid buying it back or will simply offer to re-acquire it at a substantially lower price.

Some oriental carpet suppliers – typically those of the 'direct import' variety – undertake to buy back (read 'exchange') a carpet or rug at its original value within a 'guarantee period' of five years. This sounds fair, but you can rest assured that any carpet offered in exchange will be less valuable than the one purchased originally.

Another solution is to offer your carpet or rug for sale at public auction. In that event, an expert will assess its value and fix a reserve price. It should be pointed out, however, that there are close contacts between auctioneers and dealers, and that the latter are not above making reciprocal arrangements to avoid 'bidding up' the price of an individual carpet at auction. In that event, unless a private collector is particularly interested in the carpet you wish to sell, it will be sold at a 'rock-bottom' price, from which you also have to deduct the auctioneer's commission in respect of catalogue expenses, insurance and so on. You should also be aware that, even if the carpet is not sold during the auction, the auctioneer will still levy what is known in the trade as 'buy-back' charges.

Selling your carpet or rug directly to a private collector is always a possibility, assuming you can find one who has confidence in you; if the private sale goes through, however, you must be alert to any ensuing liability for capital gains tax. Failure to declare any profit may attract a fine.

Appraisal

Having your carpet or rug appraised by an authorised expert is always worthwhile, particularly in the case of a gift or legacy. Generally speaking, the expert will probably be a carpet merchant, in which case you are best advised to say you require the item to be appraised for insurance purposes. This should cost anything up to 10% of the estimated value but, in return, you will receive a photograph of your carpet or rug, together with a certificate of authenticity detailing its provenance, age and maximum insured value.

Bear in mind that a prospective buyer will almost never suggest how much he or she is willing to pay but will require you to name your selling price. If your expectations are unreasonable and your opening price is too high, there will be interminable and often fruitless discussion. Clearly, if you place too low a valuation on your carpet or rug, the merchant will be more than happy to agree to it. What you must never forget is that, as with antique furniture, there is a gap of between 30 and 50% between insured price and market value. This shortfall represents the dealer's potential profit margin after expenses.

The recessionary climate of the 1980s obliged many people to sell a carpet or rug for which they paid a substantial amount some years before. To their consternation, some discovered that their expensive acquisition had no comparable resale value because it was either a fake or a replica. The lesson here is self-evident: make sure you proceed to an appraisal before buying, so that you are not only covered in case of theft but also protected when it comes to subsequent resale. Appraisal is particularly important in the case of an old carpet with a high nominal value; in the case of carpets or rugs purchased for, say, £500 or less, commissioning an appraisal represents an unnecessary expense.

If the value of your carpet or rug has not been previously assessed, take a look at trade journals such as *Hali* or the *Oriental Rug Review* before approaching a dealer. These journals will indicate current prices at international sales. Each ancient carpet or rug sold is illustrated, and full details are given of age, provenance, dimensions, place and date of sale, and estimated and actual sale price. This information should be sufficient to enable you to 'guesstimate' with some degree of accuracy the current value of the carpet or rug you propose to offer for sale. Remember, however, that every specimen is unique and that major international sales listed in *Hali*, for example, relate to goods of exceptional quality.

There is always a tendency to believe that the carpet or rug you are selling is a rare item. In the real world, it is important to see and touch a carpet before making a value judgement. Moreover, it is essential to make a distinction between a collector's item and a piece that is destined for day-to-day use.

Generally speaking, it is far from easy to sell a carpet or rug. The best advice is to hold on to the item in question for as long as you possibly can, for the simple reason that, even if it was bought new, a good-quality carpet will hold and eventually appreciate in value. In the interim, you can enjoy the privilege and pleasure of ownership.

These words of caution may give an unduly pessimistic view of the situation, but they are justified inasmuch as they point up certain pitfalls that parallel those in the art world. Rest assured, however, there are many well-known and reputable international carpet dealers whose probity and expertise are beyond reproach when it comes to buying *and* selling a carpet or rug. The truncated list annexed to this guide is indicative rather than definitive, and the carpet lover is advised to develop his or her own professional contacts.

Further reading

A wealth of source material and commentary on carpets exists in several languages. Only a very short selection is given below.

Arts Council of Great Britain, *The Eastern Carpet in the Western World* (exhibition catalogue), 1983

Azadi, Siawosch, *Turkoman Carpets*, Duckworth, 1975

Bennett, Ian (ed), *Rugs & Carpets of the World*, Quarto, 1981

Black, David (ed), *World Rugs & Carpets: A Comprehensive Guide to the Design, Provenance and Buying of Carpets*, Country Life, 1985

Cootner, Cathryn M., *Anatolian Kilims: the Caroline & H. McCoy Jones Collection*, with contributions by Garry Muse, Fine Arts Museums of San Francisco, 1990

Curatola, Giovanni, *Oriental Carpets*, Souvenir Press, 1982

Farr, Christopher, Matthew Bourne and Fiona Leslie, *Contemporary Rugs: Art and Design*, Merrell, 2002

Gans-Reudin, E., *The Splendor of Persian Carpets*, Rizzoli, 1978

Gantzhorn, Volkmar, *The Christian Oriental Carpet*, Benedikt Taschen, 1991

Herbert, Janice Summers, *Oriental Rugs: The Illustrated Handbook for Buyers and Collectors*, Macmillan, 1982

Hull, Alastair and José Luczyc-Wyhowska, *Kilim: The Complete Guide*, Thames & Hudson, 1993

Iten-Maritz, J.: *Turkish Carpets*, Kodansha, 1975

Justin, Valerie S., *Flat Woven Rugs of the World*, Van Nostrand Reinhold, 1980

Opie, James, *Tribal Rugs: Nomadic and Village Weavings from the Near East and Central Asia*, Laurence King, 1998

Redford Walker, Gordon, *Oriental Rugs: An Introduction*, Prion, 1999

Sherrill, Sarah B., *Carpets and Rugs of Europe and America*, Abbeville, 1996

Siriex, Françoise and Jacques Sirat, *Tapis Français du XXe Siècle*, Édition de l'Amateur, 1993

Journals:

Hali, London

Oriental Rug Review, Meredith, New Hampshire

The Textile Museum Journal, Washington, D.C.

Specialist galleries/museums

The first part of this section lists by country a brief selection of specialist galleries which deal in carpets and kilims. There are, of course, many other dealers whose professionalism and reputation are impeccable and apologies are in order to all those who are not listed here. In most instances, the telephone directory or the Yellow Pages will list carpet merchants in a given location. In every case, however, it is strongly recommended that the potential buyer proceed with prudence to establish the credentials of the individual or firm in question. The second part of this section lists a selection of specialist carpet museums and museums with carpet collections.

Specialist galleries

AUSTRIA

Graz
White Giant, Enge Gasse 1, 8010 Graz

Salzburg
Bernhard Voloder (ancient carpets and kilims), Steingasse 35, 5020 Salzburg

Vienna
Kelimhaus Johannik (ancient kilims), Langegasse 27, 1080 Vienna
Vartian (contemporary carpets), Rotenturmstrasse 15, 1010 Vienna

AUSTRALIA

Bangalow
Milton Cater Oriental Carpets, The Rug Shop, 11 Byron St, Bangalow

Port Douglas
Persian Carpet Gallery, Shop 45, Marina Mirage, Port Douglas, Queensland

BELGIUM

Antwerp
Kailash Gallery (ancient carpets and rugs), Komedieplaats 7-11, Antwerp

CANADA

Edmonton
Sheikh's Oriental Rugs, 2812 Calgary Trail South, Edmonton, Alberta

Montreal
Ararat Rug Co, 3457 Park Ave, Montreal, Quebec H2X 2H6
Tola Carpets Inc, 235 Laurier West, Outremont, Montreal, Quebec H9X 3K7

DENMARK

Copenhagen
Galerie Hans Elmby, Kronprinsessegade 40, 1306 Copenhagen

FRANCE

Cannes
Emir, 52 rue d'Antibes, 06400 Cannes

Lille
Jean Maniglier (contemporary carpets and rugs) 89 rue de la Monnaie, 59000 Lille

Lyon
Galerie Emir (ancient Persian and Chinese carpets and rugs), 7 rue République, 69001 Lyon
Galerie Girard (ancient carpets and rugs), 32 rue Auguste Comte, 69002 Lyon

Marseilles

Tapis Misraki (contemporary carpets and rugs), 39 rue Grignan, 13006 Marseilles

Montpellier

La Yourte (Habib Haider; Afghani nomad carpets and kilims, Turkish kilims and Chinese carpets and rugs), 14 rue des Soeurs Noires, 34000 Montpellier

Paris

Galerie Blondeel-Deroyan (ancient carpets and rugs), 11 rue de Lille, 75007 Paris

Galerie Triff (ancient and contemporary kilims and gabbeh), 35 rue Jacob, 75007 Paris

Hadjer et Fils (ancient carpets and rugs), 102 rue du faubourg Saint-Honoré, 75008 Paris

Kashani & Siamac (antique and decorative rugs), 138 Rue des Roiseres, St Ouen, 93400 Paris

Nissim, Artsigners (contemporary hand-tufted carpets and rugs and ancient oriental carpets and rugs), 32 rue du faubourg Saint-Antoine, 75012 Paris

Saint-Rémy-de-Provence

Les Mains d'Or (ancient carpets and kilims), 21 avenue Fauconnet, 13210 Saint-Rémy-de-Provence, Isles-sur-Sorgue

Several specialist firms offer restoration and cleaning services for ancient carpets and rugs; in France, for instance, rare and delicate carpets and rugs can safely be entrusted to **Maison Chevalier**, 64 boulevard de la Mission Marchand, 92400 Courbevoie.

GERMANY

Berlin

Galerie Neiriz (ancient kilims), Kurfürstendamm 61, 1000-Berlin 15

Bochum

Jan Kath (contemporary carpets), Hasenwinkelerstrasse 213, 44879 Bochum

Düsseldorf

Werner Bäumer GmbH (nomadic and village carpets and kilims; oriental carpets), Berliner Allee 30, 40212 Düsseldorf

Hamburg

Akhavan – Farshchi (Persian carpets and rugs), Brooktorkai 3, 20457 Hamburg

Galerie Azadi, Deichtorstrasse 24, 2000 Hamburg

Hans Eitzenberger (antique carpets), Alstertor 20, Ecke Ballindamm, 20095 Hamburg

Mannheim

Franz Bausback, 9 Kunststrasse, 68161 Mannheim

Munich

Frauenknecht (antique rugs, textiles and flatweaves), Steinsdorfstrasse 21, 80538 Munich

Ruppenstein (antique carpets and rugs), Seitzstrasse 17, 80538 Munich

Wildenberg

Markus Voigt Galerie, Siegenburger Strasse 26, 93359 Wildenberg The DOMOTEX world carpets trade fair held each January in Hanover features carpets and rugs from some 40 countries. The fair affords an opportunity to view the rich and diversified gamut of knotted-pile carpets made in each of the production centres covered in this Guide. Unfortunately, admission to the +/-85,000 m² exhibit – a veritable Aladdin's Cave – is reserved exclusively to trade buyers.

ITALY

Florence

Boralevi di Daniele, Boralevi & C. (ancient carpets and rugs), Piazza S Felice, 50125 Florence

Milan

ABC Oriental Arts (contemporary carpets), via Labriola 54/56, Casalpusterlengo, 26841 Milan

Daniele Sevi (ancient carpets and rugs), via Fiori Chiari 6, 20121 Milan

Davide Halevim (ancient carpets and rugs), via Borgo Spesso 5, 20121 Milan

Emil Mirzakhanian (ancient carpets and rugs), via Bagutta, 24 Palazzo Melzi, 20121 Milan

Mohtashem (antique carpets and rugs), via Manzoni 40, 20121 Milan

Svettini Antichita (antique carpets), via G Morone 6, 20121 Milan

Perugia

Ottoman Art (ancient carpets and rugs), via della Sposa 10, 06100 Perugia

Turin

Cohen (ancient carpets and rugs), Fiora Maria, Galleria S. Federico 41, Turin

Venice

Rascid Rahaim and Co., via XXII Marzo, St Marco, 2380 Venice

NETHERLANDS

Amsterdam

Davoud Amsterdam (antique and old carpets), Adm. De Ruijterweg 46–50, 1056 GK, Amsterdam

NEW ZEALAND

Christchurch

Pazyryk Rug Co, 18 Bealey Ave, Christchurch

Oriental Carpet Palace, Shop 2, 166 Gloucester Street, Christchurch

Newmarket

Eastern Rug Gallery, 404 Khyber Pass Road, Newmarket, Auckland

Remuera

Mary Kelly Kilims, Ranui Road, Remuera, Auckland

SWEDEN

Bastad

Galleri Orient (ancient carpets and rugs), Köpmansgatan 96, 26900 Bastad

Stockholm

J. P. Willborg (antique rugs and textiles), Sibyllegatan 41, 11442 Stockholm

SWITZERLAND

Berne

Atelier Irmak (ancient oriental carpets and rugs), Kramgasse 47, 3011 Berne

Muttenz

Galerie Nomade (nomadic carpets), Hersberger AG, Hauptstrasse 89, 4132 Muttenz

Zumikon

DreamTex (rare old and antique kilims and rugs), Räspweg 12, 8126 Zumikon

Zurich
Galerie Koller, Hardturmstrasse 102, 8005 Zurich
Mardiros Madayan (old and antique carpets and kilims),
Freilagerstrasse 47, block I, 8043 Zurich

UNITED KINGDOM
Bath
Haliden (antique rugs and carpets), 98 Walcot Street, Bath BA1 5BG
Christchurch
Christchurch Carpets, 55–57 Bargates, Christchurch, Dorset BH23 1QE
London
Aaron Nejad, Antique and Decorative Rugs, 403–405 Edgware Road, Staples Corner, London NW2 6LN
Alexander Juran and Company, 74 New Bond Street, London W1Y 9DD
Bernadout and Bernadout, 52 Pimlico Road, London SW1W 8LP
Christie's, 8 King Street, St. James's, London SW1Y 6QT
Christopher Contemporary Rugs and Carpets, 212 Westbourne Grove, London W11 2RH
Clive Loveless (carpets and ancient ethnic kilims), 54 St Quintin Avenue, London W10 6PA
Covent Garden Oriental Carpets Ltd (specialists in old tribal and village kilims and rugs), 20 Earlham Street, London WC2H 9LG
David Black Oriental Carpets (ancient carpets and kilims), 96 Portland Road, London W11 4LN
Joseph Lavian (ancient and contemporary carpets and kilims), Building E, 105 Eade Road, London N4 1TJ
Joss Graham Oriental Textiles, 10 Eccleston Street, London SW1W 9LT
Oriental Carpet Centre, 105 Eade Road, London N4 1TJ
Rug Store (Oriental and decorative new and antique carpets and kilims), 637 Fulham Road, London SW6 5UQ
The Textile Gallery, 12 Queen Street, Mayfair, London W1J 5PG
Top Floor (contemporary carpets), 2/6 Chelsea Harbour Design Centre, London SW10 0XE
Zadah Gallery (ancient carpets and kilims), 35 Bruton Place, London W1X 7AB
Oxford
Oriental Rug Gallery, 15 Woodstock Road, Oxford OX2 6HA

UNITED STATES
California
Arte Textil (South American textiles and works of art), 904 Irving Street, San Francisco, CA 94122
Oriental Carpet Gallery, George F Gilmore, 2150 Newport Boulevard, Costa Mesa, CA 92626
Tony Kitz Gallery (antique carpets and textiles), 2843 Clay Street, San Francisco, CA 94115
Ziegler and Co (contemporary carpets), 408 North Robertson Boulevard, West Hollywood, CA 90048
Florida
Heirat Ltd (Edward Koch), 7024 South West 114 Place, Miami, FL 33173
Georgia
Rugs by Robinson (contemporary carpets), 351 Peachtree Hills Avenue, Suite 133, Atlanta, GA 30305
Illinois
The Nomad's Loom (ancient carpets and rugs), 3227 North Clark Street, Chicago, IL 60657

Massachusetts
Collins Gallery (old and antique Persian rugs), 11 Market Square, Newburyport, MA 01950
Equator Gallery (South American textile art), 218 Newbury Street, Boston, MA 02116
Minnesota
Oriental Rug Company, 3947 Excelsior Boulevard, Suite 107 St Louis Park, MN 55416
New Jersey
Ronnie Newman (ancient carpets and rugs), P.O. Box 14, Ridgewood, NJ 07451
New Mexico
William Siegal Galleries, 135 West Palace Ave #101, Santa Fe, NM 87501
New York
Antiquarius (antique Persian and tribal rugs, new handwoven rugs), 484 Broome Street, New York, NY 10013
Asha Carpets (contemporary carpets), 94–98 Nassau Avenue #360, Brooklyn, NY 11222
Christie's (ancient carpets and kilims), 20 Rockefeller Plaza, New York, NY 10020
Entrée Libre, 66 Crosby at Spring Street, New York, NY 10012
F J Hakimian (distinctive carpets and tapestries of the past for the future), 136 East 57th St, New York, NY 10022
Hagop Manoyan, 106–15 Queens Boulevard, #6A Forest Hills, New York, NY 11375
Looms of Persia/Apadana (Persian carpets and rugs), 25–27 East 31st Street, New York, NY 10016
Obeetee Inc, 126 Fifth Avenue, New York, NY 10011
Persian Gallery Co. (period tapestries and antique decorative carpets), 36 East 31st Street, 5th Floor, New York, NY 10016
Warp & Weft (antique and decorative carpets), 145 Madison Avenue, New York, NY 10016
Pennsylvania
Woven Legends (carpet production and restoration), 4700 Wissahickon Avenue, Philadelphia, PA 19144
Virgina
Purcell Oriental Rug Company, 107 West Main Street, Charlottesville, VA 22902

Producer Countries

CHINA
Copies of traditional Persian and Anatolian models predominate (as in Pakistan, see below), although some firms and certain autonomous regions such as Tientsin offer all-silk designs and are making an effort to develop a modern Chinese-design carpet industry.
Tourist-oriented exhibitions and sales outlets are generally found in the vicinity of the major hotels in Beijing and Shanghai. There is also a large selection of carpets and rugs at the Beijing Carpet Trade Centre, 90 Weizikeng, Liangjiazhuang, at the Huaxia Arts & Crafts Store, 293 Wangfujing Dajie and at the Marco Polo Carpet Store, 2/F China World Shopping Arcade, Beijing-Lufthansa Shopping Centre, 52 Liangmaqiao Road.

Department stores in major European cities usually stock superior-grade Chinese carpets and rugs.

EGYPT
Oriental Weavers (contemporary carpets), 8 Zakaria Khalil Street, Heliopolis, Cairo

HONG KONG
Al-Shahzadi Persian Carpet Gallery (ancient carpets and rugs), Ground Floor, 265 Queen's Road East, Hong Kong
Mir Oriental Carpets, 52 Wyndham St, Central, Hong Kong
Tai Ping Carpets Ltd, 26/F Tower A, Regent Centre, 63 Wo Yi Hop Road, Kwai Chung, NT

IRAN
Bayat Nomad Gaminchi (contemporary carpets), No. 4, Second Alley, Kaj St., Fatemi Avenue, Tehran 14147
Tavakoli Carpet (wide selection of Gabbeh, Senneh, etc.) 97 Vozara (Khaled Eslamboli) St, Tehran
Maison de l'Ira (a selection of contemporary Iranian carpets and rugs), 71 avenue des Champs-Elysées, 75008 Paris
The Samin Group in Tehran exports Persian carpets in a range of styles and qualities
Modam (contemporary carpets), Sepidan Road, Shiraz
Zollanvari (carpets and kilims from the Shiraz region), 37 Vakil Mosque Avenue, Shiraz

JAPAN
Morita (Japanese antique textiles), 5-12-2, Minami Aoyam, Minato-Ku, Tokyo 107-0062

LEBANON
Hassan Maktabi & Sons (antique, classical and nomadic carpets), Raouchef, Beirut
Iwan Maktabi (antique and decorative carpets, kilims and textiles), Charles Malek Avenue, Quantum Tower, Beirut

MOROCCO
In addition to cooperatives noted in the major carpet production centres, other cooperatives specialize in hand-woven New Zealand wool carpets and rugs destined primarily for the export market. Among these are The Traditional Factory, 14 avenue d'Alger, Rabat, Berber Carpet (Rabat), Bouchaid el Hadadi (Le Tapis Royal, 42 rue Allai Ben Ahmed Amlik, Casablanca), or Mocary, rue Ezzarbia Salé, Kilometre 4, route de Meknès.

PAKISTAN
A great number of factory-outlet merchants operate out of Lahore and Karachi; as a rule, however, they produce mainly copies of Persian and Central Asian designs. Among them are Bukhara House, 25 Empress Road, Lahore and the Asian Carpet Palace, 13 Ekneck Street Saddar, Karachi.
Many European houses and department stores import Pakistani carpets and rugs for retail sale. There is a requirement that the provenance of the carpet or rug be clearly indicated on the reverse.

TURKEY
Antalya
Tuzcular Mahallesi (decorative antique oriental carpets and kilims), Pasa Cami Sokak No. 26, Kaleici, Antalya

Konya
Hali Han (vegetable-dye carpets and kilims from the Konya region), Mevlana Müzeri, Karsisi, Konya

Istanbul
Didim Halicilik Tic. Ve San (ancient and contemporary kilims), Gazi Sinan Pasa Sok, Kultu Han No. 14/2-3-5, Cagaloglu, Istanbul 34440
Durusel Carpets (contemporary carpets and kilims), Durusan Ltd., Piyerloti Cad No. 2, Cemberlitas, Istanbul 34400
HAK, Peykhane Cad No. 15/17, Cemberlitas, Istanbul 34400
Hali Ticaret Gallery, Istanbul Carpet Bazaar, 31 Eminönu, Istanbul
Has Hali (contemporary carpets), Serefefendi cd. No. 38, Cagaloglu, Istanbul 34440
Mavro's (carpets and kilims), Al Meydani Tavukhane Sok No. 25–25, Sultanahmet, Istanbul 34400
Mehmet Cetinkaya Gallery, Kucuk Ayasofya Caddesi Tavukhane Sokak No. 7, Sultanahmet, Istanbul 34400
Mustafa Kayhan (contemporary carpets and rugs), Terzioglu Ihracat Turism ve Pazarlama, Peyhane Cad 8, Cemberlitas, Istanbul 34400
Süsler Hali Pazarlama Ticaret (Hereke and all-silk carpets and rugs), Nuruosmaniye Caddesi (Bazaar) 59–61, Cagaloglu, Istanbul 34400

Izmir
AK Kilim, San ve Ticaret Ltd (contemporary Turkish carpets and kilims), 928 Sk No. 51, Z10 Turist Han, Izmir
Arko Hali, Atatürk Caddesi 174/A, Izmir
Dagtekin (contemporary kilims and soumaks), 35220 Alsancak, Izmir

Specialist museums and collections

AUSTRIA
Österreichisches Museum für angewandte Kunst (Austrian Museum of Applied Arts), Stubenring 5, 1010 Vienna
Museum für Volkerkunde (Museum of Ethnology), Neue Burg, Vienna 1001

AZERBAIJAN
National Carpet Museum, 123 Neftchilar Avenue, Baku

CANADA
Textile Museum of Canada, 55 Centre Avenue, Toronto, Ontario, M5G 2H5
Royal Ontario Museum, 100 Queens Park, Toronto, Ontario, M5S 2C6

DENMARK
Davids Samling, 30 Kronprinsessegade, 1306 Copenhagen
Danske Kunstindustrimuseum (Museum of Decorative Art), Bredgade 68, 1260 Copenhagen

EGYPT
Egyptian National Museum, Midan-el-Tahrir, Kasr El-Nil, Cairo

FRANCE
Musée du Tapis et des Arts Textiles, 45 rue Ballainvilliers, 63000 Clermont-Ferrand
Musée Historique des Tissus-Musée des Arts Décoratifs, 34 rue de la Charité, 69002 Lyon
Musée des Arts Decoratifs, Palais de Louvre, 107 rue de Rivoli, 75001 Paris

GERMANY

Museum für Islamische Kunst (Museum for Islamic Art, Am Kupfergraben, Bodestrasse 1-3, 10178 Berlin-Mitte
Oriental Carpet Museum, Georgstrasse 54, 30159 Hannover
Staatliches Museum für Völkerkunde (National Museum for Cultural and Social Anthropology), Maximilianstrasse 42, 80538 Munich
Museum für Ostasiatische Kunst, Universitätsstrasse 100, 50674 Cologne

GREECE

Benaki Museum, 1 Koumbari str & Vas. Sofias av. 10674 Athens

HUNGARY

Museo d'Arti Applicate (Museum of Applied Arts), Ulloi ut 33-37, Budapest 10
Museum of Ethnology, Kossuth tér 12, 1055 Budapest

INDIA

Calico Museum of Textiles, Ahmedabad, Guyarat

IRAN

Carpets Museum of Iran, Karagar-e Shomali Avenue, Tehran
Rassam Arabzadeh Carpet Musdeum, #7, Boostan 1 St, Pasdaran Avenue, Tehran

ITALY

Museo Bardini e Galleria Corsi, 1 Piazza dei Mozzi, Florence 50122
Museo Nazionale del Bargello, via del Proconsolo 4, Florence 50100
Museo Poldi Pezzoli, via Manzoni 12, Milan 20100

NETHERLANDS

Rijksmuseum Amsterdam, Stadhouderskade 42, Amsterdam 1071

RUSSIA

Museum of Ethnography, Inzhenernaya Ulitsa 4/1, St Petersburg 191011 (houses one of the most important Turkmen rug collections in the world, as well as the Dudin collection)

SPAIN

Instituto de Valencia de Don Juan, Calle de Fortuny 43, 28010 Madrid

SWEDEN

Goteborgs Etnografiska Museum, Norra Museum, Norra Hamngatan 12, Goteborg 41114
Nationalmuseum, Sodra Blasieholmshamnen, Ostermalm, Stockholm

SWITZERLAND

Museum Rietberg, Gablerstrasse 15, 8002 Zurich

TURKEY

Carpet and Kilim Museum, Imperial Pavillion, Blue Mosque, Sultanahmet, Istanbul (houses Usak, Bergama and Konya carpets dating from 16th–19th century, as well as the best examples of 13th–20th century Turkish carpets)

TURKMENISTAN

Carpet Museum, 5 Gorogly Street, Ashgabat (houses a large collection of antiques and world-renowned Turkmen carpets, as well as the largest hand-knotted Turkmen carpet in the world)

UNITED KINGDOM

Burrell Collection, Camphill Museum, Queen's Park, Glasgow G41 2EW, Scotland
Fitzwilliam Museum, Trumpington Street, Cambridge CB2 1RB
Victoria and Albert Museum, Cromwell Road, South Kensington, London SW7 2RL

UNITED STATES

Art Institute of Chicago, 111 Michigan Avenue, Chicago, IL 60603
Brooklyn Museum, 200 Eastern Parkway, Brooklyn, New York, NY 11238
Denver Art Museum, 100 W 14th Ave, Denver, CO 80204-2788
De Young Museum, 75 Tea Garden Road, San Francisco, CA 94118 (from Spring 2005)
Frick Collection, 1 East 70th Street, New York, NY 10021-4967
Indianapolis Museum of Art, 4000 Michigan Road, Indianapolis, IN 46208-3326
J Paul Getty Museum, 1200 Getty Center Drive, Suite 1000, Los Angeles, CA 90049-1687
Los Angeles County Museum of Art, 5905 Wiltshire Boulevard, Los Angeles, CA 90036
Metropolitan Museum of Art, 1000 Fifth Avenue, New York, NY 10028-0198
Museum of Fine Arts, Avenue of the Arts, 465 Huntington Avenue, Boston, MA 02115-5523
Nelson-Atkins Museum of Art, 4525 Oak Street, Kansas City, MO 64111-1873
Philadelphia Museum of Art, Benjamin Franklin Parkway and 26th Street, Philadelphia, PA 19130 (houses a significant collection of classical carpets)
The Newark Museum, 49 Washington Street, Newark, NJ 07102-3176
The Textile Museum, 2320 S Street, NW, Washington DC 20008-4088

Index

INDEX

Acknowledgements

Over the years, many people have shared with me their passion for and knowledge of carpets and kilims, and have contributed enormously to my initiation into this richly diverse and fascinating world. Many of those same friends and colleagues proved instrumental in helping me assemble the illustrative material featured in this book. I owe them all a deep debt of gratitude for their generous and unstinting support.

I wish to put on record my particular indebtedness to the following:
• To the Chevalier Gallery and, in particular, to Nicole Chevalier, for helping assemble documentation on rare and precious carpets; and to Jacques Chevalier, a friend of long standing, an acclaimed carpet expert, and a consistent apologist for the French carpet industry.
• To François Ollivier, who heads the carpet department at Au Bon Marché, the first-ever French department store to have sent a buyer to Turkey, Iran and the Caucasus in order to assemble the initial selection of Oriental carpets exhibited for sale in Paris in 1973 and 1974. Under his direction, the store has donated magnificent specimens of ancient carpets to the Museum for the Decorative Arts in Paris. François Ollivier continues this tradition to this day, personally acquiring carpets for sale in the store. Little wonder then that his knowledge of urban and nomad carpet-weaving is unparalleled. The background documentation provided by him and Au Bon Marché proved invaluable.
• To the Centre Français des Tapis de l'Orient and its dedicated director, Franck Sabet, who graciously allowed me to select from and photograph examples of contemporary carpet design that are particularly interesting in terms of technique, quality and price. The centre is intended as a meeting-place for carpet lovers and as an exhibition centre featuring specific themes, including an initial and highly successful UNESCO-sponsored project in 1994, The Silk Road: The Road to Dialogue.
• To the TRIFF Gallery, the 'gallery of the textile arts' run with such commitment and expertise by Henri and Jacqueline Daumas. Since its establishment, the 'TRIFF' has regularly organised major exhibitions and has long been in the vanguard in promoting the art of the kilim, which has been so often undervalued by merchants and collectors alike.

• To Omar Amine Benabdallah, Director of Crafts and Craftsmanship at the Moroccan Ministry for Social Affairs, who was instrumental in providing me with copious documentation on current carpet production and specialist sources throughout Morocco. My thanks also goes to the Moroccan Crafts Delegation in Paris, which provided me with access to its carpet collection, and to the Moroccan Weaving Co-operative (CTMA) in Casablanca, and the Paris-based National Office of Tunisian Crafts, which provided excellent documentation.

A number of other organisations and individuals also furnished me with invaluable illustrative material, among them:
• Habib Haider, who heads the Montpellier-based Galerie la Yourte, which boasts a selection of Afghan carpets woven by nomadic tribesmen.
• Françoise Siriex (formerly of Leleu), who procured documentation on French 20th-century designers and production houses (including Canovas, Tisca-France, Flipo and others).
• Artcurial, the leading contemporary production house and gallery.
• Marcel Zelmanovich of the Diurne Gallery, who specialises in contemporary Tibetan-knot designs woven in Kathmandu (Nepal).
• Professor Onder Küçükerman, for providing documentation on the Isparta factory in Turkey,
• Claire Rado and Madame Ramses Wissa Wassef, for access to Harrania kilim-tapestries.
• The photographer Jean-François Camp and the Dupon processing laboratory.
• The photographer Jean-Pierre Lamirand, both for the quality of his work and for his infinite patience.
• Other persons too numerous to name, including passionate collectors and merchants who encouraged and helped me in my labours – not forgetting Jean-Pierre Girard of Lyon, who taught me how to 'read' a carpet as one reads of written text ...

My thanks must also go to the directors of the various museums cited in this book. Not least, of course, my gratitude extends to all those – named and unnamed – who have designed and woven carpets and kilims. Without them and their prodigious skills, the present guide would have proved a futile exercise.

CARPETS

PHOTOGRAPHIC CREDITS

First published by Hachette-Livre
43 Quai de Grenelle, Paris 75905, Cedex 15, France
© 1994, Hachette-Livre
Under the title Le Grand Guide du Tapis
All rights reserved

Language translation produced by Translate-A-Book, Oxford
Typesetting by Organ Graphic, Abingdon

© 2003 English translation, Octopus Publishing Group Ltd, London
This edition published by Hachette Illustrated UK, Octopus Publishing Group,
2–4 Heron Quays, London, E14 4JP

Editing (French edition): Muriel Lucas
Design: GRAPH'M
Illustrations: François Charles

ISBN: 1-84430-012-9
Printed in Singapore